The Jews of Germany

The
Jews of Germany

A Historical Portrait

Ruth Gay

With an introduction by Peter Gay

Yale University Press

New Haven and London

Set in ITC Garamond type by The Composing Room
of Michigan, Inc.
Printed in the United States of America by Arcata
Graphics-Halliday, West Hanover, Massachusetts.

Library of Congress Cataloging-in-Publication Data
Gay, Ruth.
The Jews of Germany : a historical portrait / Ruth
Gay : with an introduction by Peter Gay.
p.   cm.
Includes bibliographical references and index.
ISBN 0-300-05155-7 (cloth)
        0-300-06052-1 (pbk.)
1. Jews—Germany—History.   2. Germany—
Ethnic relations.
I. Title.
DS135.G3G32   1992
943′.004924—dc20   91-30235 CIP

A catalogue record for this book is available from
the British Library.
The paper in this book meets the guidelines for
permanence and durability of the Committee on
Production Guidelines for Book Longevity of the
Council on Library Resources.

10   9   8   7   6   5   4   3

To Gaby in Berlin

R & P

Contents

Introduction

Peter Gay

Jews in the German lands have always lived double lives. Or almost always: for a few heady decades, another scenario became plausible. In the 1870s and after, enjoying complete civil rights, Jews could hardly be faulted for wondering whether the centuries-old tension between German society and its Jews might not evaporate at last. The time seemed near when they might fully enter the German economy, German civil service, and German high culture as accepted fellow citizens. The web of German culture was made up of many diverse strands; by 1900, the Jewish strand seemed almost inextricably interwoven with it. Before the First World War, when the German-Jewish philosopher Ernst Cassirer made a pilgrimage to the Goethe House at Weimar, a guard stared at the tall, handsome, blond young man as though he were Goethe come back to life. Cassirer took this as a perfectly natural tribute. Was Goethe not his favorite poet too?

Not all Jews, to be sure, welcomed the prospect of total acculturation. A sizable though shrinking minority of the Orthodox deplored it as a threat to their identity; later, a far smaller but no less audible minority of Zionists denounced the much-touted disappearance of all boundaries between gentiles and Jews as a self-deluding fantasy. To the Orthodox and Zionists alike, *assimilation* was no word of praise. Yet the majority of German Jews, even devout ones, could only cheer the signs of growing mutual understanding, of increasing integration. Early in the nineteenth century, in a remark as poignant as it is cynical, Heinrich Heine had called conversion to Christianity an entrance ticket to Western civilization. After 1871, with the founding of the Reich, and even more after the turn of the century, during the years known as the German-Jewish symbiosis, Jews believed that one could remain a Jew and be a good German at the same time. Whatever their attitude toward this development, whether they lauded it as a realistic appraisal, greeted it skeptically as a fond pipe dream, or feared it as a nightmare, the fantasy of the German Jews' double life merging into one was shattered forever on January 30, 1933, with the accession of Adolf Hitler to the chancellorship of the Weimar Republic.

The hopeful interlude for German Jews during the empire and the Weimar Republic lasted some three-quarters of a century—a short time compared to the almost two-thousand-year-long history of Jews on German soil. But the many centuries that preceded it are no less problematic, no less open to divergent interpretations. The history of Jews in Germany has been vulnerable to a hypnotic dwelling on a chain of disasters. More than half a century ago, the eminent historian of Judaism Salo Baron called this preoccupation the "lachrymose" view of the Jewish past. In sharp contrast, the Jews in Germany (like those in Eastern Europe) have also been exposed to sentimental readings in which they appear, as soon as they are given the opportunity, as the unrivaled makers of high culture, while the Jews of the stetl appear both as helpless victims and as rich in the melancholy wisdom of the ages, clustering in romantic villages where life is with people. In these texts, they have always either fiddled on the roof or cowered in the cellar. And professional historians have not failed to heed Baron's warning against this tearful interpretation of the Jewish past. But in the popular view, Jews in Germany have for centuries walked unawares the stony road to the Holocaust.

This is too simple. To reduce German Jewish history to an unrelieved sequence of outrages is to slight the times of tranquillity and the reality of Jewish achievement. For the first seven centuries of their stay in the German lands, Jews lived in peace and, indeed, often with enviable privileges. Their time of affliction started with the First Crusade. Even then it was marauding adventurers from far away rather than the Jews' neighbors who did the killing and the burning as fanatical bands lurched across Europe on their quixotic quest for the Holy Land. There can be no minimizing the travail of German Jews through the ages. Denial is as unacceptable as self-pity. Subject to arbitrary exactions and capricious oscillations between tolerance and persecution, exposed to rabid zealots, vulnerable to the bloodthirsty rhetoric of Jew-haters from Martin Luther to Richard Wagner, the Jews of Germany often lived lives of deprivation and danger. They were not free of justified anxiety even in the overestimated reign of Prussia's King Frederick II, known as the Great, a ruler whose definition of enlightenment evidently did not include the Jews.

All of these times of troubles were real enough, and all of them have necessarily found a place in the pages that follow. But as we penetrate the curtain of horrors, we see that these times do not exhaust the Jewish experience in the German lands. The discriminatory taxes, the blood libels, and the pogroms are a part of the story—far too large a part. But across the centuries, Jews managed to build a sturdy culture in their German settlements, partly independent of their gentile neighbors, partly intertwined with them. Jewish learning, however isolated; Jewish prosperity, however precarious; Jewish public service, however limited; even Jewish participation in a wider society, all claim our attention. After all, even the language they developed—Yiddish—wrongly despised as a mere dialect and ridiculed as a debased version of German, was a remarkable venture in adaptation in its own right, with an impressive literature to its credit.

Two dates of disaster have often been allowed to dominate the history of the Jews: 70 and 1933. The first marks the destruction of the Temple in Jerusalem by Roman troops, a ruthless act of war that scattered the Jewish people across the known world, including German territory; the second, the accession of Hitler to power, which foreshadowed the end of Jewish life in Germany. But it is essential to fill in the spaces between these terrible moments in order to rescue for posterity a life lived to the full within bounds, whether constricting or comfortable. Attentive to this often forgotten wealth of the German-Jewish experience, this book seeks to do justice to that experience, to the daily life Jews carved out for themselves in the ghetto: their self-governing communities, their religious institutions—from ritual bathhouses to cemeteries—their commercial activities, both within the compass of Jewish communities and with a larger trading civilization. It was in this complex way, as Jews interacted with the Christian German society and then withdrew to their Jewish street, that they lived their double lives.

Frequent as these contacts were, theirs was a largely encapsulated existence. If one imagines an observer visiting a German ghetto in the fourteenth century and then returning in the eighteenth, that visitor would have found few changes. The handful of Jews who escaped to the wider world, notably the court Jews who flourished in the seventeenth and eighteenth centuries, were such spectacular exceptions that they only underscore the unvarying life they had left behind. In the small German-Jewish settlements, history passed its inhabitants by. Then in the 1750s and 1760s, in the time of Moses Mendelssohn, the greatest culture hero German Jews can boast, the Jews began to reclaim their share of history. With all its intellectual blinders, the Enlightenment touched the Jews both within their own circles and from without. It provided a mounting number of Jews with an incentive to rethink their frozen religious ritual; they were invited—or, rather, a few bold spirits among them invited themselves—to participate in the critical intellectual style of the *philosophes,* who were showing rebellious Jews the way by performing skeptical operations on Christian teachings. What is more, the Enlightenment gave some Germans a cause: the liberation of the Jews from their confined existence and from the laws that kept them chained to the status of second-class subjects. Moses Mendelssohn's good friend the poet, playwright, and critic Gotthold Ephraim Lessing was only the most conspicuous, and least bigoted, of this minority among eighteenth-century Germans ready to treat Jews as fully human. A new dispensation seemed at hand.

The age of emancipation, bringing the once parallel and distant lines of gentile and Jewish life closer together than they had been for many centuries, was the work of the nineteenth century. But it was not a sudden leap from crippling disabilities to full equality. Gentile Germans were too much at odds with one another to let the "Jewish question" resolve itself so quickly. An episode dating from around 1800 may illustrate this tension. At about sixteen, the young Bettina Brentano, later to become a collector of great men like Beethoven and Goethe and a prolific liberal polemicist, reported to her somewhat older half-brother, the poet Clemens Brentano, that "the young girl who is teaching us to embroider is a Jewess, she is called Veilchen." She found Veilchen (Violet) a "really caressing name." One morning, Bettina had gone to visit her and found her Jewish friend, broom in hand, sweeping in front of her door. So Bettina Brentano took a turn and did some sweeping herself. This impulsive gesture was reported to her aunt, who was much offended. Just think, she said, to be seen in public sweeping the sidewalk, and in the company of a Jewess!

Bettina thought the story amusing, for she found Veilchen pretty, clean, admirable, and always helpful. Veilchen loved flowers, Bettina told her brother, slaved for her family, and was desperately poor. Clemens Brentano, much taken with his sister and, displaying the wisdom of a twenty-year-old, intent on forming her, was not pleased. Earnestly, he tried to dissuade her from so close an association with a Jewish girl. But Bettina would not listen to him and remained on the friendliest terms with Veilchen. She even read to her friend the letters her clever brother sent her. "Look," Clemens remonstrated with her, "how you lower yourself handing out these confidences." This made Bettina a little angry, no matter how much she admired her brother, who, after all, knew so much more of the world than she did. "You say of her," she replied, "'she may be a good creature, to whom I lower myself with my confidences.' Who then am I, that I should condescend to a good creature when I take her into my confidence? Am I an angel?" She doubted it. "I believe that I raise myself to her rather than lowering myself!"

The nineteenth-century debate among gentiles on the shape German-Jewish life should take proceeded along the line of this family squabble: the Bettinas pressing for increased integration, Clemens and his allies advocating continued segregation. The issue was fought out within the Jewish community as well, so often a mirror, however distorted, of the larger society. And more than a mirror, for Germany's Jews were no longer merely the pliant playthings of their gentile masters. The Wissenschaft des Judentums, launched in the early nineteenth century, was a systematic effort at joining the cultural world in which Jews had so long lived as outsiders, all too often as pariahs; a scholarly, modern study of Jewish sacred texts, history, and communal life in all its phases including religious ritual, it reflected, and shared in, the intellectual effervescence generated by gentile researchers and philosophers.

As those who applauded the Wissenschaft des Judentums recognized, one entrance ticket to Western civilization was learning. Another, and one that a number of German Jews took in the course of the nineteenth century, was very different: conversion to Christianity. The majority of German Jews took no such drastic steps; they continued in their accustomed ways, glad of the opportunities that a slowly opening society was offering them. The passage of years gave realistic grounds for their hopes; slowly but distinctly, state after state expanded the rights of Jews until they were assimilated to the rights of all German citizens in 1871.

This optimistic appraisal should not be read to imply that the passage of time made the choices German Jews faced particularly easy. The new racial anti-Semitism transformed the slander against the Jew as Christ-killer to the slander of the Jew as exploiter and subverter. A poisonous mixture of pseudo-science and sheer assertion that secured substantial popular support late in the nineteenth century, it proved particularly hard to combat. To lend the appearance of scholarship to their bigotry, some anti-Semites gathered mountains of dubious, often manufactured materials proving that the wicked Jews had a stranglehold on economic life or were poisoning the population by intermarrying with "Aryan" women. Others, needing no evidence for their imaginative constructions of the Jew as devil, made it virtually impossible for sound evidence to dismantle their fantasies. If race is indeed a defining, unalterable human reality, as millions of educated and uneducated people alike came to believe, then no amount of kindness to Jews could change their real nature. If a Jew displayed certain unpleasant qualities that anti-Semites liked to associate with Jews—greed, loud behavior, dishonesty, sexual rapacity—these were taken as proof of the racist charge. If they were not in evidence, their absence only testified to Jewish cleverness.

In this uncertain atmosphere, gentile writers confronted their Jewish fellow citizens with stark alternatives. In 1855, the influential critic and, later, famous novelist Theodor Fontane offered such uncomfortable choices in a review of Gustav Freytag's enormously successful novel with a consummate Jewish villain, *Soll und Haben*. Fontane, who had many admiring Jewish readers, observed that the Jews belonged to Germany, "constituting an essential part of our society, our state. Granted, it would be better if they were not there or were different from what they are." But whatever, "there are only two ways of getting rid of them: the medieval *hepp!*

hepp! with scaffold and stake, or that gradual amalgamation which is the quiet blessing of tolerance and freedom." The respected Austrian sociologist Gustav Ratzenhofer put it more curtly half a century later, in 1907, in his posthumously published treatise, *Soziologie:* "The assimilation of intelligent Jewry would be for the other races, and the assimilation of poor Jewry would be for its own race, a benefaction, even salvation. The disappearance of Jewry is a presupposition of civilization." As gentiles tried to settle their fate, Jews in Germany did not simply stand by; they debated these suggestions, often fiercely. And the parties divided in ways I have noted before: there were many Jews who thought that total assimilation—dressing, speaking, celebrating holidays, and educating one's children precisely as Christians did—was the ideal solution to the "Jewish question"; they were challenged by others who were not impressed with a salvation that was tantamount to the Jews' disappearance into the general population.

Read after the revelations about Nazi Germany, the choices that Fontane and Ratzenhofer offered the German Jews appear particularly ominous. But thrown as they were into an ever-improving situation for these Jews despite all setbacks, such proposals made little impression in the years of the Jewish-German symbiosis. As more and more Jews attended German schools, spoke perfect German, and associated with Germans in business, they indulged their passion for German culture. Kant, Goethe, and Schiller were their writers, Bach, Beethoven, and Schubert their composers. Although a certain glass wall remained to separate most Jews from most gentiles even during the years of the closest intimacy, that wall seemed a mere brittle survival from more primitive days. Strongly dissenting from this cheerful vista, the Zionist Gershom Scholem warned early in the 1920s that the love affair between Jews and Germans, a matter for widespread self-congratulation before the war, was pathetically one-sided: the Jews loved the Germans, but the Germans did not love the Jews. It is hard to argue with him today. But was he right?

This question raises the most delicate issue of all, one that sparked the very writing of this book. The book is history above all, but it is also

history as a rescue operation. The Jews of Germany have had a bad press. They have been held at least partly responsible for their fate. Had they not, in the late nineteenth and early twentieth centuries, attempted to deny their Jewish heritage? Had they not fawned upon a people that did not really want them and in the end proved ready to murder them? These rhetorical questions have at times been asked with malicious intent. Did not Hitler's expulsion and murder of the German Jews serve them at least partly right? The Nazis as agents of an outraged God— it sounds bizarre, even inhuman, but it is often implied, and sometimes openly suggested.

That perspective on the Jews in German lands is not only cruel; it is unhistorical. If we put ourselves in their place—and a historical study can do no less—if we attempt to relive in our minds the experiences and read the signals to which they were exposed, we will, I think, arrive at a less censorious conclusion. To begin with, those signals were confusing and, around 1900, largely positive. The anti-Semitic political parties that had sprung up after the founding of the Reich were losing their appeal and their voters. The continuing obstacles to a career in the university came to seem relics of an earlier, less enlightened time. In 1887, the year before the accession of Emperor Wilhelm II, the prominent Jewish social psychologist Moritz Lazarus spoke for most of his coreligionists when he called the "Jewish question" a "German question." He saw it as a remnant of barbarism that Germany's Jews and Germany's gentiles must erase together. In any event, he added, "we are Germans, we must speak as Germans." If there were those who continued to deny Germany's Jews the right to speak as Germans, there were many others who were glad to grant it to them. Who was to say— before 1933—that Bettina Brentano did not represent the majority of her fellow citizens?

In short, the categorical charge that German Jews had betrayed their heritage is simply false. Many of them who were atheists made no secret of their Jewish background. Besides, not many Jews actually converted, whether from religious conviction or from craven opportunism. As the pages that follow leave no doubt, there have always been several ways of being Jewish, and in modern times the choices had become more diverse than ever.

And yet the history of German Jewry ends in a minor key. The world that seemed theirs is gone forever. Of the half-million Jews living in Germany when Hitler came to power—many of them under the laws of the Weimar Republic not Jews at all—some 170,000 were killed in the camps, and only a few thousand survived the war in hiding or by passing in Germany, often hidden by non-Jews. The fortunate remainder was dispersed to the far corners of the earth, finding a haven in the United States, Palestine, Britain, or South America. A small colony spent the war years in Shanghai, for a time the only place in the world that would have them. When refugees meet and exchange stories about their escape from Hitler and their lives abroad, each has a unique story to tell, yet each story is like all the others: a life bravely made over but also a dream lost forever. The German civilization they helped create, the pool of Jewish talent fed by a fostering few decades, are now things of the past. Present-day Germany is the poorer for it. The Austrian-Jewish novelist and essayist Friedrich Torberg put it bluntly but well: "With the destruction of part of European Jewry, a part of Western civilization, too, has been destroyed."

The remnant of Jews in Germany today is not a saving remnant but at best a fragile germ of a new community. Some forty thousand Jews live in the country now, but only a handful of them are German Jews. Most of them are the children, and the grandchildren, of East European Jews who came out of the camps in 1945, sat on their suitcases for some years certain that they would never live in Germany, and then drifted into staying. A few, a very few, of the refugees who saved themselves from Hitler decided to return, and they are now dying out. Some of the old synagogues, torched in November 1938, have been restored and are in use, but they hear other melodies and see other observances. Like the Easter Island statues, they mutely evoke a past that is fast slipping from living memory, suggesting by their very scale a great culture that no longer exists. For that culture, along with its creators, fell victim to the Nazi regime and to the camps and, like the Yiddish-speaking culture of Eastern Europe, is little more than a memory.

In an old German-Jewish tradition, this is a memorial book, but it has not been content with reciting the names of the dead. Rather, it wants to remember those who lived, the world they made, the lives they led, and the vitality they brought to German civilization. The horror of it all remains vivid: a culture that had been in the making for 1,600 years was destroyed in twelve. In that November night of 1938, the Kristallnacht, twelve hundred synagogues went up in flames, and in the next few years, Germany's half-million Jews were dispersed or exterminated, as Jewish neighborhoods were destroyed, and with all that, a whole way of life and being, with its quarrels, factions, schools, publications, businesses, theaters, and orchestras, passed out of existence. When war broke out in September 1939, some 200,000 Jews were still trapped in Germany, and only a few of them managed to flee to safety.

Yet the tragedy should not cast its shadow over the whole German-Jewish experience. This book, which also records the end, is principally a report on robust everyday life, the struggles and rewards of each epoch. Its gathering of quotations from contemporary letters, memoirs, newspapers, poems, and books of manners carries the voice of the past as the illustrations convey its images. It is a mosaic in time, with its account of a ninth-century Jewish agent performing ambassadorial services on a mission for Emperor Charlemagne; a thirteenth-century Jewish minnesinger; impressive medieval Jewish scholarship; a seventeenth-century pogrom in Frankfurt in which gentiles helped save their Jewish neighbors and the leading rioters were executed. It recalls the narrative ballad in Yiddish that the Frankfurt pogrom inspired as well as lines from the charming eighteenth-century memoir of Henriette Herz agonizing over whether as a respectable married woman she would have to wear an ugly wig to cover the beautiful hair of which she was so proud. Its earliest document is a fourth-century decree by the Roman emperor Constantine permitting Jews to hold office in Cologne. Among its latest are letters from Betty Scholem in Berlin writing during the Nazi years to her son Gershom in Palestine as the noose around the Jewish community was tightening. Without indulging in idealizing nostalgia or unhistorical criticism, we can see them as part of a long story, moving, terrifying, and exhilarating, a story now over.

The Jews of Germany

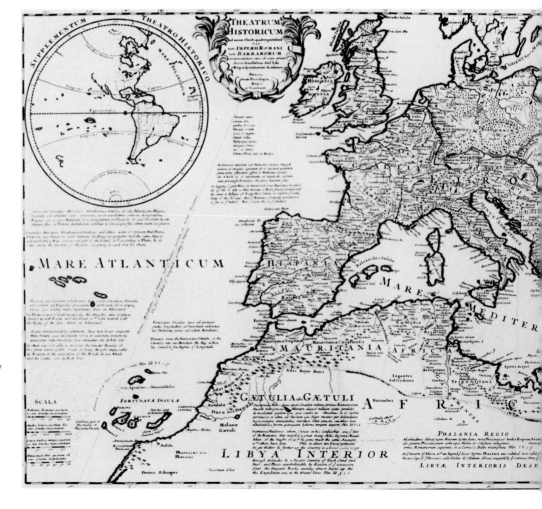

"A historical map of the Roman Empire and the neighboring Barbarous Nations in the year of our Lord Four Hundred . . . by William Del Isle . . . Paris, 1709." The map shows the Roman Empire as it looked when the first Jews were recorded in Germania.

Chapter One

Origins

Beginnings on the Rhine

Legends of beautiful Jewish maidens captured by Goths or Roman legionaires and brought from Jerusalem to the banks of the Rhine are the first sources for the antiquity of the Jews in German lands. Then there is the tale of a rabbinical council in Trier at the time of the trial of Jesus which responded to an inquiry from Jerusalem by advising against any severe measures. But these stories apart, the pivotal event underlying the Jewish presence in Germany was the fall of Jerusalem in 70 C.E., when the Roman legions destroyed the city and dispersed its population.

By then, some Jews had already had five centuries of experience with Diaspora living. The first dispersion dated from 586 B.C.E., when the victorious Nebuchadnezzar brought his Jewish

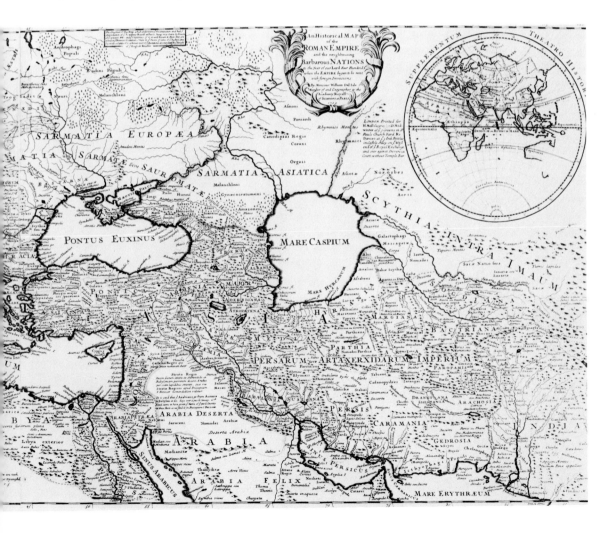

A fifteenth-century depiction of Roman Cologne. Hartmann Schedel, *Liber Chronicarum,* Nuremberg, 1493.

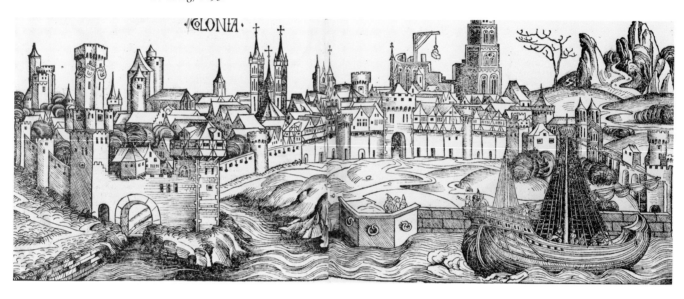

captives from Jerusalem to Babylon, where they founded a durable, illustrious community. The second dispersion, following the Roman victory, coincided with the planting of a new Roman colony on the Rhine. Established only two decades earlier, in 50 C.E., by veterans of the Roman legions, it was called Colonia Agrippinensis; later, the Germans called it Köln (Cologne). The colony functioned as the administrative headquarters for the Romans on the Rhine and rapidly grew into a thriving trade center as well as an agricultural settlement.

In the scattering that followed the Roman conquest of Judea, most of the Jews moved east, deeper into Mesopotamia, the old center of exile, and the bordering lands, Persia, Syria, and Arabia. Paradoxically, some also joined long-flourishing colonies in Italy and then moved with the Roman legions into the Rhineland. Cologne, the new colony, was a promising stopping place for the Jewish exiles, then essentially an agricultural people. By the third century, some Jews had become significant wine growers while others had established themselves as merchants, artisans, or doctors. Some may even have served in the Roman legions.

The first document establishing the antiquity of the Jews in Cologne is a decree by Constantine the Great in 321 ordaining that Jews could be called to the Curia, the city's governing body. This apparent honor had its hidden sting: as officials, members of the Curia were required to forward to Rome the revenue from taxes levied on the colony by the central treasury. Rich landowners and merchants had grown expert in evading exorbitant imperial taxation, and the poor had little to give. But Rome was not to be denied. Members of the Curia had to make up from their own pockets any shortfall between what they collected and the amount demanded by Rome. It was not an office, therefore, that anyone wanted or could evade; the decurion was almost a prisoner of his position, forbidden to move or sell property. His only escape was to transform drastically his status. Some victims, in desperation, chose to become monks or even serfs; others turned outlaw, joining bands of brigands in the countryside. This was the dubious privilege that Constantine bestowed on the Jews.

A second decree of 331 specifically exempted rabbis, especially the *Archisynagogis,* or Chief Rabbi, and officials of the Jewish community from curial service. Although these decrees tell no stories and name no names, we can extrapolate a picture of the Jewish community in the

Rhineland. The very fact that Jews were appointed to the Curia was a sign that enough of them were sufficiently prosperous to be squeezed for money. Since it is unlikely that their fortunes were made overnight, they must have been settled in Cologne for some time. And since the exemption of 331 refers to various rabbinical and communal officers, they must have lived in an organized community with a functioning synagogue.

These references in imperial decrees, scattered provisions of Roman law, accounts in chronicles, church records, municipal ordinances, archaeological excavations, local legends, and rabbinical sources all attest to the presence of Jews, but the intimate details of their lives remain in shadow. Only a few fixed points bridge the centuries after Constantine's decrees. The earliest comes in the form of a broken oil lamp in the Roman style found at Trier and dated to the fourth century C.E.

The next bit of evidence comes from the time of Charlemagne, some four centuries later. Isaac, a Jew of Aachen, was chosen by the emperor to accompany two emissaries to Harun al Rashid, the caliph of Baghdad. One aim of this embassy was to secure safe access for Christian pilgrims to the holy places in Jerusalem. Isaac, an experienced traveler in the Near East, was most likely sent as a guide and interpreter for the mission. On the return trip in 801, Charlemagne's two emissaries died, and it was left to Isaac to convey Harun al Rashid's gifts to the emperor when he finally got back in July 802. Sumptuous as they were in workmanship and materials—ivory chessmen, vessels of gold and silver, embroidered robes, ingenious clocks—nothing could compare with the sensation caused by the supreme gift, a young white elephant named Abulabaz. The elephant survived until 810, much loved and deeply mourned by Charlemagne. Its death was recorded in the Annals of the Kings of France (see plate 1)—but Isaac vanishes from history.

Two centuries later, two entries in the chronicles of Cologne record that the Jews built a synagogue in 1012 and that in 1075 they joined in mourning the death of Archbishop Anno, who insisted on his deathbed that his not-inconsiderable debts be paid in full whether the creditor was a Christian or a Jew. Ill-assorted as these scraps of history are, they yield a picture

Decree of the Emperor Constantine to Decurions at Cologne, December 11, 321. The text reads: "By a general law We permit all municipal senates to nominate Jews to the municipal council. But in order that something of the former rule may be left to them as a solace, We extend to two or three persons from each group the perpetual privilege of not being disturbed by any nominations." Clyde Pharr, ed., *The Theodosian Code and Novels and the Sirmondian Constitution,* New York, 1969.

Oil lamp showing a seven-armed terra-cotta candelabrum between palm leaves. Trier, fourth century.

of Jews living as an identifiable group in many of the communities along the Rhine. In these early centuries of Christian rule, as the pagan Roman order and pagan hegemony gave way to the church, the Jews emerged as only one of many peoples—Romans, Franks, Lombards, Saxons, Bavarians, Thuringians—making up the Holy Roman Empire. Whatever hostility early Christians had shown them had subsided into general acceptance, and under Charlemagne, Jews even enjoyed a certain favor.

In early medieval times, when the Catholic church was still fighting strong residues of paganism in Europe, Judaism was tolerated in a continuation of Roman and Carolingian policy. Carolingian law sought only to prevent Jews from proselytizing among Christians or subjecting their Christian servants to Jewish customs. At the same time, Jewish law was recognized as binding within the Jewish community, thus preserving for Jews, with their highly developed legal system, a significant measure of autonomy. With the death of Charlemagne and the collapse of his empire at the end of the ninth century, the importance of local princes, temporal and ecclesiastical, grew apace. Bishops were more than the spiritual leaders of their flocks; they were political rulers as well, concerned with such mundane matters as taxation, commerce, and defense. Although the church was careful to protect its newly won parishioners from any attempts to Judaize them, many centuries elapsed before Jews came to be treated as outcasts in a Christian world.

The decay of Roman rule had consequences beyond drastic changes in popular religion. As the imperial administrative network gave way, each principality was forced back onto its own resources rather than counting itself as part of a vast interlocking domain. Commerce was the first to suffer from this fragmentation. With no responsible authority to care for them, Roman roads and bridges fell into ruin and travel became not only physically punishing but dangerous, as bandits preyed on travelers. In consequence, the isolation of towns from one another made the merchant who would venture abroad particularly desirable. Recognizing the usefulness of the Jews for building up commerce in particular and the economy in general, at the end of the ninth century the bishops of Augsburg, Regensburg, and Salzburg invited Jews to settle in their domains. This was the beginning of a pattern to be repeated many times in later centuries.

During the Carolingian period, Jews had performed vital functions as importers of goods from the East. Isaac of Aachen was only the most prominent of a coterie of enterprising merchants whose arduous and dangerous expeditions separated them from their families for years at a time. In an otherwise closed-in world, they maintained the lifeline of trade between Western Europe and the East, venturing to Levantine centers of trade, such as Constantinople, Baghdad, Damascus, and beyond to India and China. From the Near East they brought slaves, furs, brocades, and swords, and from China spices, herbs, and other Eastern specialties.

By the tenth century, as the bishops increased their temporal power, "the Jews and other merchants" are mentioned in their edicts governing their cities. Among those cities were a number of important Jewish centers in the old Roman settlements along the Rhine: Cologne, Mainz, Speyer and Worms. The river was the artery along which people as well as goods moved, and new Jewish settlements continued to be founded up and down the Rhine into the fourteenth century, with major Jewish centers at Frankfurt am Main and Regensburg on the Danube as well. Dispersion, however, meant that outside the major cities only a few families were settled in each community. Estimates of the number of Jews in the German lands at the end of the fourteenth century range from 20,000 to

The initial B from a commentary on the Psalms written in St. Denis in the ninth century. The elephant head, bottom left, is probably Abulabaz drawn from life. (Color plate 1.)

An excerpt from the Chronicle, *written by Einhard of Franconia, Charlemagne's scribe and biographer.*

[In 801] the Emperor traveled to Pavia and there he received the news that the ambassadors of the Persian king, Harun al Rashid, had arrived in the harbor of Pisa. . . . They reported that the Jew Isaac, whom the emperor had despatched to the king of the Persians four years earlier with his ambassadors Lanfrid and Sigismund, was on his return journey, laden with great gifts. Lanfrid and Sigismund had both died on the way. Thereupon the emperor sent his notary Erkanbald to Liguria to prepare a fleet in which the elephant and whatever else was expected could be shipped. He himself, however, . . . returned to Gaul. In October, the Jew Isaac returned from Africa with the elephant and landed at Porto Venere, between Genoa and Leghorn. But because of the snow, he could no longer cross the Alps and remained over the winter at Vercelli. . . . On the twentieth of July [802] Isaac arrived [at the palace in Aachen] with the elephant and the other gifts of the Persian king and gave them to the emperor. The elephant was called Abulabaz.

Einhards Jahrbücher, *Leipzig, 1888.*

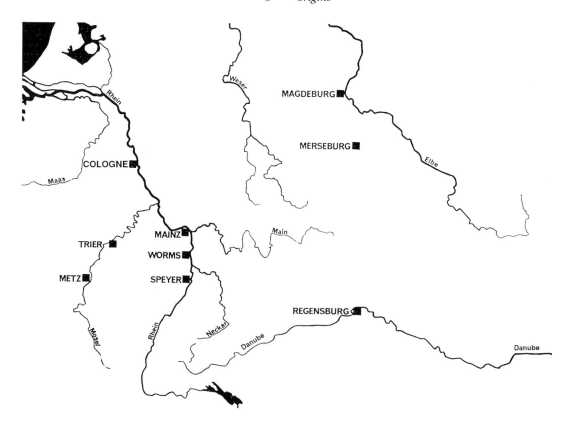

Major Jewish settlements in Germany up to the time of the Crusades. *Monumenta Judaica. Katalog,* Cologne, 1963.

50,000. In all of the Holy Roman Empire, including Switzerland and the Low Countries, there were 100,000 Jews, less than 1 percent of the total population of 12 million.

Despite their small numbers, Jews had an important place in the economy. Along the Rhine, they were active winegrowers. In addition to their activities in trade, they were skilled craftsmen—carpenters, masons, jewelers, and bookbinders—and this made them valuable additions to a town with an ambitious lord. In 1084, following a disastrous fire in Mainz, Bishop Rüdiger of Speyer, intent on transforming his hamlet into a seat worthy of his office, invited the Jews of Mainz to settle in his town. The effect of their presence, he declared, would be "to increase the luster of the city a thousandfold." That the Jews who accepted the bishop's invitation fully met his high expectations was demonstrated six years later. In February 1090, when Emperor Henry IV came to visit the dying Bishop Rüdiger, he took the opportunity to present to the emperor the leaders of the Jewish community, hoping to ensure continuation of the "privilege" he had issued on the Jews' arrival.

These much coveted "privileges" were both a form of protection and a license for exploitation. Although they guaranteed the safety of the

Jewish community, they also made it subject to the needs or whims of their overlord, who could tax or expel them at will. At Speyer, in fact, the privilege was renewed, and in the same year Henry IV issued a similar privilege to the Jews of Worms. It was bestowed on them through the leader of their community, Salman, whom the Germans called the Jewish bishop. This office, a symbol of Jewish autonomy, was widespread in German towns throughout the Middle Ages and continued in some places into the nineteenth century. (See the portrait of the last *Judenbischof* of Worms, p. 35.)

Such a pattern of privilege, protection, and intercession established a mode of Jewish life in the German lands that lasted well into modern times. But as a distinct community, the Jews of Ashkenaz (the Hebrew term for Germany) were only at the beginning of their extraordinary odyssey. In Ashkenaz they created a new language, a new culture, and a new center for Jewish life.

The Crusades

Memory, as the analyst Martin Bergmann has said, is a form of revenge, a resource Jews have long relied on. Eyewitnesses have held it their duty to record the martyrdom of those who died for the Sanctification of the Name, and Jewish prayer books to this day carry poems of mourning for events that occurred a millennium ago.

The Crusades gave Jews all too much to remember. The shock of the First Crusade of 1096, in which five thousand Jews fell to fanatical attacks on major communities on the Rhine, produced an unprecedented outpouring of literature, and not from Jews alone. In 1140, two retrospective accounts of these assaults were composed: one in Latin by a monk, Albert of Aachen, and one in Hebrew by Salamo bar Simeon, a Jew of Mainz. Remarkably, the two narratives corroborate each other in every detail. Albert relates how, after the pogroms, in their progress across Europe, the Crusaders were ignominiously routed by the Hungarians, who would not allow them to cross their land. Having condemned the bloodshed and plundering by the Crusaders all through his account, Albert finds in their defeat evidence of "the hand of God against the pilgrims who had sinned in the face of God in their unchastity and outrageous shamelessness." The Crusaders "had bloodily

Initial with a Crusader on horseback, from a manuscript copy of Albert von Aachen's history of the First Crusade (1096–99). Written in Latin around 1140, it appeared in Mönchengladbach under the title *Historia Hiersolymitana.*

The mass suicide at Worms, 1096.

A Christian and a Jew tell of the mass suicide at Worms, 1140.

When the Jews saw how the Christians advanced on them and their children and spared no one because of age, they seized their weapons and turned them against their own children and wives, mothers, and sisters, and killed one another in murder. It is a sin even to tell how mothers pierced and cut the throats of their nursing babes. For they preferred to die by their own hands than by the weapons of the uncircumcised.

Albert von Aachen, Geschichte der ersten Kreuzzugs, *Jena, 1923.*

The enemy took off their clothes, dragged them along the ground, and tossed them into a heap. They left no one alive except those few who were unwillingly forced into baptism. Eight hundred was the number of those murdered on that day, and they were all brought naked to their grave.

Salamo Bar Simeon, in A. Neubauer and M. Stern, eds., Hebräische Berichte über die Judenverfolgungen während der Kreuzzüge, *Berlin, 1892.*

The taking of Jerusalem, 1099. Johann Ludwig Gottfried, *Historische Chronicken . . . mit . . . Kupferstücken geziert und verlegt durch Mathaeum Merian,* Frankfurt, 1633.

A description of the capture of Jerusalem from a seventeenth-century German chronicle.

After Antioch and the greatest part of Syria were in Christian hands, the Crusade went directly on to the city of Jerusalem. The whole army celebrated Easter, which fell on the tenth of April, in Tripoli and Pentecost in Caesarea. On June 6 [1099] forty thousand foot soldiers and fifteen hundred horsemen laid siege to Jerusalem and with an attack on July 15, it was conquered. All the Turks and Saracens who were within the walls were cut down. The city was not plundered; instead the soldiers maintained the houses and everything that was in them in order to occupy them.

Johann Ludwig Gottfried, Historische Chronicken . . . Frankfurt, 1633*.*

murdered the homeless Jews." Even if the Jews "were the enemies of Christ," he believed, the Crusaders had acted "more out of greed than out of fear of God. For God," Albert concludes, "is a just judge, and he does not wish anyone to come under the yoke of Catholic belief against his will or through force."

The first Crusade was initiated by Pope Urban II at a church council at Clermont-Ferrand in November 1095. The pope, says Salamo bar Simeon, "let a call go out to all the people who believe in Christ" to "gather together and march on Jerusalem and conquer the city." But then "Satan came and mingled among the people," and they gathered "like one man in order to carry out the order. In numbers they were like the sands at the edge of the sea as they came by, and their voices resembled the roar of wind and storms."

That the horde was a deadly menace for the Jews along the Rhine emerged only after it appeared on their doorstep. At first, the Jews thought they would be required only to provide food and drink and pay tribute, as their brethren in France had done. But there was neither money enough among the Jews nor discipline enough among the Crusaders for such restraint to last long. Even the intervention of Emperor Henry IV, who was then in Italy and had put the Crusaders on notice that the Jews lived under his protection, could not stem the violence. For the Crusaders demanded not only plunder but the conversion of the Jews.

It was the call for conversion more than anything else, Salamo wrote, that led to grisly scenes as trapped Jews slaughtered one another rather than fall alive into the hands of their tormentors. Unlike many medieval chronicles, which are often highly stylized, Salamo bar Simeon's vivid report was based on interviews with survivors. "I inquired after all these events from the old people," he writes, "and have written down every fact in an orderly manner, according to their answers."

Salamo's account shows that the Jews were part of their world as in city after city they were defended by the ruling bishops or took refuge with their Christian neighbors. Yet most of the time the invading forces were too powerful to be stopped. Cologne, Mainz, Speyer, and Worms saw pitched battles; the greatest carnage was at Mainz, where eleven hundred Jews killed their families and themselves rather than accept baptism.

The bloody events of 1096 were an omen of the cruel anti-Semitism of the next century. The Crusaders themselves, trekking thousands of miles to rescue the Holy Land from the Muslim infidel, discovered that this infidel was the custodian of a sophisticated civilization. Not content with fighting a battle and drifting away, the Christian invaders stayed to build fortresses and castles and to administer their newly conquered lands.

In time they established trading posts in the Near East, exported goods to the West, had Arabic works of philosophy, science, and mathematics translated into Latin, and even added some of the manners of the Levant to Europe's courtly tradition. But what opened the world for Christians circumscribed it for Jews. In Near Eastern trade, where the Jews had once been a major force, the Crusaders who had taken up residence in the Holy Land preempted their place as traders. Indeed, over the next two centuries, the Jews' position in Europe was radically altered. Once a recognized if distinct element in the cultures in which they lived, they became literally marked men and women. They were pushed off the land, expelled from international trade, and channeled more and more into moneylending, that despised activity forbidden to Christians. By the end of the Crusades, early in the thirteenth century, Jews were no longer neighbors but the supreme infidels of Europe.

A People Apart

A New Language: Yiddish

Since the overwhelming evidence about Jewish life in the Middle Ages is religious—prayer books, ceremonial objects, synagogues, tombstones—it is easy to overlook the fact that the Jews shared the everyday world with their neighbors, spoke their language, and absorbed their culture. Yet one of their poets, Süsskind von Trimberg, was perhaps unique in his time as a troubador, traveling from court to court. He died in 1250, but six of his poems have survived, all written in the contemporary Middle High German. With their melancholic and philosophical themes, they reveal a courtly singer who avoided such favorite Christian subjects as

I would be but a fool

To pursue my art

When the lords no longer sustain me.

So I will flee their court.

I will let my beard grow long

With all its gray hairs,

And I will now go on through life

In the old Jewish manner,

In a cloak, long and broad,

With my hat pulled low,

Timid and with a humble mien.

And will but seldom sing courtly songs,

Banished from the favor of the lords.

Friedrich Heinrich von der Hagen, Minnesinger, Leipzig, 1838.

Süsskind von Trimberg in 1225 as he appeared in a court case relating to family property in Würzburg. He stands before an abbot who holds a bishop's crook, with the banner of his order over his head. Although Süsskind is richly dressed in a fur-lined cloak, he wears the yellow funnel-shaped Jews' hat and a long beard.

Marriage scene with jesters. Yahuda Haggadah, German, mid-fifteenth century.

earthly and heavenly love and instead chose to sing of poverty, the passage of time, sin, and the grace of God.

But in 1221, his wanderings came to an end as Emperor Frederick II enforced the rulings of the Lateran Council of 1215. In that council, cardinals and bishops had devised distinctions between Jew and Christian which had not previously existed in Europe—most notoriously the identifying badge that Jews were compelled to wear. This symbolic exclusion from European society put an end to Süsskind's career as a troubador, a fate he commemorated in a poem depicting his transformation from a courtier to a humble, bearded Jew.

Although Süsskind von Trimberg seems to have been unique among the Jews of his time, minstrels were not. Well into the nineteenth century, no German Jewish wedding or other festivity was complete without minstrels to sing, play, and improvise verses about the principals. Paradoxically, these performers, who were an indispensable part of Jewish popular life, were actually transmitting and preserving the courtly style long after the Middle Ages, long after the disappearance of the courts that had known Süsskind. The *Spilman,* or minstrel, composed his own songs as well as adapting the songs and poetry of his day for his Yiddish-speaking audiences. So ingrained was this institution that when German Jews began migrating to Poland in the thirteenth century, the *Marshalik,* or *Badchan,* as he was later called, became no less a fixture in East European life.

Yiddish emerged as a language on the Rhine around the ninth century composed of Germanic, Latin, and Hebrew elements, it soon became the private language of the Jews. By the thirteenth century it had developed a character and literature of its own, although much early Yiddish prose consists of adaptations of current romances, poems, and legends. The appetite for popular romances was extremely eclectic, drawing on Spanish, Italian, French, English, and Near Eastern sources as well as such German staples as the Nibelungen saga. These tales traveled rapidly from German into Yiddish, first being transmitted orally, then being committed to paper in manuscript form, and much later appearing in print. The legends of King Arthur's court turned up in German verse in the thirteenth century and began circulating in Yiddish, in rhymed couplets, a century later. In the Yiddish translation, of course, all pious Christian elements were excised, and domestic themes, the family and conjugal love, took on new prominence. Despite the disdain of learned Jews for this frivolous literature, the Arthurian cycle went through many Yiddish versions, so that as late as 1789, a new edition imaginatively transformed the son of Sir Gawain into a Chinese prince.

The equally durable saga of Sir Bevis of Hampton underwent a similar transformation. It went first into French, where the hero became Beauvais, then into Italian as Bovo, and finally emerged in fifteenth-century German as the *Bovo Buch.* From this version it was translated into Yiddish as the *Bovo mayse* (Bovo tale). The title, which in time became *Bobo mayse,* is used in Yiddish to this day to describe any tall tale.

In a period when few except clerics or learned men could write, the high level of literacy among Jews created an instant audience for printed works. But it was a special audience. Like their gentile counterparts, who spoke the vernacular but wrote about philosophy or theology in their sacred language, Latin, educated Jews wrote in *their* sacred language, Hebrew. The audience for popular Yiddish literature, therefore, was made up chiefly of women, who were generally excluded from higher learning, and of men without advanced Hebrew erudition. That these works were considered somehow tainted emerges from a ruling by the mystic Rabbi Judah ben Samuel late in the twelfth century that pious books were not to be bound in parchment on which the verses of romances had been written. (See pp. 15 and 18.) Nevertheless, romance literature continued to flourish. The intimate relationship between its public and the writers is attested by innumerable prefaces

An illumination from a Pentateuch dating from ca. 1300, showing how Jews saw the knights who figured in their ballads. The text, from Numbers 54, reads, "The Israelites shall camp each with his standard under the banners of their ancestral house." (Color plate 2.)

The opening verses of a Yiddish version of King Arthur's Court

All my days, I have heard much of King Arthur's court,

As in the old proverb,

"Here things go on as if it were King Arthur's court."

And although I have traveled through many lands,

I have never been able to find or read a book

About the way it really was

Until one day, in my father's house, I found such a one. . . .

It is called "King Arthur's Court or Sir Wieduwilt"

And is worth its price, telling

How this Sir Wieduwilt strove and struggled

With many a powerful giant and dragon.

And of what sort of man he was, you will get to read in this book.

Therefore come quickly and buy this pretty tale.

Johann Christoph Wagenseil, Belehrung der jüdisch-teutschen Schreibart . . . *Königsberg, 1699.*

An example of Weiber-Teitsch from a minhag book printed in Fürth in 1692. Minhag books, which were instruction manuals on how to observe the holidays, used the square type for the Hebrew prayers and the headings but Weiber-Teitsch for the main text.

caressingly promising readers that the work is "as tasty as milk and cake."

In a seventeenth-century edition of the Arthurian romances, the author is quite frank about the fading position of Hebrew in popular use:

Listen here, dear people,
Because the time has come
When people do not read gladly in the Holy Tongue
And enjoy Yiddish instead.

Another seventeenth-century author recommends his version of *King Arthur's Court* as a guide to behavior in royal and courtly society. "From it," he says in his preface, "one can learn how to speak correctly on every occasion with lords and princes and noblemen."

For all the widening stream of Yiddish literature, it remained for centuries a second-class literary medium, although it was securely the language of everyday Jewish life. An index of its standing was the way printers dealt with it. Although essentially German in its vocabulary, Yiddish was written in Hebrew script, but in popular works intended for women, printers set the text in a special semicursive type instead of the square Hebrew font used for prayer books and learned works. This special type was called *Weiber-Teitsch,* "women's Yiddish."

The plebeian standing of Yiddish romances could not restrain the popular appetite. At the same time, authors progressed from adaptations to original compositions drawing upon time-honored Jewish sources. Yet even these were embedded in the literary conventions of the period. The strophes of the Nibelungen saga were put to work relating the adventures of such Jewish heroes as David, Samuel, and Samson. By the sixteenth century, collections of tales culled from rabbinic literature as well as stories built around biblical figures and famous rabbis achieved considerable circulation. One collection, the *Ma'aseh Buch* (Story book) even features Rabbi Judah the Pious, the same Judah ben Samuel who had inveighed against this form. At a time when gripping events were captured by broadsides featuring lurid pictures with accompanying verses, Jews also resorted to poetry about events in their lives, composing long ballads to be sung to popular tunes. Yiddish was very much of, and in, the world.

Yiddish was the vehicle, too, for histories, moral and religious tracts, and memoirs. Heading the list of religious works was, of course, the Bible, translated into Yiddish for use by women as early as the fifteenth century. But far surpassing it in popularity was the *Ze-enah u re-enah*, from the verse in the Song of Songs (3:2) beginning, "Go out and seek." This compendium first appeared at the end of the sixteenth century and maintained its place as the preeminent version of the Bible for women into the twentieth century. It contained the text of the Scriptures divided to conform to the portions that were read each week in the synagogue, an annual cycle whose completion was celebrated with the holiday of Simhat Torah. A woman who never attended the synagogue was thus able to keep in step with the portion of the week, which was embellished for her in the *Ze-enah u re-enah* with exegetical comments, parables, and homilies. The book offered, in effect, a home-study course. Having appeared in more than two hundred editions across the Yiddish-speaking world by the nineteenth century, the *Ze-enah u re-enah* proved one of the most enduring of Yiddish works, making the sacred a familiar part of everyday life.

Learning and Pietism in Ashkenaz

Although the mainstream of Jewish learning descended from the academies in Babylonia and Palestine, the proliferation of the Diaspora communities dispersed centers of authority no less than people. Just as the Spanish Jews developed their philosophy, poetry, and theology in response to the surrounding Spanish and Arabic culture and the systems of Greek philosophers, the Jews of Ashkenaz constructed an intellectual world of their own by weaving old traditions into new patterns. Ancient practices brought from Palestine survived for generations in the new Diaspora settlements. In tenth-century Cologne, for example, the same four tones were still blown on the shofar on the Day of Atonement as were once heard in the Temple. Such customs, while forming the basis of Jewish life and belief, could not remain frozen for all time. Although the Jews of Ashkenaz were noted for their observance of commandments, the stresses of external events and the natural ferment of ideas produced revisions and inventions.

For centuries, the Jews along the Rhine had looked to the Italian Jewish communities, among the oldest in the Diaspora, as their spiritual mentors. "Learning comes from Bari," they said, "and the word of God from Otranto." Indeed, at the end of the tenth century, the study of the Talmud received a new impetus as the Kalonymus family of Mainz, originally from Lucca, imported scholars from Italy. The new arrivals brought accurate texts and interpretative skills.

Yet the German communities did not remain in a state of tutelage. By the end of the tenth century, Rabbi Gershom of Mainz had emerged as a leader in Jewish thought. Known as the Light of the Exile, he issued legal decisions that had a powerful effect on Jewish life across Western Europe. Most famous among them are the prohibitions of bigamy and of divorce against the wife's will, and his declaration that personal correspondence is inviolable.

It is one of the marvels of Jewish life in the Diaspora that without a secular arm to enforce judgments, without sanctions stronger than moral authority, the Jews of Western Europe built a durable, highly regulated form of self-government. Rulings and opinions echoed from community to community as students traveled to distant places to seek out famous teachers. The best known of these teachers is Rashi (an acronym for Rabbi Solomon ben Isaac), born in Troyes in 1040, who around 1060 went to study with the illustrious scholars in Worms. Upon his return to Troyes, he wrote one of the most enduring commentaries on the Bible and founded his own influential school, which became a major force in Jewish thinking all across Europe.

Jewish learning is both narrow and deep; for more than two millennia it has been occupied with the single task of interpreting the Bible. But the forms of interpretation have varied greatly: theological, legal, popular, mystical. All these found their expression in Ashkenaz. Among them, mystical teachings, regarded with awe and fear, remained distant from the mainstream of theological and legal readings of Scriptures. They were so closely associated with magic that their study was restricted to those considered old and sage enough to withstand the dangers. Known as *kabbalah* (a Hebrew term meaning "that which was received"), these mystical works formed a secret tradition handed on through the generations by its initiates.

The house of study (*Bet ha-midrash*) adjoining the synagogue in Worms where Rashi studied. He left in 1065 to return to Troyes, but a chair thought to be his was preserved until 1938, when the synagogue was destroyed during the Night of Broken Glass, November 9–10.

When a pietist school of interpreters grew up in the German lands in the late twelfth century, it was a true innovation in Jewish learning, but its founders claimed to trace their lineage as far back as Sinai, thus endowing their work with the prestige of antiquity. The founder of this movement, known as the Hasidei Ashkenaz (Pious of Germany), was Rabbi Samuel of Speyer, a member of the revered Kalonymus family. Although his movement shared some of the hallmarks of the mystics—secrecy, selectivity in the transmission of ideas, interpretation of numbers and letters to penetrate the hidden meaning of the sacred texts, and penitential exercises—the doctrine was straightforward. At Sinai, God had handed down three kinds of law: the explicitly written, meant for all Israelites; that which forms the basis of the legal rabbinic tradition; and the esoteric teaching transmitted through generations to those found worthy. The righteous therefore need to seek out the hidden law, the secret will of God, by going beyond the commandments sufficient for ordinary Jews. Central to the Pietists' practice was a system of penances for every infringement of the law: but in return for this severity, the Hasidei Ashkenaz, like other religions of the meek, promised joy and honor in the world to come.

Better known than Rabbi Samuel was his son, Judah the Pious, who became the model for the movement and a legend almost within his lifetime. The rigorous demands of his sect and its addiction to number mysticism kept it to a small elite. Their distinctive habits and esoteric pace—they would pause during services to contemplate and interpret the mystical meanings of individual words—soon isolated the "Pious" from other Jews, and led the "Good" to found their own synagogues. They married among themselves and even insisted that they not be buried next to "the Wicked"—other Jews. Striving for personal perfection, they insisted on high moral standards; the book associated with Rabbi Judah, the *Sefer Hasidim* (Book of the Pious), is filled with cautionary tales and ethical exhortations.

What had been secret doctrine until Rabbi Judah's death in 1217 was opened to the world by his disciple Eleazar of Worms, also of the Kalonymus family, who published all that had been concealed. In this and other respects Eleazar smoothed the way for reconciling Pietism with conventional Jewish life. Rather than insisting on separate communities of the elect, he shifted the emphasis to personal striving for perfection that did not require isolation and in fact made allowances for the long-standing customs of Jewish communal life.

Such policies, coupled with Eleazar's efforts to popularize Pietism, made it accessible and acceptable to Jews in Ashkenaz. In time, Rabbi Judah and Rabbi Samuel became the heroes of tales relating their pious deeds and miracles; four centuries later, in 1602, these tales were collected in a book of popular stories printed at Basel in Yiddish. The days of the Hasidei Ashkenaz, as the righteous outsiders in Israel, were over as the austere rabbis Samuel and Judah

***From the* Sefer Hasidim *(Book of the Pious), "About Relations
with People: Business Connections, Marriage Ties, Attitudes
toward Servants and Animals":***

*One recognizes three types in three situations: the humble in anger,
the hero in battle, and the friend in time of need. If you want to be
friends with someone, first find out what company he keeps. If you
speak at night, lower your voice; if you speak during the day, look
about and take care even though there is a wall behind you; if your
foot stumbles, then one can mend the damage, but if your tongue
stumbles, then death may be the consequence.*

Moritz Güdemann, Geschichte des Erziehungswesen und der Cultur der abendländischen Juden,
Vienna, 1880.

Opening page of the
Sefer Hasidim, writ-
ten in Germany in the
late thirteenth cen-
tury. This is from the
only surviving manu-
script of the work.

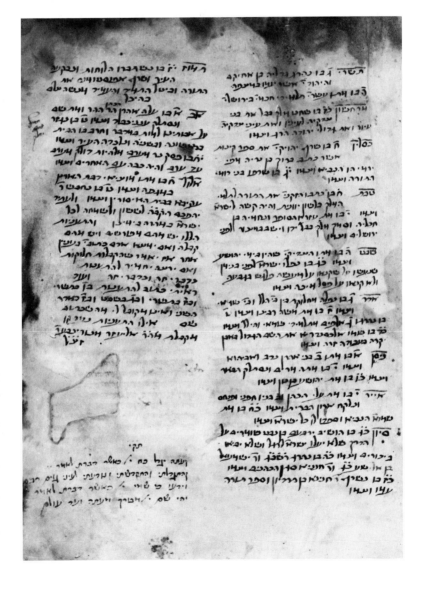

were metamorphosed into folk heroes who took their place by the side of biblical patriarchs and talmudic sages.

In a world in which both Christians and Jews took for granted the presence of demons and ghosts, good and bad spirits, angels and celestial voices, where amulets, incantations, and spells were a regular means of coping with sickness and misfortune, the distance between the magic of the mystics and the magic of daily life was easily bridged. For Jews, the ever-recurring question of just when the Messiah would come was the subject of intricate mathematical calculations by mystics whose conclusions were eagerly received by the uninitiated. While scholars ruminated and speculated in a remote world of their own, their ideas found a ready echo in the lives of ordinary Jews. Still, mystical doctrines were, for the Jews of Ashkenaz, an underground stream that surfaced only at special moments. Ultimately, it was not the esoteric doctrine of the Hasidei Ashkenaz that survived but its ethical teachings, incorporated into German Jewish life through legend and precept. It was mysticism with a difference, mysticism in the service of morality.

Dress: From Distinction to Dishonor

Long before the yellow badge and other demeaning requirements set them apart, the Jews were distinguished by their dress. This was hardly exceptional in the Middle Ages, when position in society was a matter of birth, and status could easily be read from what one was allowed—or required—to wear. Such formal regulations were part of the medieval legal arsenal. Beginning in the fourteenth century and surviving for four hundred years, sumptuary laws were a fact of life for everyone in the German lands. An orderly society was a hierarchical society, divinely ordained, and the apparel that distinguished one order from the other was its palpable demonstration. A farmer, no matter how prosperous, must not wear velvet and furs.

In this world, the Jewish man, dressing in accordance with biblical injunctions, was easily identified by his untrimmed beard and his hat. Although married Jewish women lived under their own constraints—especially that their hair be covered—the men were particularly conspicuous. Indeed, Jewish merchants setting out on a journey would try to avoid trouble by taking care to dress in uncharacteristic fashion: sometimes they even disguised themselves as clerics. But it was not until the thirteenth century that the Jewish difference in attire was made a matter of compulsion rather than choice.

In November 1215, some twelve hundred cardinals, bishops, abbots, and priors met at the Church of San Giovanni in Laterno in Rome. This Fourth Lateran Council, presided over by Pope Innocent III, sought to establish the visible power of Christianity on earth. Innocent, who ten years earlier had proclaimed the "eternal servitude" of the Jews in the Christian world, now went a step further, into the realm of sexual connection. "It happens at times," states canon 68, "that through error Christians have relations with the women of Jews or Saracens, and Jews or Saracens with Christian women. Therefore, that they may not under pretext of error of this sort excuse themselves in the future for the excesses of such prohibited intercourse, we decree that such Jews and Saracens of both sexes in every Christian province and at all times shall be marked off in the eyes of the public from other people through the character of their dress." From then on, Jews were compelled to wear some distinctive emblem, a certain style of hat, cloak, veil, or footgear. It was not until the fifteenth century, however, that the yellow badge was introduced in Germany. The ordinance was first enacted in Augsburg in 1434 and broadened in 1451 at a provincial synod in Bamberg to include nine additional cities. Distinction had become dishonor.

The fateful Lateran decree, gradually taken up and variously enforced across Christendom, endured for some four centuries. It made the Jew into an outcast. "The Jew badge," the liberal nineteenth-century German-Jewish historian Heinrich Graetz observed, "was an invitation to every street-urchin to insult the wearers, and to bespatter them with mud; it was a suggestion to stupid mobs to fall on them, to maltreat and even to kill them; and it afforded the higher classes an opportunity to ostracize the Jews, to plunder them, or to exile them." Perhaps worse, Graetz added, was the demoralization it caused among Jews, who felt their distinctive attire to be onerous in the extreme. As long as the badge was required, they made serious efforts to buy

The Lateran Council.
Hartmann Schedel,
Liber chronicarum,
Augsburg, 1500.

themselves free by bribing their local lord. At times they succeeded.

But meanwhile their own sumptuary laws—regulating how much affluence could be displayed in clothing, in ornament, at banquets—provided the Jewish community with some protection. These self-imposed decrees were intended to moderate the grossest differences within the community so that the poor would not be shamed by their meager feasts or by the contrast in attire. But they also served to reduce Jewish visibility to the outside world by prohibiting ostentation. It was one way of surviving in a censorious, often bitterly hostile gentile world.

"A yellow ring on coat or cap, not covered over, shall always and publicly be worn by Jews for their identification." J. C. Lünig, *Des teutschen Reichs-Archivs . . .*

Leipzig, 1713. Drawing by Johann Jacob Schudt, *Jüdische Merckwürdigkeiten,* Frankfurt and Leipzig, 1714. Reproduced at actual size.

Jews of Worms in the second half on the sixteenth century, with the yellow ring on their cloaks.

The yellow badge for Jews was first generally required in Germany in 1530 with the publication of section 22 of the Imperial Police Code.

Concerning the Dress of Jews

1. The Jews shall wear a yellow ring on their coat or cap wherever they go, unconcealed and publicly, so that they may be recognized.

2. And in order that this regulation and statute concerning their clothing and ornaments may be more firmly observed and enforced, we require . . . that when anyone has transgressed and violated this law . . . then he shall be punished with confiscation of the clothes or ornaments and by a fine twice the value of the clothes or ornaments.

Johann Christian Lünig, Des Teutschen Reichs-Archivs . . . *Leipzig, 1713.*

Anti-Semitism

How Jews were seen over the centuries by their neighbors in the German lands tells us a great deal about the neighbors and not very much about the Jews, since each age invented the creature it tilted against. During the first millennium, when newly made Christians in the Rhine valleys and Bavarian forests listened dutifully to the missionaries, doctrine served to define the place of the Jews in the Christian community. The Jews, said Saint Augustine, had major significance for Christian life: they served as a constant reminder of the error of the synagogue in not recognizing the truth of Christian teachings and the divinity of Christ.

This perspective governed the first thousand years of European Christianity. Jews were hardly corporeal villains. Even their wicked rejection of Christ was part of the divine scheme. In church portals, in stained glass, and in paintings, the synagogue was portrayed as a standing female figure, her bandaged eyes demonstrating that she has not yet seen the true light. Similarly, scenes of the Annunciation showed Mary with a book falling from her hand, to indicate that now, with the advent of the Saviour, she could discard the Old Testament. The Jew, then, had a place in the Christian world as an admonitory figure of proselytizing yet to be done.

Although spiritually excluded from the gentile community, a stranger to the ways of his neighbors, living by a different code, the Jew nevertheless participated in daily life. Despite the outrages that accompanied the Crusades, it was not until the thirteenth century that the parallel existence of Jew and Christian suddenly became charged with the fury that would poison Jewish existence. In a single century, distinctive Jewish dress was introduced, the blood libel was invented, and Jews were first depicted as Satanic figures. In the German lands alone a particularly disgusting portrait emerged: the Jew as the familiar of the pig. As Christians were aware, Jews felt a special repugnance toward pigs, whose flesh was forbidden food. Linking the two therefore had a particular appeal for malevolent caricaturists in Germany.

In the fatal thirteenth century, too, Jews were banished from England and from many parts of France. In 1242, the first burning of the Talmud took place in Paris after a formal theological disputation between Christian clerics and learned Jews—a disputation that the Jews, not surprisingly, lost. Twenty-four wagonloads of copies of the Talmud and other Hebrew manuscripts were brought to a square in Paris and ceremoniously incinerated. This was one of the more spectacular Talmud burnings, but not the only one, and it explains why so few Hebrew or Yiddish manuscripts dating from before the thirteenth century have survived. The oldest *mahzor* (festival prayer book) still extant was written in 1290 in Esselingen.

In the German-speaking lands, the Franciscan friar Berthold von Regensburg, a compelling orator who preached in earthy and eloquent German to enraptured audiences, made the Jews his special target: they were allies of the devil and obstinate in their refusal to accept Christ. Further—and here he sounded a note taken up by later anti-Semites—Jews were a danger to Christians, with their low morals in business and their private libertinism. While Berthold was scoring rhetorical triumphs in the towns of Germany, Switzerland, Austria, Bohemia, and France, brother friars in his home monastery at Augsburg were preparing legislation against the Jews. The new code they devised for Bavaria, called the *Schwabenspiegel,* hemmed in the Jews with new, humiliating restrictions. Jews were, for one thing, no longer permitted to bear arms. In a martial society, this left them defenseless not just against brigands on the road but also against unlawful attacks on their person or their property. Unarmed, in a class with women and priests, the Jewish man naturally gained a reputation for cowardice across Europe.

The thirteenth century, then, transformed the Jewish condition. In part, the Jews' deteriorating status stemmed from the struggle between the papacy and the temporal powers. The rulers of the Catholic church wanted to exert control not only over the souls but also over the society of Christians. In such a society, there was no room for heretics, pagans—or Jews. The Jews found allies of sorts in the Holy Roman emperor and in certain princes who regarded their beliefs and practices as less important than their ability to pay taxes. Under the emperor's direct protection, the Jews became *servi camerae,* serfs of the imperial chamber. This status proved immensely valuable to them, since it freed them from the tyranny of their local lord or city coun-

A statue representing the Synagogue, originally in the west portal of the Liebfraukirche in Trier, carved ca. 1250. This figure and its counterpart, Ecclesia (the Church), are the oldest of the very few surviving portal figures in the Rhineland. Blind to the new dispensation of Christianity, the Synagogue is shown as a woman with her eyes bound. Divested of the symbols of her former majesty, her crown falling from her head, she holds the broken scepter in one hand and the overturned tables of the law in the other.

In popular broadsides, the Jew was depicted sucking the milk of a pig, drinking its urine, or riding on its back, often in the devil's company.

The Esslingen Mahzor, a book of prayers for the holidays, is the earliest dated Ashkenazic manuscript. Completed in 1290 in the town of Esslingen, it contains the prayers for Yom Kippur and Sukkot. Until recently it was thought that only the portion at the Bibliotheca Rosenthaliana in Amsterdam had survived. In 1989, Evelyn Cohen, Curator of Prints at the Library of the Jewish Theological Seminary in New York, recognized the remarkable similarity between the Esslingen Mahzor and an undated manuscript in the Seminary Library, and they were brought together for an exhibition in Amsterdam in 1990. Upon comparison, the volume in the Seminary Library proved indeed to be the missing first part of the Esslingen Mahzor.

A devotional poem for Yom Kippur, from the Esslingen Mahzor in Amsterdam.

"The mighty king." A page from the Esslingen Mahzor in New York.

Desecration of the host at Sternberg, 1492. George Liebe, *Das Judentum in der deutschen Vergangenheit*, Leipzig, 1903.

bleed. The irony of these libels is that, just as the pig is strictly taboo in Jewish law, so is blood, because, according to Leviticus 17:14, it contains the spirit of life and must be poured away.

The blood libel first appeared in Germany in 1235 in Fulda, when several children died in a fire at a mill at Christmas. Jews were accused of having murdered the children in order to make healing potions from their blood. In retribution, thirty-two Jews were killed on the spot under the orders of the prince abbot of Fulda. The Jews who survived protested to Emperor Frederick II against the injustice while the abbot, in turn, sent the bodies of the children to the emperor as supporting evidence. Frederick remained skeptical about the Jews' guilt and initiated a thorough investigation, inviting baptized Jews among others to testify on Jewish practices and beliefs. A year later, the emperor absolved the Jews of every suspicion of guilt and renewed the Privilege originally issued by Henry IV in 1157, declaring them under his direct protection. Yet though Frederick's absolution cleared the Jews for a time, and in 1247 Pope Innocent IV issued a further proclamation against the blood libel, the idea survived and flourished.

The most sensational case, that of the infant Simon of Trent, neatly combining the themes of crucifixion and blood libel, exploded in Italy in 1475 and reverberated across Europe. A widely circulated and imaginatively illustrated account in the Nuremberg Chronicle, that universal history of the world published in both Latin and German in 1493, relates that one Passover, Jews in the city of Trent, in northern Italy, found themselves without the "Christian blood they needed for their unleavened bread." So "they secretly brought this child," the infant Simon, "into the Jew Samuel's house," crucified him, gathered his blood, and "hurried to their evening meal," eating "their unleavened bread made with the blood, while reviling Christ our Saviour." Then they "threw the corpse into a body of flowing water near their house." At the trial, Samuel and a number of other Jews—including several German Jews who were visiting Trent—confessed under torture and were executed. Skeptical of the convictions, Pope Sixtus IV ordered two additional trials, in which it emerged that a Swiss who had lost a lawsuit against Samuel was the probable murderer and accuser. But the deadly libel had developed a

cil. But such favors came at the price of tribute money, and the protection they provided was limited. Succeeding generations of Jews, blamed for natural and manmade catastrophes, faced ever greater constrictions and mounting persecutions. Finally, in the fifteenth century, the city of Frankfurt instituted the ghetto, into which its Jews were literally locked up every night.

In these turbulent centuries, two accusations against the Jews took root and were acted upon in a series of spectacular trials. The first charged Jews with ritual murder, an obscene parody of the crucifixion. The second, which caught the popular imagination with exceptional vividness, charged them with blood libel, letting the blood of a kidnapped Christian child for magical, healing, or ceremonial purposes. Related to both was the accusation of piercing the Host, which, as the living body of Christ, would then

An imaginary reconstruction of the murder of Simon of Trent, published two decades after the event. The conspirators, whose names are written over their heads, are shown collecting Simon's blood in a basin. The man on the left wears the Jew's hat, and all have the yellow ring on their cloaks. Hartmann Schedel, *Liber chronicarum*, Nuremberg, 1493.

momentum of its own. In Frankfurt, the story so captured the city fathers' imagination that they commissioned a depiction of Simon's martyrdom even more gory than the one illustrated in the Nuremberg Chronicle. It was painted on the Bridge Portal at the entrance to the city complete with a cartoon reviling the Jews. Then reports of miracles attributed to the murdered child began to circulate, and in 1575 he was beatified by Pope Gregory VIII.

Medieval and early modern anti-Semitism, then, had various roots: superstition, fear and antipathy toward the stranger, and the ineradicable animosity of devout believers against the crucifiers of Christ. Combined, they made a potent brew with intoxicating results. Gentiles also had less purely irrational reasons for finally setting the Jew apart: he was a business competitor and yet outside the restraining guild system. Moreover, he was the ubiquitous moneylender, plying a trade forbidden to Christians and making himself their creditor. It was only too tempting to banish or burn the Jew when debts became too heavy. By the time the Black Death scourged Europe, the time was ripe to cast out the Jew entirely.

The Black Death

The plague that swept across Europe in 1348 and 1349 took its toll not only among those afflicted with the disease. Seeking causes for the calamity that carried off between a quarter and a half of Europe's population, rumor mongers pointed to the Jews. The first explanation of the epidemic advanced by scholars was an unfavorable astrological conjunction. But this proved unsatisfactory, and other causes—bad air, contagion, the devil—were proffered. As the bubonic plague spread, bands of Flagellants made their way through the Rhineland, conducting public rituals of self-mortification. They deeply impressed the populace. Bystanders even ran to collect the blood, reported to possess marvelous healing powers, from the wounds of these holy men. The leaders of the penitents, however, were also preachers spreading a particularly virulent form of Jew-hatred. New accusations proliferated: the Jews seemed curiously exempt from the plague, fewer of them died, and, most damaging of all, they had caused the plague by poisoning wells.

Retribution was swift and terrible. In Strasbourg, two thousand Jews were burned on orders of the city council. There were massacres of Jews in 350 towns, and in 210 of these, every single Jew was murdered. Motives were mixed: in Strasbourg in February 1349, as the ashes cooled at the place of execution, townspeople pawed through the charred remains hoping to find jewelry that might have survived the fire. With the introduction of printing, the portrait of the Jew as the enemy of Christianity became fixed in the European mind. In the Nuremberg Chronicle, he plays his usual contradictory roles—as the heroic figure in tales from the Old Testament and as the villain in contemporary times, usually meeting a gruesome end. "The wretched, miserable, and desperate people, the Jews," as the chronicle terms them, were seen finally through their putative crimes against Christianity.

Those Jews who could escape from this charnel house fled, and the founding of populous communities in Eastern Europe owes its impetus to the refugees from the massacres that followed the Black Death. There were only nine Jewish settlements in Poland at the end of the fourteenth century; in the next century, fifty more were established, amounting to a population of some 10,000 to 15,000 souls. This was a substantial loss for the Jewish communities in Germany which, early in the fifteenth century, numbered no more than 50,000. By the next century, there were more than two hundred Jewish communities in Poland, Lithuania, and Russia. Although some of this population included refugees from Spain and Portugal, German Jews were the dominant element and formed the basis of Jewish life in Eastern Europe for the next five centuries.

Martin Luther

In the sixteenth century, as the darkest kind of anti-Jewish bigotry began to recede, officially at least, a new kind of Jew-hatred—colder, angrier, more calculated—came on the heels of the Protestant Reformation. In his early attacks on the Roman church, Martin Luther had justified Jewish resistance to conversion by the coarseness and stupidity of the Catholic hierarchy: "Had I been a Jew and seen such fools and knaves who think they are governing and teaching the

Meer
Kleve
Emmerich
Rees
Wesel
Xanten
Goch
Rheinberg
Essen
Dinslaken
Duisburg
Geldern
Mülheim
Uerdingen
Werden
Kerpen
Kaiserswerth
Dülken
Neuss
Eller
Gladbach
Wevelinghoven
Dor-
Wassenberg
Grevenbroich
magen
Monheim
Erkelenz
Stommeln
Köln
Kaster
Mülheim
Rödingen
Bergheim
Deutz
Jülich
Kerpen
Lövenich
Aldenhoven
Brühl
Lechenich
Siegburg
Düren
Heimerzheim
Bonn
Beuel
Zülpich
Machenburg
Aachen
Blankenberg
Nideggen
Euskirchen
Königswinter
Remagen
Linz
Ahrweiler
Sinzig
Heimbach
Münstereifel
Altenahr
Montabaur
Andernach
Sayn
Mayen
Lay
Koblenz
Diez
Münstermayfeld
Kobern
Bop-
Lahnstein
pard
Braubach
Gerolstein
Garden
Camp
Cochem
Ehreburg
Oberwesel
Beilstein
Bacharach
Lorch
Eltville
Wittlich
Cröw
Rheinböllen
Trabach
Winkel
Kirchberg
Bingen
Bernkastel
Kreuznach
Bretzenheim
Neumagen
Kirn
Obermoschel
Trier
Sobernheim
Alzey
Saarburg
Kusel
Zell
Worms
Odernheim
Laden-
ST. Wendel
Leiningen
burg
Kaierslautern
Wachen-
Dürkheim
heim
Speyer
Neustadt
Deidesheim
Germersheim
Landau
Zabern
Weissenburg
Selz
Lauterburg
Wörth
Bisch-
weiler
Neuweiler
Hagenau
Zabern
Maursmünster
Wolfisheim
Strassburg
Aschenheim
Molsheim
Oberkirch
Rosheim
Ehnheim
Offenburg
Erstein
Benfeld
Haslach
Schlettstadt
Rheinau
Kestenholz
Ettenheim
St. Pilt
Rappoltsweiler
Endingen
Kenzingen
Bergheim
Markholz-
Waldkirch
Reichweiler
Kollmar
heim
Kaysersberg
Türkheim
Breisach
Münster
Sulzbach
Freiburg
Rufach
Gebweiler
Sulz
Wattweiler
Ensisheim
Thann
Sennheim
Maasmünster
Mühlhausen
Waldshut
Altkirch
Pfirt
Basel
Rheinfelden
Säckingen
Aarau
Baden
Aarburg
Zofingen
Biel
Bern

Biedenkopf
Siegen
Westerburg
Wetzlar
Giessen
Münzenberg
Nidda
Limburg
Friedberg
Weilnau
Assenheim
Büdingen
Kronberg
Rödelheim
Mül-
Gelnhausen
Königstein
heim
Hanau
Frankfurt
Steinheim
Offenbach
Seligenstadt
Mainz
Loubenheim
Oppenheim
Babenhausen
Dieburg
Freuden-
Klingenberg
berg
Tauberbischofsheim
Küls-
Grünsfeld
Bersheim
heim
Königheim
Amorbach
Lauda
Heppenheim
Waldürn
Weinheim
Buchen
Schries-
Eberbach
heim
Krautheim
Heidelberg
Mosbach
Wiesloch
Neudenau
Eppingen
Bruchsal
Bretten
Pforzheim
Sinzheim
Herlisheim
Radolfzell
Ueberlingen
Ravensburg
Ailin-
gen
Friedrichshafen
Konstanz
Diessenhofen
Lindau
Winterthur
Zürich
Homberg
Rapperswil

Legend:
- ■ before 1200
- ▬ between 1200 and 1300
- ● between 1300 and 1349
- ▲ 1349

Jewish settlements on the Rhine before the Black Death and the dispersion of 1349. Monumenta Judaica, *2000 Jahre Geschichte und Kultur der Juden am Rhein. Katalog,* Cologne, 1963.

This account of the consequences of the Black Death for the Jews was set down in a chronicle by a French Carmelite monk, Jean de Venette, who was head of the order's French province between 1342 and 1366.

Some said that this pestilence was caused by infection of the air and waters, since there was at this time no famine nor lack of food supplies, but on the contrary great abundance. As a result of this theory of infected water and air as the source of the plague, the Jews were suddenly and violently charged with infecting wells and water and corrupting the air. The whole world rose up against them cruelly on this account. In Germany and other parts of the world where Jews lived, they were massacred and slaughtered by Christians, and many thousands were burned everywhere, indiscriminately. The unshaken, if fatuous, constancy of the men and their wives was remarkable. For mothers hurled their children first into the fire that they might not be baptized and then leaped in after them to burn with their husbands and children.

Richard A. Newhall, ed., The Chronicle of Jean de Venette, *New York, 1953.*

Plague patient showing a boil under the arm, one of the first symptoms of the disease. Conrad von Megenburg, *Das Buch der Natur,* Augsburg, 1499.

Jews being burned to death. Hartmann Schedel, *Liber chronicarum,* Nuremberg, 1493.

Christian faith, I should rather have become a sow than a Christian." Luther also tried to woo Jews to Christianity by declaring them to be closer than they knew, being blood kin of Jesus. "After all, are we not all good Christians?"

For their part, some Jews saw Luther's attack on the Catholic church as one of the many wonderful signs foretelling the coming of the Messiah. Isaac Abrabanel, the Spanish philosopher, had in fact computed his coming for 1532. But it was *their* Messiah whom Jews awaited, and they were unmoved by Luther's invitation. Hence, Luther's sympathy with the obstinate Jews vanished. In 1543, near death, he could no longer contain his exasperation and wrote two pamphlets vituperatively denouncing them: *On the Jews and Their Lies* and *On the Shem Hamphoras—the Ineffable Name.* Succinctly, they lent prestige to themes to be taken up again and again by anti-Semites in modern times: the Jew as the enemy and exploiter of the Christian, the Jew as "vermin" and a "calamity" for the Christian community. Luther recommended that the Jews' schools and synagogues be burned, their houses destroyed, their prayer books and Talmud taken away from them, and their money and jewelry confiscated. They themselves should be set to hard labor. Above all, he urged that, following the Spanish and French example, the Jews "be driven out of the land." His proposals were to enjoy a long and sinister afterlife.

Martin Luther. Engraving by G. Scott after a painting by Lucas Cranach.

Chapter Two

The Institutions of Jewish Life

Communal Organization

Self-Government

Until the early nineteenth century, only the exceptional Jew enjoyed legal standing as an individual. Bishops and ruling lords negotiated with the representatives of a *community* when they arranged for a Jewish settlement in their cities. It was the community that was bought and sold by the local princes, the community that was held responsible for the dereliction of an individual Jew, the community that paid the taxes.

Each local Jewish council functioned, then, as a complete government, responsible for the secular as well as the religious ordering of Jewish life. Even before the Frankfurt ghetto was established in the fifteenth century, Jews had always clustered in one area, often near the city walls. They had good reasons. As soon as there were enough Jews to guarantee a permanent settlement, they built institutions to accommodate their needs—a cemetery, a synagogue, a house of study, a slaughterhouse, a bake house, a ritual bath, a hall for weddings and other festivities, and, in the largest communities, a hospital and an almshouse for the poor.

All this required a structure governed by an elected council. Generally consisting of seven men, the council levied and collected taxes and administered the community's day-to-day affairs. It oversaw the construction and repair of public buildings, paid the salaries of their employees, and enacted such nonreligious ordinances as the sumptuary laws. A remarkable self-discipline underlay such a system, a genuine social compact, best illustrated by the Jewish court, the Bet Din. Jews felt a distinct repugnance against taking their legal differences to a Christian court. The Bet Din used Jewish religious law to adjudicate disputes over contracts, inheritances, and property. Its authority rested on the assumption that although it had no real powers of enforcement, the members of the community would abide by its rulings. The ultimate weapon in the hands of the community was not civil action—imprisonment or physical punishment—but a theological verdict—excommunication or, for lesser offenses, a range of fines. But the compulsion to comply came from within.

One of the most visible—and audible—employees of the council, a symbol of social regulation, was the beadle with his *Schulklopfer,* literally, synagogue knocker. Every morning he awakened the community, knocking on doors with a wooden mallet to remind the inhabitants that it was the hour for morning prayers. In the event of a death, the beadle also made his rounds, the dull sound of his knocking at an unexpected hour eloquently conveying the news. The supreme religious authority was the local rabbi, who held a kind of advisory and general veto power over the council's deliberations. But his special domain was rendering decisions based on Jewish law. His appointment was entirely an internal matter, and he could be dismissed at will.

The "Jewish bishop," on the other hand, held his office for life. Sometimes a rabbi but often a layman, he was appointed by the local authorities as the official representative of the community. As a symbol of his authority, he was entrusted with the key to the gates of the Jewish quarter. He also presided over the ceremonial exchange of annual gifts with the ruling power, as a sign of Jewish fealty. In Trier, the *Juden-bischof* was required to lend the archbishop of the city ten marks every year, without interest,

A medieval town as depicted in a Passover Haggadah of 1428, showing the Jewish houses clustered near the wall. Although the figures in the foreground are supposed to represent the Jews as slaves in Egypt building the cities of Pithom and Rameses, the setting is local, including the figure of a Jew wearing a pointed hat and carrying a bundle and staff. (Color plate 3.)

Seal from a document from Augsburg, dated August 23, 1298, in which the Jewish community agrees to build a wall around its cemetery at its own cost. It is the earliest seal of a Jewish community to survive.

A *Schulklopfer* (beadle's hammer) from the eighteenth century. Although the hammer shown is from Hungary, this shape was also used in Germany. This one has a hole for hanging it at the narrow end. The two Hebrew letters recall the first words of the "rules concerning arising in the morning" from the *Shulhan Aruch.* The carved eagle and stag refer to the verse in the *Sayings of the Fathers:* ". . . swift as the eagle, fleet as the stag . . . to do the will of thy Father."

while the archbishop presented him with a cow, a cask of wine, two measures of wheat, and an old, discarded cloak.

Jewish communities were no isolated enclosures. There had long been a tradition of soliciting the opinions of eminent rabbis, often from far places, on difficult questions. In addition, along the Rhine, at Cologne, fairs convened three times a year, providing opportunities for talk across communities. Leaders of Jewish settlements took counsel with one another on political matters and legal issues concerning marriage, education, and aid to the poor. In time, these informal gatherings were convened as synods. The first, held at Troyes in 1150, called by Rabbi Tam, Rashi's grandson, brought together rabbis from France and Germany. The independent German synods, meeting at irregular intervals until the seventeenth century, were originally devoted to the interpretation of Jewish law, but over the years they began to concern themselves no less with the current position of the Jews. Thus the blood-libel case of Simon of Trent led to a special meeting in Nuremberg.

With the waning of the Middle Ages, Jewish communities were no longer as tightly knit as they had been, nor did they accord the later synods the authority the earlier ones had enjoyed. In the Christian world, too, these meetings evoked suspicion; the last synod of Frankfurt in 1603 brought accusations of high treason. Although the rabbis were acquitted, it was obvious that the institution had outlived its time.

Usually governments tried to keep Jews invisible, either by confining them to ghettos or by prohibiting them from living in the town proper. In the mid-seventeenth century, Jews were not permitted to live in Hamburg although they conducted business there every day. Instead they lived in two adjoining villages, Altona or Wandsbeck. In Nuremberg, after long oscillations between admission and expulsion during the Middle Ages, Jews began returning in the seventeenth century for trading ventures but were required to pay a special tax (*Leibzoll*) every time they entered the city. Another device for limiting the Jewish population was to restrict the number of marriages as well as residence permits or to limit the number of grown children in each family allowed to settle in the city.

Because the fundamental security of resi-

Portrait of Michael Gernsheim, the last Jewish bishop of Worms, eighteenth century.

The Frankfurt Jewish council, 1716. Johann Jacob Schudt, *Neue Franckfurter jüdische Kleiderordnung* . . . Frankfurt am Main, 1716.

Between 1200 and 1223, three synods met in cities along the Rhine, with some 150 rabbis in attendance. Here is a sampling of the ordinances approved at the meeting in Speyer in 1223.

That a Jew shall not cut his hair or shave his beard after the fashion of gentiles.

That if one is summoned to court, he shall respond in three days.

That no Jew may accept religious office at the hands of gentile powers.

That no one shall divorce his wife without the consent of the three communities [Speyer, Worms, and Mainz].

That every member of the community shall pay his tithe for the support of communal institutions.

That the young men escorting the bridegroom shall receive only six denier from him, and shall not be permitted to steal chickens or anything else, even in play.

That if in any community the amount collected for educational purposes is found to be insufficient, they shall use for this purpose any bequests left the community by philanthropic individuals, unless the bequest was left for a specific purpose.

Louis Finkelstein, Jewish Self-Government in the Middle Ages, *New York, 1964.*

dence was always in doubt, Jews were profoundly dependent on their communal organizations. They might grumble about taxes and precedence, but in the end the elected heads of their government who served as intercessors had their value.

Education

For Jews in the Middle Ages, especially those in the German lands, education was inseparable from religion, and formal education was quite specifically intended for boys. It meant learning to read the prayer book and studying the Old Testament and the commentaries. The problem with this curriculum, which remained unchanged in religious schools into modern times, was that it left no room for secular learning. For a long time, in fact, pious Jews were deeply suspicious of all nonreligious study as a diversion, even a temptation to immorality. Nonetheless, Jews needed to reckon or to read German, and they learned to do so, even if through irregular byways. Wealthier families kept private tutors, or parents taught their children worldly subjects, sometimes in secret.

The sacred aura surrounding study was heightened by the elaborate customs making the first day in school memorable for a Jewish boy. The course of study was no less stylized. From his entrance into school at the age of five until he became a full-fledged participant in the religious community at thirteen, a boy followed a clearly defined path. The first three months were devoted to the alphabet. Then he was set to reading the Pentateuch, and the method was simplicity itself: each word was read and immediately translated into the vernacular. By the age of ten, he would have completed the entire Old Testament and begun to study the commentaries, the Mishnah and the Talmud. Those who continued to study after their thirteenth year entered a yeshiva for a more intense analysis of the commentaries and usually traveled from their homes to enroll in the academy of a prestigious rabbi.

How well a boy was taught depended, then as now, on his instructor. Learned men used the Scriptures to impart grammar and history and to draw moral lessons. For many children, however, education consisted of mere rote learning, almost imposed by the scarcity of books and the often untrained men who undertook the task of

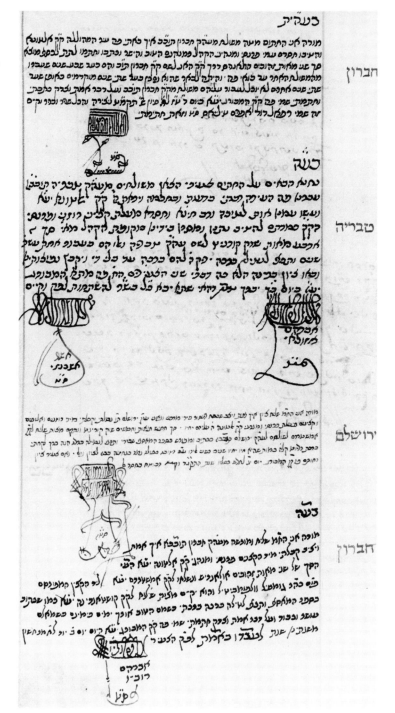

One of the functions of the community was to dispense alms. Here is a page from the receipt book of Altona-Hamburg-Wandsbeck, ca. 1789, showing the signatures of the emissaries from the "four holy cities"—Jerusalem, Safed, Hebron, and Tiberias—acknowledging a donation.

A page from the *Mah-zor Lipsiae,* written ca. 1320. The illu-mination, which shows a boy's intro-duction to schooling, follows in exact detail the ritual outlined in the twelfth-century *Mahzor Vitry,* com-posed in France by a follower of Rashi.

The ceremony illustrated here was prescribed in the eleventh century Mahsor Vitry, ***a book of prayers for the festivals and rules of religious observance.***

And when a man initiates his son into the study of the Torah, the let-ters [of the alphabet] are written for him on a board. He is washed and clean clothes are put on him. Three cakes of choice flour in honey are kneaded for him and a virgin kneads the dough. Three eggs are boiled for him and he is given apples and other fruit. A wise and important person is sought to take him to school; he covers him with his mantle and brings him to the synagogue. He is fed of the cakes, eggs, and fruits, and the letters are taught to him. Then the board is covered with honey and he is told to lick it.

Cited by Bezalel Narkiss, "Commentaries," in Mahsor Lipsiae, *Hanau/Main, 1964.*

schoolmaster. Despite evidence that some women were learned in Hebrew as well as Yiddish, the instruction of young girls was neither well regulated nor ceremonious. Much depended on the willingness of parents to find teachers or to teach their daughters themselves.

What Jews knew—indeed, what Europe knew in those centuries—was narrowly circumscribed. History was intertwined with myth, the geography of far places pictured them as populated by demons and dragons, and astronomy was hardly separated from astrology. Yet their educational system produced a remarkably literate Jewish population in the Middle Ages, however restricted its body of knowledge. Without access to the classics or the work of Arab mathematicians or astronomers, a few rabbinical scholars laboriously rediscovered what the Greeks had already known. But the core of Jewish learning lay in its preoccupation with ethical and legal questions, resolved through the interpretation of sacred texts.

Literacy in the service of theology was not enough. If in medieval times the Jews were among the most learned people in Europe, by the sixteenth century they had fallen behind as the gap between their traditional educational system and gentile culture around them widened. Those with business in the world at large had to seek outside their schools for the training that would fit them for traffic abroad. Certainly by the seventeenth century, the court Jews (see chapter 3) had transcended the limitations of ghetto learning; they and their families were educated in both cultures. Other Jews would follow suit.

Ritual Slaughter

Jewish dietary laws have had a double effect on Jewish life. They have separated Jews from their Christian neighbors and aroused the distrust that difference always brings. But they have also united Jews as they sought communal solutions to assure a regular supply of ritually acceptable meat, bread, and wine. And the sale of meat, not incidentally, benefited the local council, which hired the ritual slaughterer and collected a tax on his transactions: it was a lucrative source of income. Communities generally negotiated permission to maintain a *shohet,* an official slaughterer—an indispensable figure in any Jewish community, often serving as teacher or sex-

The courtyard of a kosher slaughterhouse in an eighteenth-century engraving. Johann Cristoph Georg Bodenschatz, *Kirchliche Verfassung der heutigen Juden* . . . Frankfurt und Leipzig, 1749.

ton as well—as part of the rights of settlement. Thus the Edict of 1671 admitting Jews to Berlin, while denying them permission to build a synagogue, explicitly mentioned the importation of "a slaughterer and a schoolmaster" as among their privileges.

The basic Jewish dietary regulations prohibit eating any animal that does not have cloven hoofs and does not chew its cud—which eliminates the pig and wild game. Jewish law also requires that the animal be slaughtered in prescribed ways: it must be lying down with neck outstretched so that its windpipe and esophagus can be cut in one stroke with a perfectly sharp knife. The Jewish view is that this is a humane method since death is instantaneous. Yet ritual slaughter, like other Jewish practices, has not escaped criticism, often virulent, by humanitarians and anti-Semites alike. The intense association of ritual slaughter with the fundamental organization of Jewish life did not escape the notice of the Nazis. It was important enough for them in April 1933, only three months after taking power, to ban it in all of Germany.

The Mikveh

The *mikveh,* or ritual bath, was another indispensable capital investment for the Jewish community. It extended to the body the rituals of purification that make up so much of Jewish religious observance. Despite their dark and cavernous ambience, the ritual baths were centers in constant use, where men came weekly on the eve of the Sabbath, and women at the end of each menstrual period. Brides came on the eve of their wedding, and new mothers at a fixed interval after childbirth. In the face of often squalid living conditions, Jews in medieval Europe probably enjoyed a higher level of cleanliness than their neighbors because of these ritual baths. It should be noted, however, that the mikveh itself was not used for actual bathing but only for a ritual immersion after the warm bath for cleansing.

Even cooking and eating vessels were drawn into the circle of sanctification. In remembrance of the Temple in Jerusalem, meals were construed as analogous to the offering of sacrifice. Thus, utensils for food had to be ritually immersed before use in order to be purified. In this closely governed life, no part of the physical world escaped notice.

Since the bathing pool dug in the ritual bath had to be fed by living water from a spring, it often required—especially in cities—a deep shaft. The mikveh in Cologne, built in the twelfth century, was nearly fifty feet underground, reached by a flight of seventy-nine steps that followed the square of the shaft. The steps leading to the bath are shown following their excavation in 1957.

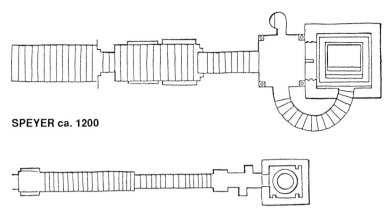

SPEYER ca. 1200

OFFENBURG ca. 1350

FRIEDBERG ca. 1260

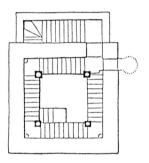

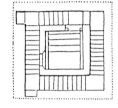

ANDERNACH 14th cent.

Diagrams of the approaches and design of medieval mikvehs in the area of the Rhine, twelfth to fifteenth centuries. Zvi Asaria, ed., *Die Juden in Köln. Von den ältesten Zeiten bis zur Gegenwart,* Köln, 1959.

An eighteenth-century mikveh. At the left we see a long flight of steps leading down to the bath. In an adjoining room is a warm bath. The dip into the mikveh, which may or may not be heated, is the last stage of ritual purification. Johann Christoph Georg Bodenschatz, *Kirchliche Verfassung der heutigen Juden,* Leipzig and Frankfurt, 1749.

Jewish gravestone in
Berlin. Dating from
1244, it was found
embedded in the wall
of the Spandau
Citadel.

Cemeteries

The first piece of communal property Jews acquired was a cemetery. Thanks to the durability
of stone, these burial places have become treasure houses of history, charting the movement
of Jews from one place to another, relating their
occupations, their wealth, their taste, and even
their degree of piety. The oldest surviving gravestones, dating from the eleventh century, are in
Mainz, in the area of earliest Jewish settlement.
But many have not endured. As Jews were expelled or moved away, their gravestones were
converted into building material. In the Spandau
citadel in Berlin, fragments of thirteenth-
century Jewish tombstones have been found
mortared into the wall. In Würzburg, when the
Jews were expelled in 1349, the cemetery was
turned into a vineyard. But wherever they have
survived, the cemeteries tell of lost communities, their dreams and fantasies frozen in
stone.

The oldest surviving
Jewish cemetery in
Germany is this one,
in Mainz. The grave-
yard was opened ca.
900, and the oldest
tombstone is from
about 1000.

A page from the
Hevra Kadisha record
book of Altona show-
ing entries from Au-
gust 1838 to February
1839.

Hevra Kadisha

The Hevra Kadisha (Holy Brotherhood), whose
members attended dying members of the community and, after death, prepared their bodies
for burial—was a society with such high prestige that the coveted places were often transferred by inheritance. Separate societies of
women washed the bodies of women and
dressed them in their distinctive grave clothes.
Also as part of their duties, these groups maintained careful records of the deaths in the community. Once a year, the members met to observe a day of fasting and prayer, which
concluded in a grand ceremonial feast. These
societies, first recorded in Germany in the fourteenth century, endured to the very end of the
Jewish community there.

Hevra Kadisha, Mann-
heim, 1925.

Religion and Ritual

The Synagogue

The synagogue has been a dominant feature in Jewish life everywhere for untold centuries. That Paul's campaign to convert the Jews took place in synagogues demonstrates how widespread this institution was as early as the first century, even before the destruction of the Temple in Jerusalem in 70 C.E. But because of that destruction and the subsequent dispersion of the Jews, the preeminent building of the Jewish community became a house of assembly, a house of study, and a house of prayer. Certain ancient terms regarding Temple ritual survived as a reminder of past glories: the word *avodah,* for one, which had originally described a ceremonial sacrifice, came to stand for the sacred prayer service.

In the Diaspora, the synagogue became the center of Jewish life. It was the place where government decrees were proclaimed to the community, where those seeking justice might make their case, and where advanced students literally ate and slept. It was the stranger's first stop on arriving in a new community. Yet as a place of prayer, it was also potentially offensive to Christian neighbors when it was conspicuous in size or ornamentation, or when sounds of the service penetrated beyond its walls. For the synagogue was not simply a house of prayer: men chatted with one another about business affairs; fathers brought their young children, who sometimes distracted their attention from prayers. Others came in dirty clothes or muddy shoes, and took snuff or spat.

Discomfited Christians were not alone in objecting to the noise in the synagogues. Over the centuries, many Jews deplored the lack of propriety during services, and community regulations repeatedly—apparently ineffectually—outlawed the most flagrant breaches of order. By the eighteenth century, with Protestant decorum as a constant example, Jewish reformers grew increasingly uneasy with the traditional standard of behavior, which had made the synagogue into a familiar house of assembly where one also addressed God.

In earlier centuries, the ruling consideration had been external safety rather than internal orderliness. In a ghetto or a dense Jewish settlement, the synagogue normally occupied a

The earliest depiction in Ashkenaz of a synagogue service. A *chazan* (cantor) stands before the reading desk, wrapped in a prayer shawl. Behind him are two men wearing Jew's hats. From the *Mahsor Lipsiae,* ca. 1320.

prominent position. But where Jews lived intermingled in gentile society, they tended to place their synagogues in courtyards, hidden from public view, and to make the exterior as neutral as possible so as not to arouse attention.

Before most crafts were closed off to them in the Middle Ages, Jews had built and ornamented their synagogues themselves. Yet apart from the absence of human and sometimes of animal figures, German Jews developed no distinctive "Jewish" architecture or decor. Rather, in every epoch the synagogues reflected the style of the surrounding culture. Thus the entrance of the eleventh-century synagogue of Worms strikingly resembles the north portal of the Worms Cathedral. Its interior, too, with its groined vaulting, double nave, and even the leaf designs carved in the capitals of its columns, paralleled local churches in structure and ornamentation. Only in their organization of space did the syn-

agogues differ markedly from churches. In the Diaspora the reading of the Torah became literally central, so that, until the nineteenth century, the reading desk was always placed in the center of the synagogue and the ark with the Torah scrolls on the eastern wall.

Another difference between Christian and Jewish forms of worship was the absence of women from the synagogue. Though men and women had been segregated even in the times of the Temple, with a separate court for each sex, this division was carried through even more stringently in the Diaspora, until synagogue builders ceased to provide space for women. Even in Worms, the earliest Jewish community to make a place for women, the women's synagogue was not added until the thirteenth century, after the men's synagogue had stood for two hundred years. At about the same time, the synagogue in Cologne provided a curtained area

Synagogue interior during New Year's service. Each man wears his *kittel,* or burial shroud, as was customary in Germany. Paul Christian Kirschner, *Jüdisches Ceremoniel,* Nuremberg, [1734].

The synagogue at Worms. The first synagogue in Worms was built in 1034 and continued to function for nine hundred years. Destroyed during the Crusades, it was rebuilt in the twelfth century. The interior shown here is substantially the way it looked from the mid-nineteenth century until its destruction by the Nazis in 1938.

where women might sit, not to attend services, but to hear the sermons. From the fifteenth century on, however, women's presence was more widely accepted. Communities began to build separate prayer rooms for them, sometimes in adjacent buildings, sometimes provided with peepholes or grilles through which they could observe the proceedings in the synagogue itself. But Jewish women had neither a Torah for their own use nor a cantor; a learned woman in their midst led the prayers.

Permission to build a synagogue became a kind of barometer of the Jews' place in the world. In 1671, when a few Viennese Jewish families were invited to start factories and develop trade in Berlin, the terms of settlement explicitly forbade them to build a synagogue, even though they were permitted to maintain private places of worship. When they finally received permission in 1712 to build a public synagogue in the Heidereutergasse, it was, characteristically, partially screened from passersby and its entrance placed in a courtyard. Otherwise it mirrored contemporary neoclassical taste (see p. 93). Similarly, when in 1789–90 the duke of Anhalt-Dessau wanted to show "his" Jews particular favor, he built them a synagogue in his park at Wörlitz designed as a kind of exotic garden folly and modeled after the antique Roman building known as the Round Temple. Piranesi's engraving of this structure, entitled *Veduta del Tempio di Cibele,* had been published in 1758 in an album that rapidly became familiar throughout Europe. A circular structure with high windows and ornamented with pilasters, the temple was reproduced almost precisely at Wörlitz, with its interior adapted to Jewish services.

In the synagogue, then, architecture could be taken as an index of the integration of German Jews into the society around them as well as of their difference. The Heidereutergasse synagogue perfectly represented the first stages. Despite its neoclassical exterior, the interior maintained the traditional organization of space in Jewish worship. The prominent reading desk, the significance accorded the Torah ark with its baroque housing, and the separation of women, who, after entering by a modest side door, sat in a separate raised gallery—all were specific to Jewish religious ideas. These public and private faces showed how the Jews would attempt to maintain their identity even as they joined the mainstream of German life.

View of the Temple of the Sibyl in the Piazza della Bocca della Verita, Rome, by Giovanni Battista Piranesi, 1761.

"The Jewish temple on the lake," constructed in the park of the Duke of Anhalt-Dessau in 1790, shown here in a contemporary etching by Israel Salomon Probst.

Circumcision

As the most fundamental Jewish rite, marking the covenant between Abraham and God that brought the Jewish people into being, circumcision is a ceremony surrounded with laws and legends. An event that carries a certain risk, it has accumulated special rituals and traditions to ward off danger. The eight days between birth and circumcision were considered especially hazardous for mother and child, who were, it was feared, beset by evil spirits. In the German lands, on *Wachnacht* (watch night), the eve of the circumcision, a company of men gathered at the mother's bedside and spent the night feasting, praying, and studying the Torah to ward off malevolent spirits, particularly the demon Lilith.

On the day of the circumcision, the boy was borne to the synagogue by his godmother and received at the door by his godfather (*sandak*), whose duty it was to hold the child during the ceremony. According to ancient legend, the prophet Elijah, the Messenger of the Covenant, is present at every circumcision. Hence the sandak sits on a bench with a double seat, or a chair is provided for the prophet.

Every *mohel* (circumciser) carried a book with the requisite prayers in which he also recorded the names of the boys he had circumcised, with the date and place. These books were often hand-lettered and exquisitely decorated with drawings illustrating the proceedings. The Mohel Book of 1741, written in Altona, Ham-

An eighteenth-century writer explains, "This is called *Kisse Eijahu*, the chair of Elijah, and it is not enough simply to set it down. One must quite explicitly say these words: 'This is the chair of Elijah'; otherwise—because he has not been directly invited—Elijah will not appear. The chair remains standing in its place for three days so that the prophet can rest after his long journey." The second seat is for the godfather, who holds the baby during the circumcision ceremony. Paul Christian Kirchner, *Jüdisches Ceremoniel*, Nuremberg, [1734]. This eighteenth-century chair is from Dermbach, Thuringia.

burg, and Wandsbeck, passed through the hands of several *mohelim* and was in use down to 1783. It records operations in places as far-flung as Prague, Hamburg, Königsberg, and Posen. One illustration shows the opening phase of the ceremony. Before the actual circumcision (*berit milah*) takes place, the child is laid for a moment in Elijah's place and then is given into the arms of the sandak. Since wine played an indispensable part in the ceremony—a touch was dabbed on the boy's lips after the operation—particular pains were taken over the decorations for the blessing that concludes the ceremony. (See plates 4 and 5.)

One custom special to German-speaking lands was the use of the *Wimpel,* or ornamental binder. A long strip of swaddling cloth, it was painted or embroidered with a prayer that the boy grow up to marry, study the Torah, and do good works. At the conclusion of the ceremony, the child was swaddled in the *Wimpel,* which was afterward presented to the synagogue. Upon his thirteenth birthday, when the boy became *bar mitzvah* (son of the covenant), it was used to bind the Torah from which he read aloud to the congregation—an act that signified his newly attained status as an adult.

The ritual that brought the boy into the community of Israel was only part of his induction into his double world. Coupled with this religious observance was another ceremony, called *Hollekreisch,* which had grown up among German Jews to mark giving the child its German name. Although the meaning of this term was lost by the fourteenth century, it continued to be used, particularly in southern Germany, into the twentieth. The most popular etymology connects the first syllable, *Holle,* with the name of the German pagan goddess who brought children into the world. The *Hollekreisch* was essentially a light-hearted celebration during which the children lifted the cradle three times into the air as they shouted, "Hollekreisch, what shall the child's name be?" Then they gave it its secular name. The Hebrew name, which the boy had received at circumcision and the girl on the first Saturday after the birth, when the mother visited the synagogue, was often reserved for ceremonial religious events or Jewish legal documents, whereas the secular name or a Yiddishized diminutive was the one in daily use.

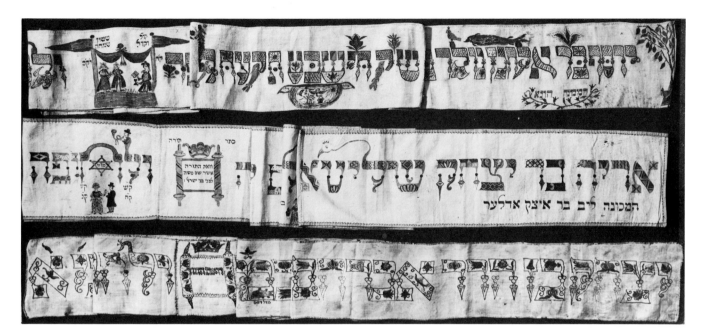

Three wimpels, or swaddling cloths, decorated in honor of the birth of a boy and later used as Torah binders. The two upper binders are from the nineteenth century and are painted on linen; the bottom binder dates from 1735 and is linen embroidered in silk.

Hollekreisch naming ceremony.

Bar Mitzvah

A velvet curtain for
the Torah ark in the
synagogue at Kassel,
embroidered in 1744
by "Bluma" in
honor of her son's
bar mitzvah.

At the age of thirteen, when a boy became bar mitzvah—responsible for carrying out the commandments—he was given a special prayer book. A wealthy family might give their son a book bound in silver like this mahzor for Passover synagogue services, printed in Amsterdam according to the Ashkenazic rite in 1667 or 1668. The text is in Hebrew, with certain passages translated into Yiddish. The cover shows the star of David on the left and Jonah entering the whale on the right.

Marriage

This picture by Moritz Oppenheim of a wedding in Frankfurt at the end of the eighteenth century was actually painted in 1861. With great attention to detail, he conveys the special customs of the German Jews. Where possible the event took place under the open sky, as here in the courtyard of the synagogue. In Oppenheim's picture, the bridal couple wear traditional silver marriage belts and, following Frankfurt usage, stand under a draped prayer shawl rather than a canopy. During the ceremony, the couple took their vows with a communal wedding ring in the shape of an elaborate house, for which a simpler ring was substituted later. The glass, which in Eastern Europe was crushed underfoot to commemorate the destruction of the Temple in 70 C.E., in Germany was thrown against a wall. (See color plate 6.)

A marriage scene from a Torah binder. Tempera on linen. Germany, 1845.

Wedding belts for bride and groom. Silver, gilt, and semiprecious stones. Germany, seventeenth century.

Ivory communal wedding ring in the shape of a house. Germany, seventeenth century.

The Bingen wedding stone. This stone was embedded in the synagogue wall in Bingen on the Rhine as the target for the wedding glass.

The Sabbath

In the life of European Jewish communities, the sequence of religious observance followed two ever-repeating rhythms: the weekly cycle, climaxed by the Sabbath, and the annual cycle with its procession of holidays commemorating historic events and seasonal changes, like the spring festival, Passover. Jews celebrated the Maccabean revolt of the second century B.C.E. at Hanukkah, as they celebrated the new-year and agricultural festivals in spring and autumn.

The sanctity of the Sabbath was so compelling that much of Jewish daily life was built around its coming and going. A Jewish peddler organized his itinerary around it, leaving his house on Sunday, making his circuit from village to village, and returning home in time to celebrate the onset of the Sabbath on Friday evening. For market women and housewives, too, it was the crown of the week, when the best food was bought and prepared in its honor. However buffeted Jews might feel in the course of their daily existence, on the Sabbath their home was meant to be a haven of peace and joy.

The German-Jewish poet Heinrich Heine—despite his conversion to Lutheranism in 1825—was struck by this transforming power of the Sabbath. With characteristic irony, he introduces into his mocking travel tale *The Baths of Lucca* the character Moses Lump, affectionately known as Lümpchen. A peddler from Hamburg, Lümpchen

> runs about the whole week in wind and weather with his bundle on his back to earn the few marks he needs; now when he comes home on Friday evening he finds the lamp lit with its seven candles, a white cloth on the table, and he lays down his bundle and all his cares, and sits down at table with his misshapen wife and even more misshapen daughter, partakes with them of fish cooked in a tasty garlic sauce, sings the most splendid psalms of King David, rejoices wholeheartedly at the exodus of the children of Israel from Egypt, rejoices also that all the miscreants who behaved wickedly towards them died in the end, that King Pharaoh, Nebuch..d-nezzar, Haman, Antiochus, Titus and all such people are dead, while Lümpchen is still alive and partaking of his fish with his wife and child—and I tell you, Herr Doktor, the fish is

delicious, and the man is happy, he does not have to worry about culture, he sits wrapped contentedly in his religion and his green dressing gown like Diogenes in his tub, he gazes cheerfully at his candles, which he does not even have to trim himself. And I tell you, when the candles begin to burn a little dimly and the *Schabbesfrau* [a gentile woman employed during the Sabbath to perform tasks forbidden to Jews on that day] whose task it is to trim them is not at hand, and if Rothschild the Great were to enter with all his brokers, discounters, dispatchers and *chefs de comptoir* with whom he has conquered the world, and he were to say: "Moses Lump, ask me a favor; whatever you wish shall be granted," Herr Doktor, I am convinced Moses Lump would calmly reply: "Trim my candles!" and Rothschild the Great would exclaim in astonishment: "Well, if I weren't Rothschild, I should like to be such a Lümpchen."

On such a night no Jew could be permitted to be without a roof over his head. Accordingly, strangers arriving at the synagogue were parceled out among the householders and received at their dwellings with ceremony and honor.

Characteristic for the observance of the Sabbath among German Jews was a star-shaped oil-burning lamp. This kind of lamp was in common use in German households until the sixteenth century and then was gradually abandoned in favor of candles, but Germany's Jews retained it as their ceremonial lamp until late in the nineteenth century, converting the homely utilitarian object into a beautiful ornament. The lamp hung from the ceiling and was lowered for lighting and then raised again by a ratchet. This lowering of the lamp, which heralded the arrival of the Sabbath, gave rise to proverbs celebrating the cessation of daily care which the Sabbath brings:

> As down comes the Sabbath lamp,
> Want and worry must decamp.

Strict observance of the Sabbath required that one refrain from work, attend synagogue, and read devotional literature. Even women were expected to read their Yiddish translations and commentaries on the sacred texts. But as regulations of the eighteenth-century community fathers in Frankfurt demonstrate, this practice was not universally observed. The regulations for-

"Sabbath Eve,"
by Moritz Op-
penheim, 1882. An
exotic-looking Sab-
bath guest stands at
the door.

Star-shaped hanging lamp. Germany, fourteenth century. Excavated in the Jewish quarter of Deutz, a city across the Rhine from Cologne.

Silver hanging lamp for Sabbath and festivals. Frankfurt, 1680–1720.

From Minhag book, Frankfurt, 1708. The woman is lighting the Sabbath candles on a lowered lamp. Note the two Sabbath loaves on the table.

דיא וייל אן חיבד מיטׂ זילי ברכה אונ׳ זונטט אחכין חי אן די אלות
טוט . חוברעט חיז דא גיט אויגׂליך . דען וון זיה זחוט דיה
ברכה אחכין חונ׳ דער נחך מן לינדן . זח דערטׂט זיה ניט דחש זילבט
חוֹת דר החגר טטעלן . דרום חלֹיגט זיה פֹחר חונ׳ טטעלט דט זילֹבֹט פון

bade unmarried women to stroll on the main boulevards or gather in the streets in groups on the Sabbath—obviously a tempting way to spend an idle afternoon. The penalties for violating these injunctions were severe indeed: the fine amounted to some twenty thalers, the equivalent of a half-year's rent for a house. In addition, the young women were warned that if they were found violating this rule, "the servants of the community . . . are empowered to fling excrement at them." The Sabbath must not be trifled with, particularly by women.

Passover

As the holiday commemorating the galvanizing flight of the Jews from Egypt—the event that made them into a people—Passover has a long history. In Europe, however, it was also a danger-

The depiction of a stag hunt in the fifteenth-century Darmstadt Haggadah. This scene was actually a mnemonic device for the sequence of blessings when the Seder fell on a Sabbath evening. Listed in order, the initial letters of the blessings made up the phrase JAKNHAZ, which closely approximates the German words for "chase the hare" (*Jag' den Has'*). Often represented by a hunting scene, based on the tapestries of the period, it sometimes showed, as here, a stag as quarry instead of a hare.

ous time of the year for Jews because its observance coincided with the most highly charged event in the Christian calendar, the crucifixion of Jesus. Anticipation was often tempered by fears of violence from an aroused, sometimes deliberately incited populace. Beginning in the thirteenth century, the belief that the Jews needed the blood of a Christian child to make matzah haunted the Passovers of European Jews, leading to accusations of murder that were often the prelude to massacres.

Passover is a unique holiday in that its celebration consists of not merely a festive meal but an entire service, the Seder, conducted at home. In its evolution it bears traces of the many stages along the way of Diaspora life. The burnt shank bone on the Passover plate is an echo of sacrifices offered at the Temple. The injunctions to recline at the table, to eat herbs dipped in salt water, and to serve small appetizers are distinct reminders of the Roman past. The Greek influence is represented in the word *epikomion*,

which became *afikomen*—the piece of matzah eaten at the close of the meal. In Germany itself, local custom continued to modify the menu of the meal, and German folk melodies were adapted to the allegorical songs that conclude the service.

The order of the Seder is in the Haggadah, a book of prayers, excerpts from the Bible, commentaries, and songs telling the story of the Exodus. Although components of the Haggadah date to the fourth century B.C.E. in Babylonia, it achieved its present form only in the eleventh century with the completion of the *Mahzor Vitry*. This prayer book for the festivals, compiled by a student of Rashi in Vitry, a town in northwestern France, was widely followed in France and Germany.

By the thirteenth century, handsomely ornamented and illustrated Haggadot were being produced, particularly in southern Germany, showing how people looked, what kind of matzah they made (small round ones), how they sat at table, what imagery fed their imaginations—and how intertwined Jewish life was with the surrounding culture.

Children are principal actors in the Seder. The four ritual questions that come toward the beginning are supposed to be asked by the youngest person present. What follows, presumably as an answer, is the tale of the Exodus with all its embellishments. At the dramatic phrase, "Pour out thy wrath upon the nations that know thee not," from Psalm 79, wine is poured into the best goblet in the house and the door is opened for the prophet Elijah, who as the harbinger of the Messiah is popularly believed to visit every Seder table. Another messianic element, the concluding phrase of the service, "Next year in Jerusalem," may be interpreted literally or as a hope for speedy redemption by the Messiah.

The Passover ceremony, which in the Diaspora is repeated on the second night, unites the participants physically in a shared community and reminds them of their collective history. The drama of the domestic setting arrayed in exceptional splendor served to give it a cherished place in German Jewish life and may have led illustrators to continue to produce handwritten and decorated Haggadot long after the invention of printing. For Passover, as we shall see, is a holiday that lost none of its force over the centuries.

Illustration from the Darmstadt Haggadah showing the Seder table under the phrase, "Pour out thy wrath upon the nations that know thee not." (Color plate 7.)

***Heinrich Heine describes the Seder in his* Rabbi von Bacherach.**

In the great hall of his house, there once sat Rabbi Abraham with his relations, students, and other guests and celebrated the evening of the Passover holiday. In the hall everything shone even more than usual; on the table lay the colorfully embroidered silk tablecloth, whose golden fringes hung to the floor, while the familiar little dishes with the symbolic foods shimmered in their setting, as did the tall wine-filled glasses whose decorations of sacred tales were executed in most intricate workmanship. The men sat in their black cloaks with their black barrettes and white ruffs; the women, in exotic glittering gowns of Lombard silk, wore in their hair and around their throats their jewelry of gold and pearls. And over the devout and contented faces of old and young alike, the silver Sabbath lamp poured its festive light.

Sukkot

Sukkot, the Feast of Booths, commemorates the wanderings of the Israelites in the desert after their escape from Egypt. Celebrants build "booths," temporary structures open to the sky, where they take their meals and sleep (weather permitting) during the week of the festival. Ingenious solutions have been devised over the centuries that take account of the climate, the materials available, and the architectural tastes of the local community while complying with the Biblical requirements. These are views of the *sukkah* (booth) of the Deller family of Fischach, in Swabia, made by the local carpenter in 1825 and painted according to the family's instructions. Note the combination of sacred and profane themes: Holy Jerusalem on one wall, the father of the family with his son, hunting rifle, and dog on the side panel. The sukkah was made of boards that could be taken apart and reassembled each year. This one was used until 1910 and is now in the Israel Museum, Jerusalem. (Color plates 8 and 9.)

Hanukkah

The ornamentation for the lamp used at Hanukkah, the most secular and historical of holidays, often drew on local themes. This Hanukkah lamp, dating from the eighteenth century, used a grenadier's hat-plate as the backing. It was an expression of loyalty to Frederick II during the Seven Years War (1756–63). Incidentally, the brass furnished an excellent reflecting surface for the Hanukkah lights.

A fourteenth- or fifteenth-century brass Hanukkah lamp. The six-spoked wheel is the emblem of the cities of Mainz and Speyer. Its incorporation in the lamp may have been a sign of gratitude for the protection of the city. The figure is that of Judith holding the head of Holofernes. According to rabbinical tradition, Judith was descended from the Hasmoneans, and she appeared frequently on Hanukkah lamps.

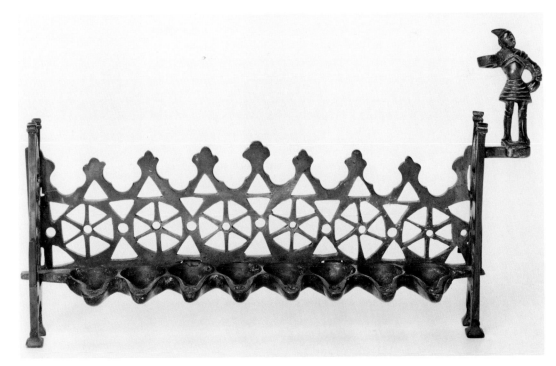

Chapter Three

From the Middle Ages to the Court Jews

The Ghetto of Frankfurt am Main

For the Jews of Frankfurt, the Dark Ages began late, in the fifteenth century. Until then some ten Jewish families, most of them headed by wealthy bankers, had lived in Frankfurt under the protection of the Holy Roman emperor and, from the fourteenth century, as subjects of the city itself. Their sudden removal by the city fathers in 1462 from the center of town to a remote and barred ghetto dramatically illustrates the swings in Jewish fortune. An outbreak of mob violence or the whim of a ruler could uproot a long-established community overnight.

The Jewish presence in Frankfurt stems only from 1150. As the site of large annual fairs, the city naturally drew Jews from all over Europe. Although most of those who settled there clustered near the Bartholomäus Church, Jews were free to buy land and build houses wherever they chose. By the thirteenth century, they had established their own cemetery, always the first sign of an entrenched community, and owned land, houses, and vineyards. In the fourteenth century, with a boldness rare in later

times, they argued that not being Christians, they need not pay tithes on their land to the church. Such confidence reflected their security—a number of Jews, both men and women, had been written into the *Bürgerbuch* of Frankfurt as full-fledged citizens.

The Black Death abruptly and violently ended this first period of Jewish residence in Frankfurt. In the wake of the plague, the fanatical Flagellants (see p. 28) were whipping an already distraught populace into frenzy. On July 14, 1349, the Flagellants reached Frankfurt and headed directly for the Jewish quarter. Although the Jews had constructed defenses, the combat proved unequal. A fire broke out, reducing to ashes Jewish houses, the Bartholomäus Church, and ultimately the entire quarter. The Frankfurt city council, calculating the costs, reckoned that with all the deaths, the value of their Jews had diminished by half. Those who escaped immolation fled the city, and Frankfurt repaid itself by selling their abandoned property.

By 1360, the Jews had reestablished their community, complete with rabbi, cantor, and

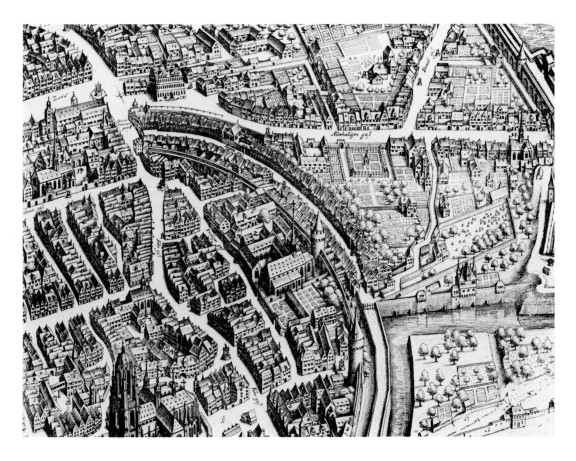

A view of the Juden-
gasse, in Frankfurt,
1646. Note the por-
tals at either end of
the street. Matthaeus
Merian, *Francofurti
ad Moenum urbis
imperialis* . . .
Frankfurt am Main,
1764 [?].

ritual slaughterer. For a century they lived in Frankfurt in the old way. But it was precisely their proximity to the rebuilt church that induced the clergy—and the emperor—to call for the Jews' removal in order to keep them from witnessing Christian ceremonies and from disturbing their gentile neighbors with their own religious observances. In 1460, responding to this pressure, the city council decreed that the Jews must move to a ghetto beyond the city walls.

Two years in the making, this ghetto at first accommodated eleven families and a surprisingly large number of communal institutions: a dance hall, a poorhouse which also served as a hospital, two inns (presumably to house Jewish visitors to the fairs), a community building with living quarters for community officials, a teacher's domicile, a synagogue, and a ritual bath. This new *Judengasse*—street of the Jews—was barred at either end by heavy wooden portals. Isolation, however, was no protection against Jew-hatred. The fifteenth century saw an abrupt change in the Jewish condition, psychologically no less than physically. A freely chosen way of living and paying taxes, once subject to negotiation, had become subject to fiat as Jews were cast into the role of the outsider—distrusted, reviled, vulnerable.

Although the Jews of Frankfurt heatedly objected to their enforced transfer (which also exposed them to marauding bands), the council remained unmoved. What began as a relatively open, spacious street meant for some sixty people eventually had to accommodate more than three thousand. Just before the great fire of 1711, which destroyed much of the ghetto, some 505 households totaling 3,024 people crowded into the 203 houses of the Judengasse.

Crowding was not the only menace. In 1612, on the occasion of an imperial election, Frankfurt's guilds, long restive, took the occasion to voice their dissatisfaction with the city council. Its policies, they charged, favored the export trade and did nothing about local unemployment and the falling value of the currency. The Jews, of course, were involved in export and money exchange, especially during the fairs, and struck guildsmen as a growing menace—literally growing, what with the ghetto's burgeoning population. Unable to enlist the newly elected emperor Matthias or the council to their

cause, the guilds continued to agitate until they could no longer be contained. On August 22, 1614, a baker named Vincenz Fettmilch gathered a mob and led an attack on the ghetto. On the mob's approach, a number of Jews fled, but those who remained entered the fray with cudgels and defended themselves energetically. Outnumbered by their assailants, they were defeated, and on the following morning the 1,380 Jews who had survived left the city to find asylum in the surrounding countryside. "Wherever we came," the poet Elchonon ben Avraham recalled, "everyone, Jew and Christian alike, showed us goodwill with food and drink and kind words. May the Blessed One reward them. But," he added dryly, "in another manner."

The triumph of the Fettmilch vigilantes was short-lived. Under the prodding of the emperor, incensed at this outrage to "his" Jews, the city council placed Fettmilch and three leading henchmen on trial. Convicted, they were hanged and broken on the wheel, their heads displayed on the city gates as a warning to all. The houses in the ghetto were repaired, and on February 28, 1616, the Jews of Frankfurt were escorted back to their old habitat by a troop of the emperor's musicians playing on silver trumpets.

Although this return to a confined existence hardly looks like a victory from a modern perspective, Frankfurt's Jews saw the restoration of their homes and businesses as a demonstration of how the powerful shielded them from persecution. To chronicle all these events and to praise the "Guardian of Israel as well as the temporal powers for their return," Elchonon ben Avraham composed a Yiddish poem in one hundred verses to be sung to the tune of *The Battle of Pavia*. For Elchonon, the Jews' reentry guaranteed both safety and freedom.

This drama led to the promulgation of a new constitution reaffirming the emperor's pledge to protect the Jews. Yet it also placed a kind of iron girdle around Jewish expansion in Frankfurt: the number of families was limited to 530; no house could have more than three stories; no couple could marry before the age of twenty-five; and no more than twelve marriages were permitted in any year. These rigid constraints led to the involuntary dispersion of many among Frankfurt's Jews.

As the ghetto became more crowded and

A contemporary chronicler reports on the plundering of the Judengasse in 1614.

This [outcry] caused a great tumult and drove the idle fellows to run about in the city with great fury and threats. Thus it appeared that they were planning something dangerous, which finally actually happened when some of the common people joined them. Together on August 22 they stormed the Judengasse and plundered a good part of it—in the course of which many of them came away with bloody heads instead of booty.

Johann Ludwig Gottfried, Historische Chronicken . . . Frankfurt, *1633.*

A contemporary engraving of the procession of the Jews into their street "with pipes, drums, and flags flying . . . as the Imperial arms are hammered onto the gates . . . 28 February 1616."

In this excerpt from his long poem on the Fettmilch uprising, Elchonon ben Avraham relates how the Jews returned to their street.

The first were a great flock of foot soldiers
With their rifles over their shoulders.
Then the cavalry, well armed.
Anything more handsomely decked out we
　　had never seen.
Then laid in their own carriage, the
　　Imperial Eagles
and thereafter pipes and drums.
Then we poor frightened children
Came next and accompanied them.
A rider with a silver trumpet rode behind us
And after him many riders and knights.
Then many people followed on foot
All well-armed with their weapons.

In every street where we turned in,
They blew on the trumpets with all their
　　power.
All those citizens who heard it
Wished that they had kept us.
With a flag flying even over the Zeil [a main
　　street in Frankfurt]
They brought us to our streets. . .
A trumpeter rode with us into our street
He blew high into the air with all his
　　strength
Until each one had gone into his house.
And then he went about his business.
With great joy, we moved into our houses as
　　we found them.
May God be praised and further protect us
　　from all sorrows,
Until the righteous Messiah appears before
　　us.

Johann Christoph Wagenseil, Belehrung der jüdischteutschen
Red- und Schreibart . . . 1699

space ever more precious, single twenty-four-foot houses were torn down and replaced with three new houses, each eight feet wide. This practice met with the approval of the city council, which received a total of twenty-four gulden in taxes for the three new houses instead of the eighteen it had received for the single larger house. But expansion came at the cost of valuable open space. Stalls meant for cows and chicken coops were built up to accommodate humans; additions were piled onto rooftops, often with an overhang blocking light and air; houses were subdivided by walls creating rabbit warrens of crooked corridors and staircases.

Although the Jewish population shrank somewhat in the mid-seventeenth century after the hardships of the Thirty Years War and the plague years of 1635 and 1636, it began to climb again by the eighteenth century, placing the ghetto inhabitants under unprecedented strain. They lived under curfew in a street less than a quarter-mile long, its gates locked every sundown. The physical confinement, the lack of air, and the hopelessly inadequate sanitary arrangements led one visitor to observe that with the "surge of such a stench rushing toward me, I knew I was in the Judengasse." Another eighteenth-century traveler was struck to see that "most of the people, including [those] in the blooming years of their life, look like the walking dead."

In 1769, when local Jews asked for permission to walk on the newly opened embankment around the city's walls, their plea was rejected as yet another example of presumption. Ten years later, they reinforced their argument, appealing for fresh air in the name of "humanity and progress in civilization." This time they obtained a minimal concession: they could leave the ghetto after five in the afternoon on Sundays, when all church services were over.

This pathetic tale of physical deprivation and systematic contempt does not, however, get at the inner truth of life in the Judengasse. The ghetto, as the American sociologist Louis Wirth once noted, is as much a state of mind as a place. The Frankfurt ghetto was not just the scene of confinement and persecution but a place where Jews were entirely, supremely, at home. When they were first forced into it in 1462, they had derisively called it the New Egypt; by the seventeenth century, they were calling it the New Jerusalem. In 1694, their community counted

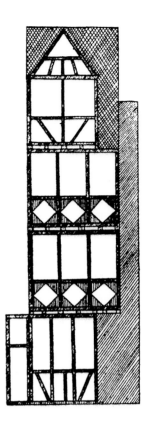

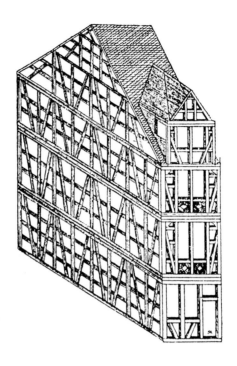

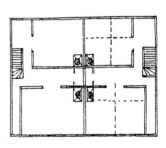

Diagrams of Judengasse buildings, clockwise from upper left: the Golden Peacock, At the Backyard School, a floor plan of the hospitals, and the facade of the hospitals. I. Kracauer, *Die Geschichte der Judengasse in Frankfurt am Main,* Frankfurt am Main, 1904.

Most of the people among the Frankfurter Jews, even those who are in the blooming years of their life, look like the walking dead. It would not be necessary to compel them to wear their short black cloaks and their collars in order to distinguish them from the others. Their deathly pale appearance sets them apart from all the other inhabitants in the most depressing way.

Bemerkungen eines Reisenden durch Deutschland, Frankreich, England und Holland, *ca. 1795, Cited in Isidor Kracauer, "Die Geschichte der Judengasse in Frankfurt am Main," in* Philanthropin 1804–1904 *[Frankfurt am Main, 1904].*

Excerpts from the New Frankfurt Jewish Dress Regulations *of 1715:*

18. Married and unmarried women are subject to the ordinance, which they are expected to follow without any slyness or deception or any attempt to evade it. Velvet garments, especially with gold and silver threads, both already made and those which may be made in the future, are all forbidden to be worn . . .

19. From today on it is forbidden that new Sabbath or festival clothing for women shall be of more than one color and shall not cost more than $2\frac{1}{2}$ thalers the length.

20. On workdays no married or unmarried woman may wear silk clothes except for a little cap of silk in only one color. Also, no gathered petticoat or skirt with flounces. Under the above-mentioned penalty [20 thalers].

27. Gold veils are forbidden except on the wedding day, when the mothers of the bridegroom and bride may wear them. But in no case may their wear veil pins. [These pins were often set with precious stones.]

28. Gold chains or gold girdles; pendants or lockets with precious stones and even more with pearls; and earrings with precious stones are entirely forbidden. Also, unmarried women are totally forbidden to wear any rings.

Johann Jacob Schudt, Neue Frankfurter jüdische Kleiderordnung *(1716), repr. Berlin, 1912.*

A Jewish man and woman of Frankfurt wearing the prescribed Jewish dress, 1703. Copper engraving by Christoph Weigel. Abraham à Sancta Clara, *Neueröffnete Welt-Galleria . . .* Nuremberg, 1703.

The controversial title page of a volume of responsa by Rabbi Joel Sirkes, published in Frankfurt in 1697. The Christian printer, using conventional ornaments, included both pagan and Christian elements in his decoration. The rabbinical council withheld its approval of this fantasy, and a different title page was subsequently printed.

Süsskind Stern (1610–1686) was a money changer and a dealer in pearls in Frankfurt. This portrait, said to be the earliest painting of a Jew in Germany, was probably commissioned by the sitter on a visit to Amsterdam in 1671. Originally the picture showed his cloak with the round yellow badge Jews were required to wear; a vestige of a badge is still discernible in the upper left-hand corner. (Color plate 12.)

The Judengasse, 1864.

eight rabbis, five cantors, one synagogue-summoner, ten schoolmasters, two physicians, one nurse, one notary, two men trained in the law, and two minstrels. A series of distinguished rabbis going back to the thirteenth century added luster to their yeshiva, which drew scholars from all over Europe. Thus Frankfurt's Jews developed a rich culture, living under their own elected government and speaking their own language. Well into the nineteenth century they issued sacred and secular texts, manuals of good conduct and religious observance, and the popular ballads that were a staple of ghetto entertainment in Yiddish. Although Frankfurt's government barred the Jews from owning printing presses, they published erudite Hebrew commentaries and, in 1720, even an edition of the Talmud, using Christian printers. The achievements of the Jews in this community shine all the more brightly for having emerged almost literally from the dungheap of their lives.

How the members of the Frankfurt Jewish community supported themselves in the face of onerous prohibitions on their economic activities is a testimony to human ingenuity. These very prohibitions shaped the profile of Jewish enterprise. The church's abhorrence of money lent at interest had turned Jews into the sole lenders. Meanwhile, the guilds barring Jews from their crafts and the municipal regulations prohibiting them from owning land conspired to force them into trade. Although a number of Jews adopted moneylending as their occupation, most Jews were engaged in some form of business or trade: buying and selling cloth and clothing, working as jewelers, tailors, butchers, horse traders, carpenters, bakers, and as dealers in spirits and wine, oil and spices, and all sorts of foodstuffs. Every generation boasted one or two physicians, sometimes even a woman physician. Specialization became so refined that there was even someone, the *Schaletsetzer,* whose job it was every Friday to deliver the pots containing each household's Sabbath meal to the communal oven. Since Jews could not open shops in Frankfurt proper, they did their business just outside the gates of the ghetto or in the densely crowded ghetto street itself.

Despite this varied activity and their ingenuity in seeking out new openings, most Jews in the ghetto made only a meager living. The top of the steep economic pyramid was occupied by a

Ludwig Börne, the journalist who was born in the ghetto in Frankfurt in 1786, describes it as it was in 1795, just before the French bombardment. The conflict within him that later expressed itself in his conversion to Christianity is demonstrated here as he alternates between irony and passionate anger.

Our readers may permit us to give them a picture of the Judengasse as it appeared twelve years ago [i.e., in 1795]. Let us take a walk through the long, dark prison into which the highly celebrated light of the eighteenth century had not yet been able to penetrate. . . . It was eleven o'clock when we entered the Judengasse, and we had chosen the Sabbath morning as the time when everything could be seen in its greatest glory. An eagle had been planted at the entrance to the street, elsewhere a symbol of freedom and pride, here the sign of servitude and powerlessness. It is an imperial eagle, which the Jews have placed there as a sign of gratitude to the German emperor because he had so often taken them under his protection against the fury of the Frankfurter citizenry. Stretching ahead of us lay an immeasurably long street, near us just enough room to reassure us that we could turn around as soon as the wish overcame us. Over us is no longer sky, which the sun needs in order to expand in his breadth; one doesn't see sky, one sees only the sunlight. An evil smell rises everywhere around us, and the cloth that is supposed to shield us from infection serves also to catch the tears of compassion or to hide the smile of malice from the gaze of the watching Jews. Tramping laboriously through the filth slows our pace enough to permit us the leisure for observation. We set our feet down skittishly and carefully so that we don't step on any children. These swim about in the gutter, creep about in the filth, innumerable as vermin hatched by the sun from a dungheap. Who would not indulge these little boys in their small desires? Indeed they have no courtyard, no little garden attached to their houses where they can carry on their childish play. In fact, if one were to consider play in childhood as the model for the reality of life, then the cradle of these children must be the grave of every encouragement, every exuberance, every friendship, every joy in life. Are you afraid that these towering houses will collapse over us? O fear nothing! They are thoroughly reinforced, the cages of clipped birds, resting on the cornerstone of eternal ill-will, well walled-up by the industrious hands of greed, and mortared with the sweat of tortured slaves. Do not hesitate. They stand firm and will never fall.

"Die Juden in Frankfurt am Main," in Ludwig Börne, Sämtliche Schriften, Düsseldorf, 1964.

The international house of Rothschild. The founder, Mayer Amschel Rothschild, is shown in the center.

handful of Jews grown rich in large-scale banking and in supplying states with weapons, uniforms, horses, and provisions. Paramount among these was the Rothschild family, which had lived in the Frankfurt ghetto since the sixteenth century. Its fame begins with the career of Mayer Amschel Rothschild, born in 1744, who brought himself to the notice of the landgrave of Hesse-Kassel, William IX, an avid collector, by procuring rare coins and antiquities for him. Together with his five sons, Mayer Amschel and the house of Rothschild became almost legendary financiers to the major powers of Europe. His sons dispersed, establishing branches of the house in England, France, Italy, and Austria, cooperating across national frontiers, and serving as bankers to their new rulers. Although they conducted transactions with the highest levels of government across Europe, the founder of the house, Mayer Amschel, continued to live in the Frankfurt ghetto, subject to all the constraints hampering his fellow Jews. When at the height of his fame he requested permission to take walks outside the ghetto for the sake of his health, the city council did not hesitate to refuse. But change—drastic change—was in the air.

Women

Jewish women in the medieval German lands were in an anomalous position. The educational system made no official room for them; according to Jewish legal custom they were treated as the minor children of their fathers or the chattel of their husbands. In religious ceremonies, the core of Jewish life, they hardly counted—perhaps even less than did women in Christianity. They could not be part of the quorum of ten (*minyan*) needed to form a congregation for prayer; they were not required to attend services; they were prohibited from studying the commentaries, the mark of a well-educated person; and their testimony was not admitted in court. When a boy was born, it was customary for the father to say, "God grant that I may raise him for the Torah, for marriage, and for good deeds." On the birth of a daughter, he said, "God grant that I raise her to sew, spin, and knit and to do good deeds." Although the home lies at the heart of both these prayers, the emphasis for girls was on domestic duties rather than education.

Yet the reality of women's situation was less oppressive than this outline might suggest. In an age when Charlemagne could not sign his name, when the greatest poet of the twelfth century, Wolfram von Eschenbach, could neither read nor write, Jewish women learned to read both Hebrew and Latin letters and formed an avid public for Yiddish literature. A conspicuous model for them was Dolce, the wife of Rabbi Eleazar of Worms, one in a long line of female breadwinners. Among the most learned wives of her age, she instructed the women of her community in the dietary laws (*kashruth*) and the order of the prayers. Her martyr's death in 1213 or 1214 at the hands of the Crusaders was commemorated in a poem by her husband praising her gentle spirit and her good works. The extensive Yiddish literature, both sacred and profane, which included treatises on ethics and conduct, all explicitly addressed to women, indicate that many were competent readers. Indeed, a sixteenth-century moral tract argues that even if Jewish women may not study the commentaries, they should be taught to read the twenty-four books of the Old Testament and the laws governing Jewish life.

The separation of the sexes showed itself particularly in language. Men wrote treatises on the law or philosophy in Hebrew and used Yiddish only when they wrote books intended for women. Most women, although taught to repeat and even to read prayers in Hebrew, did not understand the words they recited. In the eighteenth century a learned Christian, Johann Jacob Schudt, who wrote a bulky treatise on Jewish customs, once confronted a Jewish woman with this anomaly. "You read like the nuns," he said. "They read the psalms in Latin and also don't know what they are saying." His respondent was not perplexed. "It doesn't matter if I understand it," she answered, "God understands it."

This reply has a certain bite, but its rationale did not satisfy many Jewish women intent on expressing their religious feelings more directly and pointedly. For this purpose there developed a form of Yiddish prayer, *tehinoth,* or supplications, which dared to invoke the merits of Jewish mothers—Sarah, Rachel, and Rebecca—instead of Abraham, Isaac, and Jacob, as was customary in the synagogue. At first these prayers were largely written by men for women, but women soon undertook to compose their own,

A view of a synagogue showing women (and children) standing in the back, behind a partition; their eyes are veiled as a sign that they are blind to Christianity. This is from an early sixteenth-century book on Jewish customs, by an apostate. Johannes Pfefferkorn, *Libellus de Judaica Confessione sive Sabbato afflictionis,* Nuremberg, 1508.

cast in a more intimate tone than the conventional supplications. They centered on marriage, pregnancy, and childbirth, asking for a safe delivery, healthy children, and for a good living. Women also came to write works of poetry and prose which served as handbooks of moral behavior and gave advice on household management and marital affairs.

Still, marriage was the principal concern for a girl. Early marriages were long a feature of Jewish life as parents attempted to provide for their daughters in the event of their own untimely deaths. In these betrothals between children (a girl could be married at twelve) neither bride nor groom had much choice. But as adults, only the husband was entitled to start proceedings for divorce. Even so, Jewish culture made some room for humane pieces of legislation. Thus in the eleventh century, Rabbi Gershom of Mainz outlawed divorce without the wife's consent, as well as polygyny.

Although keeping multiple wives was exceedingly rare in Europe in Gershom's day, his decree played a part in 1196 when a German Jewish synod met to adapt Jewish marriage law to changed conditions. The Bible had laid it down that a woman whose husband dies childless should be taken to wife by her husband's brother. If the brother refused, a ceremony called *halizah,* designed to shame him, required the woman to loosen "a shoe from off his foot, and spit in his face and say, 'So shall it be done unto the man that doth not build up his brother's house'" (Deuteronomy 25:8). By the Middle Ages, however, this biblical tableau had become irrelevant to Jewish realities. In a society where Christians and Jews alike outlawed polygyny, the biblical injunction ran into immediate difficulties if the brother was already married. If the widow was reluctant to marry, an unscrupulous brother-in-law had an opportunity to extort money as the price for withdrawing his claim. The work of the synod, therefore, in regulating the amounts due to the widow, as well as to her late husband's brother, offered women a measure of economic and personal protection—a significant step in advancing the rights of a woman before Jewish courts. She was no longer being treated as a chattel to be handed on with her husband's estate, entitled only to her dowry as her inheritance.

Lacking the legal rights of full adults—that is,

of men—proved to be no deterrent to vigorous economic activity among Jewish women in the German lands. From the earliest times, they engaged in trade on many levels and in many areas. They indirectly "profited" from the high esteem accorded to study in Jewish life, which encouraged the husband to devote himself to scholarship, leaving the wife to earn the living for the family. Where the husband was the breadwinner, the home and the place of business were often the same, and the wife frequently worked as her husband's assistant. She worked, too, in her husband's absence. Even before the Crusaders had established a permanent beachhead for Christian merchants in the Near East, Jewish traders had plied the routes between Europe and the Levant, and during these journeys (often lasting several years) the wife, who had stayed at home, needed to secure some means of livelihood. These commercial expeditions were so hazardous that some husbands left behind a conditional bill of divorce permitting their wives to remarry if they had not returned by a specified date. This was to prevent the tragic situation of a wife becoming an *agunah,* a woman whose husband's death could not be proved and who therefore remained in a kind of legal limbo.

Accepted—even honored—though their commercial role was, Jewish women rarely received any formal training. Yet in addition to being literate, as businesswomen they must have known the rudiments of arithmetic. And in some pursuits they had more systematic preparation. In the Middle Ages, Christians and Jews alike found a special place for the wise woman, the herbalist who could prescribe potions or poultices for the sick.

In time, Jewish women expanded their traditional role as midwife and herbalist to that of physician. Between 1389 and 1497, fifteen Jewish women were recorded in the archives of Frankfurt as practicing medicine, particularly ophthalmology. In fact, of the four ophthalmologists in thirteenth-century Frankfurt, three were Jewish women. Yet although they were accorded certain privileges—in Frankfurt one Jewish woman physician could live outside the ghetto—their practice was by law confined to Jewish patients. As the number of noble lords with Jewish physicians attests, this ban was by no means always observed.

The halizah ceremony in an eighteenth-century engraving. The widow removes a special shoe worn by the man, spits on the ground, and says a certain formula. This frees them both from the obligations of a levirate marriage. Also shown is the halizah shoe. J. C. G. Bodenschatz, *Kirchliche Verfassung der heutigen Juden sonderlich derer in Deutschland,* 1749.

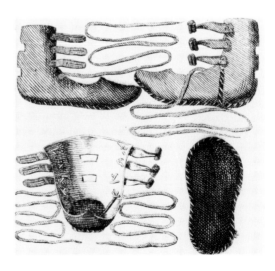

Medicine was not the only liberal profession Jewish women could practice. They took on the onerous occupation of traveling musician, playing and jesting at weddings; and they worked as printers and, even more frequently, writers. But whether she worked or not, the main arena for a Jewish woman's activity—like that of her gentile sisters—was the home, where she played many roles from caretaker to teacher, stage manager to high priestess. The Jewish household was in itself a kind of temple dedicated to the domestic aspect of the Law. What was forbidden and what permitted were instilled in the little Jewish girl through precept and observation, and carrying out these requirements to the letter would be among her most serious responsibilities as a wife. Since the major Jewish holidays have their public and domestic faces, her ordering of the household to manage their celebration was as important a task for her as attendance at synagogue was for her husband.

If we count the names in the lists of martyrs kept by medieval Jewish communities, the women are hardly outdone by the men in their steadfastness to their faith. Clearly, though, they shone not in death alone. Women were the vital force transmitting the daily observance of Judaism and the carriers of the vernacular culture. In songs, poems, stories, legends, even in the superstitions woven into the texture of daily life, they preserved *mama loshen* (the mother tongue)—Yiddish. They were the first teachers of their sons, sometimes the only teachers of their daughters. Working at home they thus joined the twin aspects of Jewish life: the religious tradition, which gave structure and rhythm to the course of the week and the year, and the vernacular culture, with its profound connection to the world around them. They managed to populate a rich universe whose echoes still reach us, most vividly of all in the long memoir by Glückel of Hameln.

Glückel of Hameln

In her own time Glückel of Hameln would have been a remarkable woman even if she had not written her autobiography. Without it, we would have known the outlines of her life from her gravestone: she was born in 1646 in Hamburg to a wealthy Jewish family; she married Hayyim of Hameln at the age of fourteen and bore him thirteen children; Hayyim died in 1689, and in 1700 she married again, this time a French Jew, Cerf Levy, whom she also outlived. She died in 1724.

Glückel came from that merchant caste that was neither court Jew nor simple trader nor moneylender, the occupations of so many Jews of the period. Glückel's husband Hayyim was a merchant, gem dealer, and banker, turning from one business to the other as the occasion offered. With careful and steady application to his work, he came to enjoy great wealth, so that in 1671, nobility—even royalty, including Frederick, later the first king in Prussia—attended the wedding of their eldest daughter, Zipporah, in Cleves. (See plate 10.)

Yet Glückel and Hayyim were Jews who lived their private lives entirely within the bounds of Jewish tradition, spoke Yiddish with each other, and watched the rich world they served always from the distance of the stranger. However splendid their lives—and Glückel describes with pride the gilded leather that covered the salon walls of her in-laws' house in Cleves—they also knew that they lived at the pleasure of the lord or of the city fathers. Much of the concern of Glückel's and Hayyim's life was to marry off their children, not only to give them good partners, but also to be assured that they would enjoy a permanent home. The right of settlement remained a scarce and costly commodity.

Glückel was fortunate not only in her wealth but also in her happiness. When she came to Hameln, a timid bride of fourteen years, "left alone in a strange land with strangers," she quickly learned to cherish her in-laws. "They were both such estimable and pious people," she wrote, "and were kinder to me than I deserved." Although her husband had been chosen for her, the marriage was marked by the most profound affection and confidence on both sides. "He was such a loving and faithful father," Glückel wrote of him, "as one seldom finds, and loved his wife and children beyond measure." Indeed, when he fell and, as it turned out, fatally injured himself, he at first refused to send for a doctor lest it be rumored that his children came from poor stock.

Glückel's piety, which permeates her memoirs, was also a measure for her judgment of others, and her husband's steadfast observance of the law evoked her greatest admiration. "He

The Hamburg Exchange and City Hall in Glückel's time, around 1680, showing a demonstration of new fire-fighting equipment. Th. Schrader, *Hamburg vor 200 Jahren,* Hamburg, 1892.

A marriage contract
(*ketubah*) such as
would have been used
at the wedding of

Glückel's daughter
Zipporah in Cleves.
Amsterdam, 1718.
(Color plate 10.)

***One of Glückel's constant preoccupations was the marriage of
her children. Here she describes the wedding in 1674 of her
daughter Zipporah to Kossmann, the son of Elias of Brandenburg, who resided in Cleves.***

*As the time of the wedding approached, all of us together, my husband
and I, with a babe at my breast, my daughter Zipporah, the bride,
Rabbi Meir . . . and our servant Handsome Samuel and a servant girl,
thus in grand suite journeyed to the wedding. We traveled from Altona
by ship in company [with others], and what a jolly trip we had, I can
hardly describe. And so we arrived happily in Amsterdam full of joy
and contentment. . . .*

*At last as we stood under the marriage canopy with the bridal pair, it
was discovered that in the great excitement we had forgotten to write
the ketubah. What should one do at this point? All the honored guests
including the young prince [later King Frederick I of Prussia] were
standing there waiting to observe the ceremony. Then the rabbi said
that the bridegroom should appoint someone to stand surety for him
and bind himself to have a marriage contract written immediately
following the ceremony. . . .*

*After the wedding, all the honored guests were brought into Elias
Cleve's grand, stately hall, all lined with gilded leather. There stood a
great table set out with the finest delicacies. . . . Then a costumed
company came in and performed all kinds of comical pieces which
added to the pleasure. And at the end they presented a Dance of Death
which was quite exquisite.*

Denkwürdigkeiten der Glückel von Hameln, *Frankfurt am Main, 1987.*

Ketubah detail. The
inclusion of human
figures was an inno-
vation in Jewish art
from the time of the
Renaissance.

was," she wrote of him, "the perfect paragon of a pious Jew." Indeed, on his deathbed, the two were prevented from a last embrace when Glückel had to admit that she was "unclean" (menstruating) and therefore should not touch her husband. By the time of Hayyim's death, when Glückel was only forty-three, she had become not only her husband's confidante but also his business partner and could carry on independently. With eight of her twelve children still to be provided for, she worked successfully, not only earning dowries for them but also arranging suitable matches.

Her second marriage, eleven years after her husband's death, seems to have been less an affair of the heart. In any event, it brought her only sorrow: her husband went bankrupt two years after their wedding, losing not only his fortune but hers as well. When he died in 1712, she became dependent on her children for support, something she had always dreaded. In 1715, after considerable hardship, she finally consented to live with her daughter Esther and her husband, Moses Krumbach, in Metz. The move proved more congenial than she had pictured it. There, she reports with great satisfaction, she was treated with the deference she so valued— always served first, with the choicest morsels.

Although her business affairs and the welfare of her children were at the center of Glückel's preoccupations, she also had a shrewd eye for what was happening in the world. We learn from her how the Sabbatean movement affected the Jews in Germany; she comments on relations between Sweden and Denmark and the consequences for the Jewish communities of Altona and Hamburg. The life of the rich and pious Jews of Western Europe is always a vivid part of the background. But most remarkable is the report of the interior life of an educated Jewish woman who lived fully, observed closely, and to our great good fortune found the occasion to write down her thoughts.

Of Glückel's many descendants, two are particularly noteworthy: the poet Heinrich Heine and Bertha Pappenheim, a pioneer in the field of social welfare. Pappenheim translated Glückel's memoirs, as well as other Yiddish writings, into German, and she sat as the model for an imaginary portrait of Glückel by the painter Leopold Pilchowski, adorning the memory of her ancestress with her finest laces.

Revivals of Mysticism

The mainstream of Jewish religion revolved around the devout reading of sacred texts, the meticulous observance of commandments, and the faithful celebration of holy days, but mystical leanings never quite disappeared. They revived with particular energy in the course of the seventeenth century and did not leave the Jews of Germany untouched.

With the expulsion of the Jews from Spain in 1492, many scholars—mystics among them— settled in Safed in Palestine, drawing others of similar persuasion to this new center of learning. There, paradoxically, the mystic Joseph Caro wrote a new codification of Jewish law: his *Shulhan Aruch* (Prepared table), became the definitive basis for Jewish orthodox practice. And there Isaac Luria developed a new approach to kabbalah emphasizing asceticism, fasting, and strict adherence to the law. These scholars persuaded many Jews that the curse born in the time of the Creation and their own suffering in exile were part of the struggle to mend the troubled divine order. The Jew in exile, the mystics argued, had a mission to defeat the forces of evil and oppression by observing the 613 commandments of the law. According to rabbinical lore, 613 was the number of parts of the human body; in Luria's scheme, it also represented the parts of the soul, whose unity had been shattered by Adam's sin. Only the restoration of the soul to its primordial harmony would bring perfection and redemption back to the world. Although he died in an epidemic in 1574 at the early age of thirty-eight, Luria's messianic message prepared the way for the Sabbatean movement, which would sweep Jewish communities across Europe, including Germany, a century later.

The Jews of sixteenth-century Europe had already witnessed the shattering of what had seemed an indivisible Christianity. Martin Luther's successful challenge to the power of the Roman church and its "idolatrous" customs brought forth a new age. Popular movements have their ebb and flow, generally stimulated by a charismatic personage, who excites the imaginations and touches the hearts of ordinary people. In Jewish life, the foundation for such a movement was the age-old longing for the coming of the Messiah, and it only awaited the leader who would call it into life.

It was the *idea* of Shabbetai Zevi rather than his physical presence that created the hysterical fervor which transformed Jewish life in the 1660s. Places where he had never set foot, including the German lands, were caught up in the conviction that he was the Messiah: the time was ripe for the restoration of the Jews to the Holy Land. Normally sensible businessmen in all parts of Germany sold their houses and goods so that they might be ready to depart when the moment came. Even Glückel's sober father-in-law was caught up in the flood of feeling; he disposed of his house, land, and furniture and sent two casks of provisions to Hamburg to be held in readiness for the great voyage. When at the height of the fever in 1666 the Jewish community of Hamburg made a contract with Altona concerning the sale of land in a cemetery, they included the coming of the Messiah and the return of the Jews to Palestine—the Redemption—as a contingency. "And if the Redemption should take place before [December 1666]," the contract specifies, "the Hamburg congregation will nevertheless pay the due amount of fifty thalers to the Altona congregation, who will give it for the building of the Temple."

The man who aroused all this fervor was a Jew born in Smyrna in 1626, whose extravagant swings of mood from total withdrawal to wild elation earned him a reputation for eccentricity. Admired for his obvious intellectual gifts, he remained restless, unsettled in his community. In 1662, at the age of thirty-six, after erratic travels in the Near East, he decided to go to Jerusalem, where a young rabbi, Nathan of Gaza, was attracting attention for his powers of spiritual healing. When Shabbetai Zevi appeared in Gaza, Nathan "recognized" him as the Messiah. On May 31, 1665, amid wild popular enthusiasm, Shabbetai Zevi proclaimed himself the Messiah and appointed a group of twelve disciples, each representing one of the tribes of Israel. Nathan, serving as his prophet, published his own revelation that at the end of 1666 the age of the Messiah would come, and he admonished Jews everywhere to use the time remaining for repentance and good works. By October 1665 the news had reached Europe, including Germany, and a frenzy caught up rich and poor, lettered and unlettered, country and city people alike.

Der Große betrieger und Falsche MESSIAS
SABATAI–SEVI,
König der Jüden
Anno 1666.

Shabbetai Zevi
(1626–1676). From
the frontispiece from
*Die Geschichte von
dem grossen Be-
trieger* . . . 1702.

A contemporary account by the English traveler Nathaniel Crouch of Shabbetai Zevi's conversion to Islam.

Sabatai appeared much dejected and failing of that courage which he had showed in the synagogue; and being demanded several questions by the grand seignor, he would not trust so far to the virtue of his Messiahship as to deliver himself in the Turkish language but desired a doctor of physic, who had from a Jew turned Turk, to be his interpreter, which was granted to him. . . .

But the grand seignor would not be put off without a miracle, and it must be one of his own choice; which was that Sabatai should be stripped naked, and set as a mark to his archers: if the arrows pierced not his body, then he would believe him to be the Messiah. But Sabatai not having faith to stand so sharp a trial, renounced all his title to kingdoms and governments, alledging that he was an ordinary chocham *[learned man], and a poor Jew, as others were, and had nothing of privilege or virtue above the rest. But the grand seignor not being fully satisfied with this plain confession, declared, that having given public scandal to the professors of the Mehometan religion, and done dishonor to his sovereign authority by pretending to draw such a considerable portion from him as the land of Palestine; his treason and crime were not to be expatiated but by a conversion to the Mehometan faith, which if he refused, the stake was ready at the gate of the Seraglio to impale him.*

Sabatai being now reduced to extremity, yet not doubtful what to do, for to die for what he knew to be false would be the death of a mad man; replied with much chearfulness that he was contented to turn a Turk, and that it was not of force, but of choice, having been a long time desirous of so glorious profession: he esteemed himself much honored, that he had an opportunity to own it first in the presence of the grand seignor.

Nathaniel Crouch, A Journey to Jerusalem, Hartford *1796.*

Jonathan Eybeschütz
(1690–1764), rabbi
of the communities of
Altona, Wandsbeck,
and Hamburg.

After dividing up the kingdoms of the world among his followers, Shabbetai Zevi set sail in December for Constantinople. But when his ship arrived there in February 1666, he was arrested and held by order of an alarmed vizier. Undeterred, pilgrims came from afar to visit him, while preparations for the messianic age continued throughout the Diaspora. Shabbetai Zevi, brought before a court attended by the Sultan, was accused of having represented himself as the Messiah and was given a choice between death and conversion to Islam. In a mood of deep dejection, he agreed to submit to the Islamic faith, in which he nominally remained until his death in 1676.

Even this betrayal did not burst the bubble of Jewish ardor. While the rabbinate tried to hush up the whole affair, true believers sought higher justifications for these stunning events, and the powerful effect of that intense messianic year, 1666, survived in Jewish culture as the core of an underground mystical doctrine that lasted into the eighteenth century. It became a public scandal in 1751, when Jacob Emden, a rabbi in Emden, accused Jonathan Eybeschütz, the eminent rabbi of Hamburg, of distributing secret amulets with Shabbatean inscriptions. Although an international council of rabbis exonerated Eybeschütz, the aura of Shabbateanism clung to him. Suspicion erupted again in 1760, when his son declared himself a Shabbatean and the yeshiva over which Eybeschütz presided was discovered to be infected by Shabbatean notions. The yeshiva was closed, but Eybeschütz remained in his post, his reputation as a preacher and scholar intact.

Another messianic upheaval, sparked by Jacob Frank, a visionary born in Podolia in 1726, attests to the vitality of mysticism. In the dawning age of the Enlightenment, however, Messianism as a literal belief could no longer command the imagination of many Jewish followers. Shabbatean, Frankist, and other messianic sects lingered on in various corners of the Diaspora into the twentieth century. But Jewry had a different agenda. Theodor Herzl, the founder of Zionism, whose frenzied followers in Eastern Europe hailed him as the king of the Jews, resembled these false Messiahs only superficially. His thought was rooted in the present and in the temporal rather than the Heavenly Jerusalem.

The Court Jew

As Jewish occupations grew more restricted and permanent residence became a privilege instead of a right, the gap between rich and poor widened. At the top were the court Jews, men summoned to serve a prince or noble lord, most often as financial advisers and bankers but also as tax administrators, suppliers of military materiel like horses, provisions, and weapons, or purveyors of jewels, antiquities, and other luxuries. These Jews, who profited immensely from their opportunities, also lived in two worlds. Dressed in the latest fashion, exempt from the onerous badge and other marks of Jewish dress, speaking several languages and well educated, they enjoyed the advantages of their wealth. Yet serving at the pleasure of a prince who might prove fickle, whose mind might be turned against them, who might suddenly die, made theirs a hazardous occupation. Always the outsider and dependent on the goodwill of his patron, the court Jew was easy game for a discontented prince and a visible target for his subjects.

The model of the court Jew was Josel of Rosheim. Although he was born in Alsace, Josel's powers of persuasion were so efficacious that he was importuned for help by Jewish communities in places as distant as Bohemia, Saxony, Silesia, and Hungary. Born Joseph ben Gershom at the end of the fifteenth century (ca. 1478), he lost his father at the early age of six. The family had paid bloody dues to the superstitions of the time: three of Josel's uncles were condemned to a grisly execution in 1470 following a blood libel in a celebrated case in Endingen. We can only conjecture about the effect of this somber background, but we know that Josel must have had a remarkable presence, because he was early prevailed upon to intercede for Jewish communities in trouble. In 1520, at the coronation of Charles V, Josel managed to procure a letter of protection from the new emperor for the Jews in German lands. Accorded honorary titles by grateful Jewish communities, he became their single most important spokesman against the recurrent blood libels, the ever more violent denunciations of Luther, and the calumnies that regularly threatened the continuity of Jewish settlements.

During the sixteenth century a rather more indirect form of attack—staged disputations between learned Christians and Jews—was at the height of its popularity. Entertainment and trial rolled into one, these disputations had begun in the fourth century, in the time of Constantine, and were often a ceremonial prelude to expulsions and the destruction of Jewish life and property. In 1530 a learned apostate, Antonius Margaritha, published a book describing Jewish belief and practices in which he claimed, among other strange distortions, that the Jews of the German lands prayed three times a day, and especially on the Day of Atonement, for the destruction of the Holy Roman Empire and the letting of Christian blood. Charles V ordered a disputation to be held in June of the same year, on the occasion of an assembly of the court in Augsburg, and Josel was bidden to appear to defend his fellow Jews and Jewish practices against the slanders of Margaritha. Unlike most disputations, this one ended with Margaritha, rather than the Jewish community, banished from Augsburg at the behest of Charles V.

While Josel earned his living as a money-changer, his commercial activities fade against his lifelong service as an intercessor. He was also, as we have seen, an intellectual representative of Jewish thought and belief to the Christian world as well as a scholar securely within the Jewish tradition. He wrote philosophical works on ethics and even an autobiography shortly before his death in 1554. Both in his influence and in the use of his powers, this remarkable man, who won such favor with Charles V that he and his family were given permission to travel and settle wherever they chose, was unique among court Jews.

Unfortunately, Josel's memory neither improved the character nor protected the life of the court Jew Lippold, the rapacious accomplice of the elector Joachim II of Brandenburg, who came into prominence at the time of Josel's death. Lippold moved to Berlin from Prague around 1550 as mint master for Joachim, collector of his taxes, and manager of the privy purse. He also charged extortionate sums for private loans—sometimes as much as 50 percent.

As the confidant of Joachim, he was appointed governor of the Jewish community. He tyrannized over the Jews, extorted money from them, and did not scruple to rob the widow and children of his brother. Although he managed to accumulate a great fortune, whether by legitimate or illegitimate means, he was not the richest of the bankers or purveyors to the court; he was only the most hated.

An example of the use of influence as late as the eighteenth century: the opening page of a document written in July 1716 in which Emperor Charles VI, at the request of his court factor, Emanuel Oppenheimer, recommends Moses Dellheimer to the city of Speyer and asks that Dellheimer and his dependents be granted the protection of the city since Dellheimer will be entering the service of the emperor.

It was Lippold's intimate personal relationship with Joachim that caused his downfall. On the night of the prince's sudden death (January 3, 1571) witnesses testified that they had seen Lippold hand him a goblet of wine. Johann, the prince's son and successor, who had reason to loathe Lippold for what he perceived as his pernicious influence over his father, needed no better evidence. On that very night he ordered the gates to Berlin barred to prevent Lippold's escape. Lippold was arrested and charged with murder; a rich arsenal of torture instruments produced a confession. Although he subsequently retracted his words, it was too late; on January 28, 1573, he was drawn and quartered in the presence of an avid multitude, and the Jews of Berlin were once again banished from the city. The fate of the court Jew was, then, no private matter; a fallen court Jew could carry a whole community down to destruction with him. However execrated he may have been, Lippold dead brought a worse fate on the heads of his fellow Jews than Lippold alive.

Perhaps the most spectacular of all the court Jews was the eighteenth-century banker known as Jud Süss. Born Joseph ben Issachar Süsskind Oppenheimer in the late 1690s, he was reared as

A sixteenth-century disputation. The Jews wear medieval Jewish hats, and each has a ring on his coat. Georg Liebe, *Das Judentum in der deutschen Vergangenheit,* Leipzig, 1903.

■

The modern reader should not be deceived by the seemingly humble tone of this appeal, a style that was conventional in such memorials. In his carefully constructed argument to the governors of Strasbourg in 1546, Josel of Rosheim first describes the events in which Jews have been attacked, not flinching from accusing high-ranking officers of acts of violence and plunder. Then he appeals to a higher sense of justice, since such violence is countenanced by neither "divine nor profane" law. Finally, he invokes the special status of the Jews, who stand directly under the Holy Roman emperor's protection, reminding the governors that this protection had been renewed only recently, at a meeting of the Reichstag in Worms. What is in form an appeal becomes, then, almost a threat backed by the higher power of the emperor.

Honorable gentlemen,

This did I hear from Regensburg upon my return home, and it seems a trustworthy report. The truth is that from among your Honors' comrades-in-arms, several of the officers and their soldiers hunted out the poor Jews in Swabia, took some of them prisoner and demanded ransom, destroyed the houses of those that escaped, plundered and wasted whatever was within, and ruined and chased away many poor widows and orphans. . . . Honorable gentlemen, in all my experience of forty years, whatever unjust and offensive things have been done to me and my brothers, we have always regarded your Honors and all your kin and dependents as our resort and with the greatest trust . . . and therefore we remain in the secure hope that your Honors are still inclined to the same graciousness and justice . . . and *will not permit any of us either collectively or individually . . . to be asked for ransom or accused, which would be against the decree of public peace and especially against the protection granted by the Holy Roman Empire and its members for all time. . . . Because one can find in no law, whether divine or profane, whether written or natural, that any one could deprive our poor selves of our possessions and drive us from our established places of abode against all recognized rights, and it is also publicly known that at the latest Reichstag in Worms [in 1545] a petition was circulated by our enemies to banish us poor Jews from Germany, but through the gracious favor of the Almighty, the electors and princes, all the estates and the most prudent representatives established and stated that such action was not to be taken, and as has long been the case, the ruling powers are to continue to grant to their Jews, without diminution, the protection and safe-conduct promised them by the Holy Roman emperor. . . . The conclusion of these matters lies with your Honors, to whom my humble pleading and request on behalf of the often mentioned poor Jews of the German nation . . . is that you will instruct your soldiers and allies that the poor Jews collectively or singly, wherever they may be found, may continue to remain unhindered and unharmed, so that those in Swabia, as well as [elsewhere], may once again enter their abodes and live there.*

[Signed] Your Honors' humble and obedient,
Joslin, Jew of Rosshein,
General Commander of the Jews

Ludwig Feilchenfeld, Rabbi Josel von Rosheim, *Strasbourg. 1897.*

Drawing and quartering of the court Jew Lippold, January 23, 1573.

a devout Jew in Heidelberg and received a traditional Jewish education. As a member of a distinguished banking family, he was sent abroad, when he was old enough, to be trained in relatives' counting houses in the capitals of Europe. In 1732, a seasoned financier, he entered the service of Duke Karl Alexander of Württemberg and quickly became his principal economic adviser. Oppenheimer with his worldly experience encouraged the duke in fiscal policies intended to build a centralized, modern, mercantile state. But since these innovations dislodged the old estates and the burghers from their former power and privileges, their anger fell on the convenient target, the court Jew. There was another thorn. Having turned Catholic, the duke also planned to raise Catholicism to equality with Protestantism in his dominions. But anxious Protestants transformed this statesmanlike proposal into a rumor that the duke would force conversion on his subjects. This hardly added to the duke's popularity among the Protestant peasants and poorer elements in the population.

Unmoved by this almost universal opposition, Jud Süss remained at the duke's side, as both his companion and his financial counselor. He even refused more lucrative offers from other courts. He was rich, clever, known for his success with women—a perfect baroque gentleman, with grand houses in Mannheim and Frankfurt as well as in Stuttgart, the duke's seat. The inventory for his house in Stuttgart alone lists three coaches and horses, quantities of fine clothing, furniture, porcelain, silver, jewels, books in French, Latin, and German, and eighty-five paintings, among

them works by Cranach, Rembrandt, Jordaens, and Rubens. His parties were legendary for their splendor, concluding with souvenirs of precious jewels for the ladies.

But when the duke suddenly died on March 12, 1737, in the midst of a night of carousing, the Jew who had been with him became the obvious target for revenge. The duke's dissolute life and unpopular policies were now all laid at the door of his court Jew, who was seized and charged with high treason, offense to the established religion, fraud, sale of offices, and many other crimes. The trial and examination of the evidence took nearly a year, during which Oppenheimer was transformed from a dapper, charming courtier to an old Jew. He grew so thin that he could slip his hands out of his manacles, and he transformed himself inwardly as well, returning to the practices of Judaism. During his imprisonment he was tortured for evidence and subjected to several attempts at conversion, which he rejected.

In December 1737 he was sentenced to death by hanging, and although the Jews of Württemberg offered 50,000 florins for his release, the new prince was not to be moved. The day of Jud Süss's hanging—February 4, 1738—turned into a folk festival with thousands crowding into Stuttgart to witness the strange event, for the ironworkers' guild had fashioned an ornate man-sized cage in which he would be hanged high above the gallows. As he climbed the fifty-two steps to his crimson-painted cage, he is reported to have recited the fundamental Jewish credo: "Hear, O Israel, that God is our God and that He is One." Broadsides with portraits of Jud Süss and his mistress, Henriette Luciana Fischer, together with depictions of the entire event appeared immediately to assist the imagination of those absent from the hanging and displayed a remarkably sympathetic view of the pair.

By the beginning of the nineteenth century, the institution of the court Jew, like drawing and quartering, was becoming obsolete. Industrialization and the modernization of finance transformed the nature of statecraft, while the gradual emancipation of the Jews changed their place in society. Although the nineteenth-century Jewish banker continued to serve kings and princes, he was more a businessman than a courtier. It was a less glamorous life than that of his predecessors, but certainly safer.

Joseph Süsskind Oppenheimer, known as Jud Süss. A contemporary engraving shows him surrounded by instruments of torture, and below him is the cage in which he was hanged. The verse rejoices that this "insolent Jew" has paid for his sins on the gallows.

How can I console you

Gallant Fischerin, dearest treasure.

I know that it will break your heart

When you think of this place.

But just the opposite when you think

Of the pleasure that we enjoyed together.

Adieu, farewell a thousand times

O gallant Jew, charming Süss.

You must pay on the gallows

For what your good sense overlooked.

Ah, if only my little boy were still alive

I would have a remembrance of you.

"The Last Farewell of Jud Süss to his Mistresses, Especially to the Former Maiden Fischer" and "The Expression of Thanks of the Former Maiden Fischer, a Mistress of Jud Süss," in Gespräch Zweyer unter dem Stuttgardter Galgen . . . von des famosen Jud Süssen Leben und Ende . . . 1738.

Berlin: A Community of Court Jews

In the seventeenth century, the position of German Jews was simple. They were treated as unequal "partners" in a transaction in which a ruler provided them with a place to live and work, and the Jews in return paid protection money—*Schutzgeld*—for the privilege of existence. In those years, both Jews and their rulers saw themselves engaged in an exchange of services, unclouded by philosophic considerations. Ideas about toleration, human rights, and mutual moral obligations had not yet come to confuse a clearly defined, if one-sided, business relationship.

The genesis of the last Jewish community in Berlin is a classic example of how the system worked. Although Jews had lived in Berlin in the early Middle Ages, the modern community was founded in 1671, benefiting from the misfortune of the Jews in Vienna. There in February 1670 some 3,000 Jews, including a group that had fled from deadly pogroms in Poland in 1648, had been notified by an order of Emperor Leopold that they must leave by the following Easter. Desperate for a place of refuge, they appealed to the representative of Brandenburg-Prussia for permission to settle in the lands of Frederick William, the Great Elector. "The very earth on which we stand, indeed the entire world, is closed against us," they wrote in their plea. They were, they said, being "treated cruelly, against all natural law."

Enhancing this appeal to natural law was the reality that Frederick William was facing a land depleted by the Thirty Years' War. He had come to the throne in 1640, eight years before the end of that war, but even after a quarter-century of his rule, his country remained impoverished and trade was at a standstill. Berlin's population had been reduced by half and in 1648 counted a mere 6,000 or 7,000 inhabitants. The Great Elector was determined to build his capital into a thriving center of commerce and beauty, laying out new streets, planting trees, constructing a fortified city wall, and rebuilding the palace, which had fallen into ruin. In the interest of promoting trade, he embarked on an extensive and exceedingly successful program of canal construction.

Hence the Viennese Jews' appeal was welcome to him: a recovering city needs people with technical skills. He cautiously told his envoy in Vienna that he was not unwilling to admit forty or fifty well-to-do Jewish families who would bring their capital with them and invest it in enterprises in Berlin. Around Easter 1671, twelve of the families took advantage of the Great Elector's offer and dispersed to three of his cities: Berlin, Frankfurt an der Oder, and Zullichau. The three families that went to Berlin were headed by Hirschel Lazarus, Benedikt Veit, and Abraham Ries.

The edict of May 21, 1671, which spelled out the conditions for admitting these first Jewish families, also specified how they were to live and make their living. The first restriction was one of time: the privilege was to run for only twenty years. But they could settle where they liked, engage in trade without restrictions, and keep a slaughterer as well as a schoolteacher. Heavy taxes were laid upon them in return for these privileges, and in order to curb the growth of the Jewish population in Prussia, each family was allowed to settle only one child in the community.

In an age of envenomed, often violent religious intolerance, Frederick William showed himself a ruler of remarkable liberality. In addition to Jews, he admitted Protestants from the Rhineland, Huguenots from France, and an assortment of religious dissidents, such as Arians and Mennonites. Like his Jews, these sects settled in segregated areas, each speaking its own language and founding its own schools and places of worship. These groups, too, were valued for the skills and trades they brought with them, the Huguenots especially for their expertise in the manufacture of textiles.

With the same energy with which he extended Prussia's boundaries from the Rhine in the west to the Baltic Sea, the Great Elector pursued his building and collecting passions at home, providing a formidable example for his son and successor, Frederick III, who in January 1701 crowned himself Frederick I, king in Prussia. The Great Elector, an avid accumulator of paintings and gems, was not alone among rulers in his preoccupation with splendor. His model was Louis XIV of France, the Sun King, whose lavish expenditures on palaces, furniture, jewels, and works of art were emulated by every monarch and princeling whether he could afford it or not. In those days the court jeweler was a busy man, and in Berlin he was likely to be a Jew.

Seventeenth-century Berlin, the capital of Prussia, made up of Berlin, Cölln an der Spree, and Friedrichswerder.

The Edict of May 21, 1671, permitting the settlement of fifty families of protected Jews in Berlin.

Jost Liebmann, who came to Berlin in 1679, succeeded to that lucrative post by marrying the widow of the former court factor, Israel Aaron. By the end of the century, Glückel von Hameln called him the richest Jew in Germany. Liebmann was also a patron of Jewish learning, supporting needy scholars and placing members of his family as rabbis in outlying towns. Yet in Berlin the court Jews, unlike their fellows elsewhere, were not unique personages. As a slowly rising population, they became a community, but an invincible rivalry made its early years anything but harmonious. The community divided into two factions whose competition was first expressed in the maintenance of two private synagogues. Jost Liebmann's was the first to be officially sanctioned, in 1687, and he appointed one of his sons-in-law as its rabbi. Ten years later the Veit-Ries faction also received permission to hold services and built a two-story brick building in the Gothic style. But when the enmity between the two parties could not be resolved, the community sought permission to build a public synagogue. This was finally granted in the Privilege of 1700—for a payment of 3,000 thalers. The new synagogue, in the Heidereutergasse, was opened on the Sabbath before the Jewish New Year in 1714 in the presence of the king and members of his court. Widely admired as the handsomest in Germany, it was said to rival in elegance the famous Portuguese synagogue in Amsterdam. For the outside world, it stood as an emblem of the solidity of the Berlin Jewish community. With its graceful neoclassical decor, it indicated that that community shared the aesthetic if not the religious convictions of the surrounding culture.

Private building by Jews enjoying permanent residence in Berlin closely followed this first public architectural statement. The richest among them vied in erecting veritable palaces furnished in the grand manner. The two most famous of these were built in the 1760s by Daniel Itzig and Veitel Heine Ephraim, both of whom had made their fortunes during the Seven Years' War minting coins for Frederick II. In the picture collections of both palaces, the secular and the religious coexist with complete ease. The Itzig house displayed paintings by Rubens, Wouvermans, and De Witt, while the Ephraims boasted Caravaggios, Poussins, and Salvator Rosas. Mixed in with genre scenes, portraits, and landscapes were paintings of Christian religious subjects: the Holy Family on the flight to Egypt (at the Ephraims) and a Saint Jerome in the desert (at the Itzigs).

But more fundamental than what hung on their walls was the way both bankers built Jewishness into their houses. In his U-shaped mansion on the river Spree, Daniel Itzig had constructed a synagogue and a room with a movable roof, which could be opened at Sukkot and filled with branches and fruits in accordance with Jewish custom. On a more secular level, one of the technical marvels of the Itzig palace was a bathroom, reputed to be the first in a private house in Berlin. Ephraim's house also had a synagogue, which occupied the entire third floor. The facade itself demonstrated the royal favor by means of eight massive columns taken from a castle at Brühl and presented to Ephraim by the king. Quite apart from their impressiveness as monuments to the wealth and cultivation of the families that had built them, the Ephraim and Itzig mansions stood as harbingers of a movement toward cultural integration that would come to dominate Jewish life in the next century.

For all its liveliness and prosperity, Berlin's Jewish community remained little better than a hostage, living under a privilege periodically renegotiated, at rising prices. In the eighteenth century, the renewal of privileges in 1700, 1714, 1730, and 1750 cost more and brought fewer rights. The last of these, granted ten years after Frederick II had come to the throne, reduced to one the number of children who could be settled and reintroduced the humiliating body tax levied on Jews and cattle entering the city gates. In the economic sphere, Jews were rigorously excluded from any branch of trade in which gentiles were established. Frederick's attitude toward his Jewish subjects was at best one of distaste; his much-advertised commitment to Enlightenment did not extend to Jews. His main concern was to inhibit the growth of the community, which was larger than the law allowed.

As early as 1731, almost six hundred Jews without residence permits had been ruthlessly expelled. By 1750, among the two thousand Jews then living in Berlin, some five hundred to seven hundred were there illegally—most of them very poor. About half of the Jewish population, some two hundred families, had perma-

Jost Liebmann, "der
Schutzjude," (Pro-
tected Jew) painted
by Anthoni Schoon-
jans in 1702. The
portrait shows him
dressed in fashion-
able and opulent
clothes and holding a
ring as the emblem of
his profession.

Interior of the
Heidereutergasse syn-
agogue. Engraving by
A. B. Göblin from a
drawing by Anna
Maria Werner, 1720.

The Itzig Palace.

The Ephraim Palace,
ca. 1885. Max Ring,
*Die deutsche Kai-
serstadt Berlin und
ihre Umgebung,*
Leipzig, 1885.

Benjamin Veitel Ephraim was a wealthy manufacturer in Berlin whom Friedrich Wilhelm II had employed as a confidential agent in France. In 1806, after Prussia's defeat by Napoleon's armies, Ephraim was arrested on vague charges based on his intimacy with the French. When the invaders occupied Custrin, where he was imprisoned, the French officers invited him to dine. The conversation took an unpleasant turn as his hosts complained that despite their emancipation by the French Revolution, the Jews continued to love money above all. Ephraim, by his own account, had a ready answer.

For the last fourteen years [Marshal Augereau said] the Jews in France have enjoyed the same freedom as the Christians and nonetheless they remain exclusively and entirely engaged in usury. I answered the marshal that after one and a half thousand years as traders, it was not the work of fourteen years to transform them into a farming people. . . . All the gentlemen asked me if I had daughters, and how much dowry I would give with them, without concerning themselves too much with any of the other essential circumstances which would go with a marriage. It shows at least that they have no aversion to the worth of money, which among young people is practically a virtue. Why, then, should one only attribute this preference to the Jews?

B. V. Ephraim. Über meine Verhaftung . . . *Dessau, 1808.*

Architectural drawing
of the Ephraim Palace,
by Laura Levy.

nent rights of residence as protected Jews (*Schutzjuden*); another sixteen families had limited tenure valid only for the lifetime of the head of the family and not transferrable to his children. Although the illegal Jewish residents particularly troubled the king, Berlin then as later proved an irresistible attraction to Jews from the provinces. Many were retained by their fellow Jews as actual or nominal servants or were taken on as employees of the community, working as teachers, slaughterers, sextons, or at whatever could be found for them. The first post held by the later-revered Moses Mendelssohn, for example, was as tutor in the house of the silk manufacturer Isaac Bernhard, where he was counted among the domestics.

For all these impecunious denizens, the Berlin Jewish community was fairly prosperous, though that profile was sustained by severe government measures: before being admitted to Berlin, Jews were closely interrogated to exclude vagrants, and those who overstayed their welcome or had entered illegally were summarily deported. The major source of Jewish commercial activity in Berlin and the major customer was, of course, the royal court. Despite the king's distaste for them, Jews continued to be general purveyors to the army and the state, manufacturers and importers of luxury goods. In 1777, in the midst of constant efforts to build his armies and defend his borders, Frederick dispatched two Jews to the king of the Tartars with a commission to buy three hundred horses. He encouraged other Jews to set up factories to supply the army. Deprived of access to traditional crafts, Berlin's Jews turned their position as outsider to advantage. Adopting innovative ways of manufacture, they became Frederick II's instruments in developing the modern Prussian state, whose hallmark was the centralization of power and procurement in the monarch's hands. Jews not attached to the court were on the whole involved in more modest occupations as shopkeepers, pawnbrokers, and peddlers. It was exactly this large and uncounted underclass in his capital city that so alarmed Frederick and led him periodically to order roundups and expulsions. To the Jews in Berlin Frederick was hardly "the Great."

As in commerce, so in their communal life, the Jews of Berlin felt themselves hemmed in by regulations and restrictions. Prussia treated

Letter from Frederick II to Schagin Geray, khan of the Tartars in Crimea, in 1777, presenting Marc Raphael and Jacob Wolff, who have been commissioned to buy horses for the Prussian army.

them as a collectivity: the annual levy of "protection money" was laid upon the whole community, which then had to divide the burden equitably among its members. Additional taxes were assessed during the year for the army, the church, and special holiday observances. Marriages, limited to ten a year, were also an expensive occasion. First the couple had to show a capital of 2,000 thalers. Then they had to buy a marriage certificate costing 400 thalers and, in addition, 300 thalers' worth of porcelain, thus subsidizing the royal factory. This hated regulation, along with the body tax, was not rescinded until 1787, a year after Frederick's death.

But Berlin's Jews, like other Jews in German lands, maintained an elaborate system of institutions fostering ritual obligations, caring for the indigent, and educating the young. When Moses Mendelssohn's gentile friend, the bookseller and philosopher Friedrich Nicolai, wrote his description of Berlin in 1786, he marveled over the extensive structure of Jewish charitable organizations, among them "a number of institutions entirely unknown among us, but in operation among the Jews for many years." The institutions Nicolai admired included a hospital; a charity distributing alms among the resident poor as well as strangers; and societies to provide dowries for indigent girls and stipends for students—even one to provide relief "in such a way that the recipient is spared the blushes of accepting charity." Following the establishment of the communal synagogue in 1714, the community also employed a series of rabbis, among them the eminent David Fränkel. Had Nicolai cared about education, he could have added the Free School started in 1778 by David Friedländer, which added secular instruction to religious training. It had eighty students, half of whom were educated without charge; the families of the others paid according to their means. However hampered, Berlin's Jewish community could serve as a model to others—and not Jews alone.

A street peddler. *Vergameling Mans en Vrouwstaden,* Amsterdam, 1833.

Chapter Four

The Return to History

The Age of Moses Mendelssohn

In October 1743, Moses Mendelssohn, then a boy of fourteen, presented himself at one of the two gates through which Jews were permitted to enter Berlin. After close scrutiny by representatives of the Prussian government and of the Jewish community, he was issued the pass of admittance. Born in Dessau in 1729, the son of a poor Torah scribe, Mendelssohn became a devoted pupil of Rabbi David Fränkel, and when Fränkel moved to Berlin to take up the position of rabbi at the Heidereutergasse synagogue, Mendelssohn followed him. His legal status was that of student, a shadowy category that depended on the acknowledgment of the community. Those who allowed him into Berlin could not have known that they were admitting a historic disturber of the peace.

For the next seven years Mendelssohn lived precariously, studying Talmud in the *beth hamidrash* (house of study) organized by his teacher and earning a little money copying manuscripts. Although these were years of privation, he took a path that later generations of Jews would follow. He learned languages—German first, then Latin, Greek, French, and English—then philosophy, mathematics, and science. Although barely introduced to Western civilization, Mendelssohn was soon writing reviews and philosophical treatises as well as establishing his place in the Berlin intellectual world. In 1750, he moved as a tutor to the house of Isaac Bernhard, a silk manufacturer who, recognizing Mendelssohn's acumen, brought him into his business as a bookkeeper and eventually made him a partner. Mendelssohn never wanted for money after joining Bernhard, but he was pressed all his life for time to pursue his scholarly work.

By 1762, he was established enough to marry. His choice was Fromet Gugenheim, a great-great-granddaughter of the Viennese court Jew Samuel Oppenheimer, although her own family lived in rather straitened circumstances. Of the ten children born to the couple in the next twenty years, six survived into adulthood, and their life histories became as much paradigms for German Jewry as their father's would be.

In the year following his marriage, Mendelssohn won a competition at the Royal Academy of Sciences for an essay on metaphysics, though Immanuel Kant was a rival. In October of the same year, exactly two decades after his ar-

Den 14 Jun. Anno 1744 kommt unter Vorzeigung eines richtigen Passes von
allhier an, der Jude
nebst
und giebt an, daß er bey
zu verrichten, und auf der Gasse
bey logiren, auch sich
Wochen 8 Tage hier aufhalten wolle.
Wannenhero er diesen Zettul sofort bey dem Commissario des Quartiers der Stadt in welchen er logiret, bey Einen Rthlr. Strafe vorweisen und unterschreiben lassen, auch wenn er wiederum von hier abreiset, gegenwärtigen unterschriebenen Zettul an der Landwehr, durch welche er ausgehet, an den dasigen Thorschreiber abliefern muß.
Berlin, den 14 Jun. Anno 1744
Thor-Schreiber. Jüdischer Thor-Steher.
Commissair de Quartier.

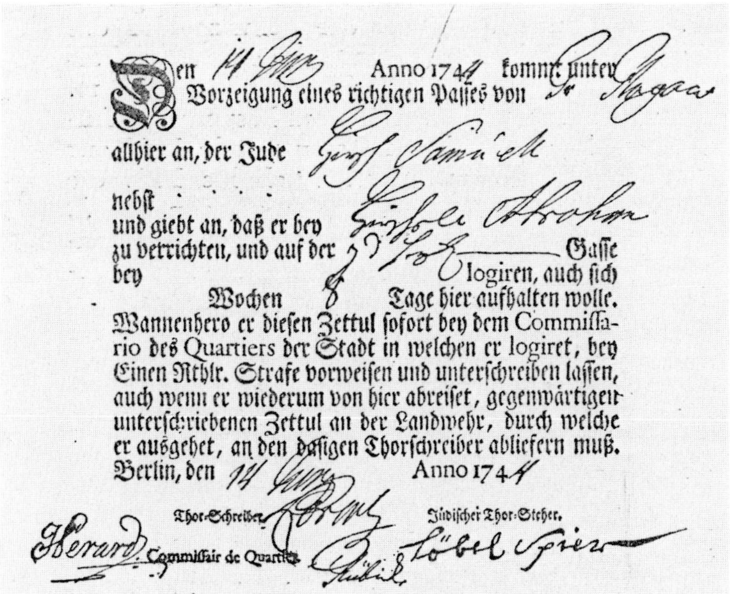

Pass of admission (*Passierschein*) of the sort that would have been issued to Moses Mendelssohn on his arrival in Berlin in 1743. This one is dated 1744. *Jüdisches Lexikon,* Berlin, 1927.

rival in Berlin, he was granted permanent residence as an "extraordinary" protected Jew. This designation carried a lesser grade of security than an "ordinary" protection since it would not pass on to his family on his death. In fact, his family was not granted the right of residence until 1787, the year after Frederick II's death. Mendelssohn's case had been made to the "philosopher-king" by the marquis d'Argens, a scholar and guest at court. "A bad Catholic philosopher," he is reported to have said, "begs a bad Protestant philosopher to grant the privilege to a bad Jewish philosopher." Frederick acceded, but he could not be moved a second time when in 1771 the Royal Academy of Sciences in Berlin presented Mendelssohn's name for membership. This was a status, implying a stipend, for which Mendelssohn was extremely eager; he longed to be freed from business cares to devote himself to his writing. But the king remained adamant, and Mendelssohn continued at the factory. Despite the lack of time and ill health, he remained prolific, rising at five in the morning to give himself three hours or so before his daily duties began.

In addition to his prizewinning essay, it was his *Phaedon,* published in 1767, a charming,

Moses Mendelssohn, painted by Johann Christoph Frisch, ca. 1780. A late portrait of Mendelssohn drawn from life. (Color plate 13.)

stylish Platonic dialogue offering a rational proof of the immortality of the soul, that gained Mendelssohn entry into the literary and philosophical world. *Phaedon* was reprinted four times in its first year and frequently thereafter and was translated into Dutch, Danish, French, and Russian. But probably his boldest literary venture was his translation, with four collaborators, of the first five books of the Bible from Hebrew into German. Intended for his fellow Jews, the German text was printed in Hebrew letters instead of the usual Roman alphabet.

Mendelssohn's Pentateuch was completed in the astonishingly short time of three years and published between 1780 and 1783. But this seemingly irreproachable enterprise instantly aroused the ire of orthodox rabbis, who condemned the translation of the Holy Book into a secular tongue as blasphemous and even threatened Mendelssohn with excommunication. Nonetheless, the work enjoyed three editions in his lifetime, and Genesis was even published in conventional German script in 1780.

Simultaneously with this translation, Mendelssohn worked on his *Jerusalem*, a summing up of his lifelong effort to define a philosophically acceptable place for Judaism in a modern world. Having spent much of his energy writing defensively, protecting both traditional Judaism and his own beliefs from the efforts of Christian clerics to convert him, Mendelssohn now presented his vigorous personal affirmation. Opposing all manner of religious compulsion, he compared Judaism to the first floor of a building on whose foundations Christianity, the second floor, had been constructed. To abandon the truths of Judaism was therefore to cause the collapse of Christianity. Judaism's revealed law, a law that only God can abrogate, Mendelssohn insisted, is the irreducible, unique element that sets Jewry apart from all other people for all time. (See plate 11.)

Though he longed for the integration of Jews into Western culture, he warned that it must not come at the price of abandoning the law. "If civil union cannot be obtained under any other condition," he argued, "we are sincerely sorry to find it necessary to declare that we must rather do without civil union." In the conclusion of *Jerusalem*, he abandoned the philosopher's tone for that of the preacher. "What good will it do you," he asked his German readers rhetori-

The opening pages of Exodus in Moses Mendelssohn's translation of the Hebrew Bible into German. The Hebrew text appears in the upper right-hand block, the German translation, spelled in Hebrew letters, in the upper left, Mendelssohn's commentary (*biur*) in the lower left, and a legal commentary in the lower right.

cally, "to have fellow citizens without conscience?"

For many Christians and Jews who would never read a line he had written, Mendelssohn became a household word in his own time. Philosophers, German aristocrats, scholars from all parts of Europe, as well as poor Polish Jews, all came to Mendelssohn's house to speak with this "German Socrates." He became a close friend of the poet, playwright, and critic Gotthold Ephraim Lessing. Indeed, Lessing probably modeled the wise and spotless hero of his last play, *Nathan the Wise,* completed in 1779, on Mendelssohn. Set in Palestine, where a knight of the Templars falls in love with Nathan's adopted daughter, the drama culminates in the parable of the three rings, giving poetic expression to the enlightened view that three great world religions—Judaism, Christianity, and Islam—are of equal worth. Mendelssohn believed that the outcry of the pious against such heresy shortened Lessing's life—he died in 1781—but Lessing's play has survived into the twentieth century as a powerful plea for the ideals of tolerance and brotherhood.

When Mendelssohn died, on January 4, 1786, he left behind a community of Jews who had already taken the first steps out of the spiritual enclosure in which they had lived for most of their sojourn in Europe. It had been a central implication of Enlightenment thought that the Jew could be elevated to a fellow human being. No longer devils, no longer social pariahs, no longer even members of a separate "nation," Jews had become—at least for some advanced spirits—citizens who simply professed another religion. This portentous difference from times past was one that the world was beginning to understand. How to live with it was a different matter.

Pressures for Change

In the closing decades of the eighteenth century, pressures for change in Jewish life began to build, from both within and without. The standard-bearer for a radically revised gentile approach to Jews and Judaism was Christian Wilhelm Dohm—theologian, Prussian diplomat, and royal archivist in Berlin. A member of Mendelssohn's circle, Dohm had collaborated with him in 1780 on a memorandum in support of the Alsatian Jews. But his claim to immortality

was his "apologia in behalf of my circumcised brethren," *On the Improvement of the Civil Status of the Jews,* published in September 1781. The slightly ambiguous title indicates that this improvement was to work both ways. The Jews must do their share by modeling themselves, it seemed, more closely on the surrounding culture. Still, in his pathbreaking treatise, Dohm urged that Jews be admitted to full citizenship and that the many disabilities under which they labored—housing restrictions, extraordinary and humiliating taxes, occupational prohibitions—be lifted. At that time, the Jews of Frankfurt still lived in a walled-in ghetto whose gates were locked every night.

Yet Dohm did not hesitate to criticize the Jews for their "too mercantile spirit" and revived the old argument that Jews were engaged in unproductive labor. "It would be better," he asserted, "if the Jew works in the shops and behind the plow." But he laid the cause of the Jews' deplorable condition squarely at the door of gentile prejudice and exclusionary policies: "Everything the Jews are blamed for is caused by the political conditions under which they now live." No doubt "we ourselves are guilty of the crimes we accuse them of." The "moral turpitude in which that unfortunate nation is sunk," he insisted, cannot justify anti-Jewish policies. Dohm's argument was rational and simple: the restrictions placed on Jews squeezed them into commerce as their only means of livelihood, into social isolation, separate school systems, and hence alienation from society. "How can we demand willing obedience and affection for the state from him when he is tolerated only to the extent of being a means of revenue? . . . How can one expect virtue from him if one does not trust him?"

Dohm published his persuasive argument a few months before Joseph II, the Habsburg monarch and Holy Roman emperor, issued his Toleration Edict, on January 2, 1782. The edict suggests, in language much like Dohm's, that a fostering approach would be more effective than a punitive one in making Jews "more useful and serviceable to the state." In practice this meant that Jews would henceforth be eligible to attend state schools, learn and engage in crafts hitherto monopolized by Christians, live where they chose, and be freed from discriminatory taxation. Taken together, Dohm's treatise and

The parable of the rings from Gotthold Ephraim Lessing's
Nathan the Wise.

In the olden, olden time
There lived an Eastern chief, who owned a
ring
Of priceless worth, had from the hands of
one
He dearly loved. The stone, an opal, flashed
The broken light in a hundred lovely hues
Upon the eye, and had the marvelous power
To make him loved alike of God and man
Who, strong in this assurance, wore the
ring. . . .
So came the ring
From sire to son, until at length it fell
To one, the father of three loving sons,
All dutiful alike, and all by him
Cherished with like regard; . . .
It grieved him sorely now that he must
needs
Defeat the hopes of two among his sons, . . .
He summons privily a jeweler,
Of whom he orders two more opal rings
After the pattern of the one he wore,
Nor cost nor pains being spared in making
these
Exactly like his own. The artist triumphs:
The rings produced, the father cannot tell
Which of the three is his. Content, resigned,
He calls his sons in turn to his bedside,
and gives to each his blessing and a ring,
And soon thereafter dies. . . .
The father dead, each son displays his ring
And would assert his place as lord of all;
Discussion follows, difference, dispute—
In vain! The true ring cannot now be
known—
As little known as among ourselves
The true religion.

Gotthold Ephraim Lessing, Nathan the Wise: A Dramatic Poem, *London,*
1868.

An imaginary meeting of Gotthold Ephraim Lessing (standing) and Johann Casper Lavater (seated right) with Moses Mendelssohn, from a painting by Moritz Oppenheim, 1856.

Moritz Oppenheim discusses his painting of Mendelssohn with Lavater and Lessing with Mendelssohn's grandson, Philipp Veit. Veit had been baptized a Catholic as a child.

[Philipp] Veit never spoke to me either about his Jewish origins or about his later acquired Catholic faith. It happened only once when we met at the Café Röder and I remarked that whenever I ate ices I often thought of his grandfather [Moses Mendelssohn]. He had so much loved to eat sweets that he regretted it when he was no longer permitted to do so. Then Veit turned the conversation to a picture that I was currently working on. It represented the well-known episode, "Lavater's visit to Moses Mendelssohn,"* in which Lavater attempts to convert him and demands, indeed, that Mendelssohn either give in to his wish that he be baptized or make public his counterarguments. I then told him, as is historically known, that this placed Mendelssohn in an embarrassing position, and how he had fretted over it because he could not express himself as he was able and with his whole heart would have wanted to. It was only to the Duke of Brunswick, who had urgently pleaded with him, that he had not concealed his arguments. When Veit heard this story, he sighed and said: "Who knows what penance he must now do for it!" Veit was otherwise a very sensible man.

Moritz Oppenheim, Erinnerungen, Frankfurt am Main, 1924.

**Despite Oppenheim's assertion, there was no actual meeting. But in 1769 Lavater had challenged Mendelssohn in writing to defend the superiority of Judaism publicly and if he could not do so to accept the consequence and convert to Christianity—Ed.*

Joseph II's edict raised the discussion about the position of the Jew in Europe to a new level.

On the Jewish side, the transformation was propelled forward by David Friedländer, who came to Berlin in 1771 from his native Königsberg and in the following year married one of Daniel Itzig's daughters. He became one of Moses Mendelssohn's disciples, visiting him daily and participating in the regular Saturday-afternoon gatherings at which Mendelssohn's followers discussed religion, education, and the human condition. After Mendelssohn's death in 1786, Friedländer apostrophized him as the "Palm of Israel, the Cedar of Lebanon." Essentially a man of action, Friedländer, acknowledged to be Mendelssohn's successor, was intent on giving his master's ideas concrete expression.

By 1778, Friedländer led in founding a Free School in Berlin aimed at giving Jewish children a secular education in German as well as providing the traditional Jewish curriculum. What had been the sticking point for Mendelssohn, the indissoluble quintessence of Judaism—the law—became for Friedländer the point at which he thought Jews must bend.

Friedländer turned his master's teachings upside down. Where Moses Mendelssohn had accentuated the primacy of the Jewish law, Friedländer stressed the primacy of fundamental Jewish ideas. In 1799, in an anonymous *Open Letter* addressed to the leading figure in Berlin's Lutheran church, Wilhelm Abraham Teller, he offered the startling proposal that Jews become a sect within Protestantism. To his mind, Jewish ceremonial law was neither rational nor compatible with life in the modern world. Its bonds were steadily loosening, and in any event, ceremonies were only the shell of Judaism. Its essence was close to Christian beliefs: Christians and Jews believe in one God; believe that the soul is spiritual, incorporeal, and immortal; believe that God created man and that man strives toward perfection. The two religions had traveled along what seemed incompatible courses for nearly eighteen hundred years, but their fundamental principles, Friedländer argued, must be recognized as points of real convergence. "The purpose that accompanies this proposal," he openly confessed, "is to reach the goal of being full citizens." The Jews' "most ardent wish is that in this way we will see the intellectual and

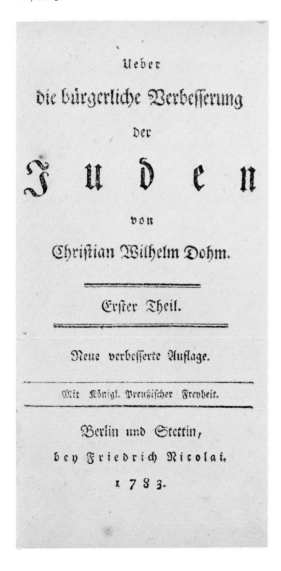

Title page of a tract by Christian Wilhelm Dohm, *On the Improvement of the Civil Status of the Jews,* Berlin and Stettin, 1783.

David Friedländer
(1750–1834).

***David Friedländer on the contemporary practice of Judaism in
his open letter to Dean Teller in 1799.***

*The religion that was taught us was full of mystical principles. The
earliest history of the world was mysterious, dark, and illogical; the
events were often so strange and so dissimilar, down to the slightest
nuance, to the world in which we lived that they all seemed practically
unbelievable. The characters, the ways of thinking and the feelings of
persons who appeared in the Holy Scriptures were not only puzzling to
us in their manner of expression, they also, for the most part, stood
in great contrast to our own feelings and modes of behavior. The
ceremonial laws were observed in our fathers' houses with the most
anxious punctiliousness. These estranged us from the sphere of ordinary life; as empty customs they produced no further effect on our behavior than to make us shy, embarrassed, and often uneasy in the
presence of people of other religions or even before servants.*

David Friedländer. Sendschreiben, *Berlin, 1799.*

physical capabilities of our descendants fully developed."

It is not surprising that Friedländer's proposal met with a roar of indignation from his co-religionists and a polite but firm rejection from Dean Teller. However farfetched such a proposal must now seem, it is an instructive barometer of the state of mind of some German Jews—or their state of confusion—as they saw a new age dawning. They had been prisoners of their birth; now they permitted themselves to hope that the cosmopolitan and humane ideas of the Enlightenment would apply to them as well. In their fantasies of the world to come, David Friedländer's proposal was perhaps extreme; but in extraordinary times, extraordinary thoughts came to free minds.

A third force acting upon late eighteenth-century German Jews was the immigration from Eastern Europe of Jews in flight from what they perceived as the benighted life around them toward the light of the Western world. The passions that moved people to leave home and family for an unknown fate cannot be better represented than in the eccentric and tragic genius Salomon Maimon. A child prodigy in his native Poland, Maimon was entirely self-taught in profane literature, learning German script secretly from printers' notes in Hebrew books and devouring whatever work in German philosophy he could find. His father sold him into a bewildering and hateful marriage at age eleven. Three years later, he was a father, yet moving from one ill-paid tutor's post to another, he could never find a means of supporting his family. In 1779, in his rage at the cruelty, ignorance, and superstition of the life around him, he left his family, his whole world, and decamped for Berlin.

In every way except his devotion to learning, Maimon was the dark twin of Mendelssohn. Mendelssohn had spent his life trying to bring traditional Jewish beliefs into harmony with Western thought; Maimon rebelled against the theocracy governing Jewish life. Mendelssohn was an exemplary paterfamilias; Maimon abandoned his wife and children without a backward glance. Mendelssohn was respected and beloved by all Berlin; Maimon, who painfully felt his boorishness, never learned to speak German properly, so that he seemed like a feral child, uttering a strange mixture of Yiddish and mis-

The conclusion of David Friedländer's *Open Letter* proposing that Judaism be accepted as a branch of Protestantism: "Without in any way wishing to anticipate your decision, Venerable Sir, we expect from the true spirit of Protestantism, that in its widest compass it will also shelter and protect us and our system [of belief] so that we may achieve our aforementioned goal." David Friedländer, *Sendschreiben . . .* Berlin, 1799.

Ohne also im mindesten Ihrem Urtheile, ehrwürdiger Greis, vorzugreifen, erwarten wir von dem ächten Geiste des Protestantismus, daß er auch uns und unser System in seinem weiten Umkreis bergen und schützen wird, auf welche Weise wir das vorgesteckte Ziel würden erreichen können.

Salomon Maimon
(1754–1800), fron-
tispiece of his
Lebensgeschichte,
Berlin, 1792–93.

pronounced German. After his dissolute habits and incurably raffish way of life became common knowledge, he was quickly abandoned by the respectable Berlin Jews who had taken him up. Yet he was a man of exceptional and obvious philosophical brilliance: when Marcus Herz sent Maimon's assessment of the *Critique of Pure Reason* to its author, Kant commended him as understanding his philosophy better than anyone else. Indeed, at first Moses Mendelssohn took him up kindly. But by 1780 Maimon, under severe criticism from his Jewish patrons, had left Berlin, wandering rootlessly—to Hamburg, to Amsterdam, back to Berlin. He died in 1800 at the early age of forty-three, his work known only to a few specialists. Yet this improbable, dissipated wanderer went significantly beyond Mendelssohn and Friedländer in exerting pressure on traditional Jewish ways of thinking. Mendelssohn, we know, had sought to stay within the accepted boundaries of the Jewish religious imagination; Friedländer, however daring, had not left the ground of theology. In sharp contrast, Maimon developed a theory of knowledge and a metaphysics that were uncompromisingly secular. His immediate influence on Jewish thought was slight, though it was marked on German romantic philosophers—including, ironically, the Jew-hater Fichte. This pathetic genius experimented with unprecedented boldness for a Jewish thinker of his day: he set out to think universal thoughts divorced from all sectarian allegiances.

Maimon also stands as an early witness to the draw of the German magnet for Jews from the East, who, leaving tightly structured Jewish orthodoxy behind, hoped not only for a better material life, but sought also for the personal freedom of the West. As they were transformed in their new homeland, they transformed German Jewish life in turn. When the trickle westward in the late eighteenth century turned into a flood of millions, East European Jews became an increasingly potent ingredient in the amalgam that was German Jewry—decades after Maimon's death, and in far less intellectual ways than his.

Emergence into Social Life: The Salons

The salons that sprang up in late eighteenth-century Berlin, a domestic version of contemporary scientific and literary associations, also marked the debut of the Jewish bourgeoisie in German society. In important ways, the salon was the first institution to transcend centuries-old barriers, and it set the pattern for Jewish life in modern Germany. The Jewish salons completely adopted contemporary forms of dress and behavior, yet they were imbued with a special quality. The major difference was that the rigid distinctions of rank ruling conventional German social intercourse were of far less consequence to a people who, by definition, stood outside accepted social hierarchies. This freedom made the Jewish salons exceptionally informal and diverse in their guests.

Their liberal hospitality was among the first demonstrations of how Jewish families entering German life would adapt and mold existing social forms to a shape agreeable to them. The gregarious intimacy of close-knit Jewish communities found a congenial counterpart in the eighteenth-century cult of friendship. Significantly, Moses Mendelssohn is always pictured in conversation with philosophers, theologians, and men of letters. There is hardly an account of a call on Mendelssohn that fails to report the visitor's staying for a meal—cheerful if frugal—with the family. Two Jewish hostesses, Henriette Herz and Rahel Varnhagen, without splendor or magnificent entertainment, drew the best minds in Berlin simply for the conversation. The company, receptive to ideas, was borne along on tides of good talk, readings from new works, presentations of scientific papers, and accounts of foreign parts by passing visitors.

In her memoirs, Henriette Herz shrewdly observed that in her time the tone in the upper levels of Berlin society was set by the court, which, under Frederick II, had excluded women and, under his successor, Frederick William II, was notoriously tedious. "Among the middle-class Christians at that time," she noted condescendingly, "one could not even speak of any intellectual interests outside their profession. They had many honorable familial virtues, but were even more characterized by their intellectual limitations and lack of cultivation." One envisions a society sinking under boredom.

By contrast, her own house in the first years after her marriage in 1779 struck her as "one of the most agreeable and sought-after in Berlin." The daughter of Benjamin Lemos, a physician of Portuguese origin, she was married at fifteen, after a betrothal of more than two years, to a thirty-five-year-old doctor, Marcus Herz. The marriage became a love match, at least on her side. And since her passion extended to the life of the mind, Marcus Herz was soon cast as the teacher as well as the husband of his young wife.

Indeed, at first the attraction of their salon was the philosophical and scientific evenings instituted by Marcus Herz. Even the crown prince of Prussia, later Frederick William III, was taken to them by his tutor. But in time, Henriette Herz herself became the center of a literary and theological circle counting among its regulars scientists and statesmen like the Humboldt brothers, the influential young theologian Friedrich Schleiermacher, the novelist Jean Paul, the witty journalist Ludwig Börne, the French statesman Mirabeau, and a prince of the royal house, Louis Ferdinand. The women guests, sometimes the hostess's good friends, were a glittering group: Dorothea Veit, Mendelssohn's daughter; Marianne, the wife of the sculptor Gottfried Schadow; Catherine von Dacheroden, later the wife of Wilhelm von Humboldt; to say nothing of that international celebrity Madame de Staël.

Henriette Herz's induction into the world proceeded on many levels. One episode reveals the kinds of choice facing young Jews from Orthodox households as their talents brought them into a wider society. According to Jewish custom, a married woman must conceal her hair lest this ornament of feminine beauty lead other men astray. But for an attractive and independent young woman, the effect of the substitutes—a huge clumsy headdress or a lifeless wig—was devastating. Henriette Herz's portrait painted just before her marriage (see plate 14) shows why she would regret bundling up or cutting what she described as her "shining raven-black hair."

In her memoirs she reports how she chafed at this demand and charts the stages to the moment when she rejected Jewish edicts in favor of her own hair. Nor was she alone in taking this step. Fanny Arnstein, the daughter of the wealthy court Jew Daniel Itzig, was married in Berlin in 1776, a few years before her friend Henriette Herz. Once she had moved to Vienna with her husband, a member of a prominent banking family, she insisted on wearing her own hair but prevailed only after a dramatic confron-

A Berlin salon in the "classical period," late eighteenth to early nineteenth century. Drawing by C. F. Zimmermann.

This passage from a widely read book of manners and morals offers an insight into the received attitude toward educated women in the eighteenth century.

I must confess that I am always somewhat chilled when I am seated in company next to a lady who makes great claims to wit or even learning. If women would only consider how much more interest they would arouse if they remained with the destiny that nature has set out for them and distinguished themselves from the mass of their sisters by the faithful fulfillment of their vocation. Of what use is it to them to compete with men in areas in which they are not equal, where they have not been instructed in fundamental principles, which have been knocked into boys from their childhood? . . . Among the forty or fifty women whom one can count in Germany today as authors . . . there are perhaps hardly half a dozen who, as privileged spirits of a higher order, have found their true calling. . . . Is it not the case with men who are authors that only a few among them are of exceptional merit? Certainly—but with the difference that the lust for fame or fortune can lead them astray; but women cannot so easily find an excuse when, with mediocre or less than mediocre talent, they undertake a course in life which neither nature nor civil society has allotted to them.

Adolf Freyherr von Knigge, Über den Umgang mit Menschen, *Hanover, 1788.*

Henriette Herz (1764–1847) as Hebe, the Greek goddess of spring. In a painting by Anna Dorothea Therbusch, 1778. (Color plate 14.)

The importance of her hair to Henriette Herz may be seen from the way she begins the account of her marriage in her memoirs, written a half century later.

Herz's hairdresser was the first person to see the fifteen-year-old wife on the morning after her wedding. . . . That evening there was a ball in my parents' house. I dressed and was not pleased with the way I looked; I changed and changed my ornaments and I was not any better pleased. The reason was that according to Jewish custom I was required as a married woman to hide my hair totally, and my headdress, which was decorated with pearls and flowers, did not suit me. I arrived somewhat later than some of the other guests, and my mother received me with annoyance and scolded because here and there my hair peeped out from under the headdress. . . ."

[Some time later she takes to her bed with measles.] "I recovered quickly and grew prettier and more blooming. My vanity received an occasion to rejoice because at this time Jewish women were given permission to wear, if not their own hair, at least false hair. Since my parents had nothing against it, a wig was made for me that was very becoming. But it was very soon laid aside and was replaced by my own raven-black, shining hair. And so I lived happy and industrious."

Henriette Herz. Berliner Salon: Erinnerungen und Portraits, *Frankfurt am Main, 1984.*

tation with her in-laws, in whose house she lived.

Such minor acts of rebellion presaged more serious breaks to come. Judaism was being tested against new arguments. These were not the great medieval disputations about fundamental truths: the questions at the end of the eighteenth century were being posed more pragmatically. Had Judaism perhaps outlived its time? Was it only a religion of laws that were no longer relevant? Was baptism the answer? The presence of Schleiermacher in the Herz salon insured that such questions would not go unexamined.

The impressionable and emotional Henriette Herz's struggles over her hair demonstrate how the gradual erosion of one detail after another of Jewish law and custom cast doubt on the entire structure of Jewish observance. Confidence in the religion itself was at risk. In a characteristic compromise, Henriette Herz converted to Protestantism in 1817, a step she had long wished to take but postponed until after her mother's death. By then, she had been a relatively impecunious widow for many years—Marcus Herz died in 1803—and although she maintained her friendship with the powerful and famous until her death in 1847 at eighty-three, she no longer presided over a salon. But in her early years, she had helped point the way for Jews to German society.

In Henriette Herz's generation, the conflicting demands of the two worlds in which Jews had lived—the ceremonial world of the past and the urgent world of their surrounding culture—grew increasingly exigent. Rahel Levin vividly demonstrates these demands, wrestling with her Jewish past until the end of her life. Born into a rich Berlin Jewish family in 1771, she was largely self-educated. Her parents spoke Yiddish, and she was taught the Hebrew alphabet only to read that language. But upon the death of her father, a jeweler, when she was nineteen, she was granted a small income by her brother, who had inherited the family business; and since she was on bad terms with her mother, she arranged for partial independence by moving into a garret apartment in the family home. There she began to entertain literary and political figures.

Along the way she had managed to acquire a formidable education, but above all she had developed into a magnetic personality and an en-chanting conversationalist. The Austrian novelist Franz Grillparzer, who visited her at the height of her fame in 1827, describes how in her presence his "weariness vanished or rather made room for a kind of intoxication. She spoke and spoke until around midnight, and I don't know whether they drove me away or whether I left on my own. I have never in my life heard better or more interesting talk."

By sheer force of character, she made the salon in her garret room into a magnet for Berlin notables. Her love life was tumultuous—two engagements failed, first to a German, then to a Spanish nobleman. But from 1804 on, when Europe, including Prussia, was at war with France, romance gave way to politics. When Napoleon's troops marched into Berlin in 1806, social life came to a stop and with it Rahel Levin's salon. Sympathetic to the French, even contemplating a flight to Paris, she nevertheless remained in Berlin. In 1808 she met Karl August Varnhagen, a minor literary figure, later a diplomat, fourteen years her junior. He was soon certain that she was the woman he wanted, but they did not marry until 1814. Even before then, she had taken two drastic steps: she had converted to Protestantism and had changed her name to Antonie Friederike.

Unlike some of her pragmatic men friends, who saw a change of religion as the only avenue to worldly success, Rahel Levin did not undertake conversion lightly. In Christianity she found the color, spirituality, and mysticism that she missed in Judaism; the Jewish mystics, who for centuries kept their esoteric teachings from women, had nothing to say to her. And in the Bible she saw only dead laws, which, she wrote, left her "totally alienated from my nation." Yet the security and tranquility of those born into Christianity, for whom their religion was part of their history, eluded Rahel Varnhagen until her death in 1833. In her twenty years as a Christian she did not cease to examine and re-examine the place of the Jew in the world and her own place in the no-man's-land of the convert. For her, being a Jew was nothing less than "a curse which the children of its adherents vainly try to flee in all quarters of the globe."

The intransigent anti-Semitism that belied the promise of Christian love, or even of simple decent acceptance, struck deep at the hearts of the new converts. They watched with dismay as

Rahel Varnhagen
(1771–1833).

Rahel Varnhagen's deathbed conversation with her husband, August, on her Jewish heritage and her Christian belief.

What a history! I am someone who has fled out of Egypt and Palestine, and find help and love and care from all of you. And you, my beloved August, I was sent to you under the guidance of God, and you to me. I think about this, about my origins, with sublime rapture, and the entire interweaving of destiny, how the oldest memories of mankind are bound together with the latest condition of things, how the most far-flung times and places are interconnected. What for such a long time was the greatest shame, the sharpest pain and misfortune—to be born a Jewess—I would not now miss at any price. . . .

O my beloved August, what a consoling insight, what a meaningful comparison. . . . My dear August, my heart is refreshed to its inmost core; I have thought of Jesus, and for the first time had the feeling that he is my brother. And Mary—how she suffered! She watched as her beloved Son suffered, and did not succumb; she stood at the Cross. I could not have done that! I would not have been strong enough. Forgive me for it, God; I confess how weak I am.

Rahel Antoine Friederike (Levin) Varnhagen von Ense, Rahel: Ein Buch des Andenkens für ihre Freunde . . . *Berlin, 1834.*

French troops, led by Napoleon, enter Berlin, October 2, 1806. Ternisien d'Haudricourt, *Fastes de la Nation Française,* Paris, [18—].

Prussia descended from its egalitarian high point, reached in 1812 when the Edict of Emancipation promised Prussia's Jews that they would "enjoy equal rights and liberties with Christians." By 1819 a wave of reaction resulted in anti-Jewish riots, and in 1831, when there was a cholera epidemic in Berlin, Rahel Varnhagen reported to her brother (who had also converted and changed his name to Robert) that the servants were saying that two Jews had poisoned the wells. In letters to him in her last years, she partly reverted to their childhood language, to German written in Hebrew script. The image of the mixed letters well represents the eternal coexistence of the two parts of herself, for Antonie Friederike Varnhagen von Ense could never totally supplant Rahel Levin.

In time, the religious solution to the admission of Jews to Europe made way in her mind to a political one. The emphasis had to shift, she wrote, from "origins" to "rights," from other-worldly preoccupations to "what improvements the earth can make for us." The conflicting claims of her past seemed equally strong, yet each found expression in language that showed the levels they occupied in her mind. Her Jewish affirmation took on the qualities of the confession to an old love which, with all its pain, remained an ineradicable part of her. But her Christianity had a wilder, more exalted quality in which she herself enters the drama of its origins as she imagines herself at the foot of the cross. Her husband, who attended her faithfully to her end, immortalized her in his diligent collection of her correspondence and in a memoir published the year after her death.

A third dominant figure in the Jewish salons of the age was Henriette Herz's friend Dorothea Schlegel. In 1783, the nineteen-year-old Dorothea, then called Brendel, had entered into an arranged marriage with Simon Veit, a Berlin banker nine years her senior. Her father, Moses Mendelssohn, had chosen Veit for her. In the Mendelssohn home, Brendel had grown into one of the best-educated young women in Berlin, yet during the fifteen years of her marriage to Simon Veit, her salon lacked the glamor and international cachet of the Herz establishment. She presided over a staid literary society that met on Thursday evenings at her house, where all the guests were Jews. One of the first visible signs of her dissatisfaction with her Jewish-centered social life was her discarding, around 1794, of the good Yiddish name Brendel in favor of the very European Dorothea.

At the salon of Henriette Herz she found the companionship and emotional outlets she craved. There, at age thirty-four, she also fell in love: in 1798 she met the brilliant literary critic Friedrich Schlegel, an incarnation of her romantic ideals and ideas. A Protestant eight years her junior whose passionate nature enthralled his contemporaries, he was soon drawn to Dorothea Veit. Within a year, she had left her husband for Schlegel.

Partly impelled by Schlegel's financial straits and partly as a means of exhibiting delight in her liberated if irregular life, she blossomed as a writer. Her novel *Florentin* was published anonymously in 1801, followed by translations from the French and articles for a journal edited by Schlegel. But it was Schlegel's explicitly erotic novel *Lucinde,* published in 1799, that truly immortalized their illicit intimacy. In their writings, both she and Schlegel were questioning the institution of arranged marriage, which was hardly confined to Jewish circles. The heart, both maintained, could not be commanded where to love: the ideal of marital happiness was changing. So was the cultural situation of Germany's Jews. By the terms of the divorce, Dorothea's two young sons were to remain with her husband, but Simon Veit allowed her to take the six-year-old Philipp with her on the condition that she not marry Schlegel. It was not a stipulation she could long obey: she and Schlegel were married in April 1804.

Prescribed respectable conduct was not the only conventional boundary Dorothea Schlegel crossed. On the day of her second wedding, she converted to Protestantism. Her search for the true religion, however, did not stop there; over the years she was increasingly drawn to Roman Catholicism, as were other romantics, as much for its aesthetic appeal as for its doctrine. In 1808, Dorothea and Friedrich Schlegel joined the Catholic church. In 1810, she made her apostasy complete when she also arranged to have her two sons baptized as Catholics. Her life as a hostess changed as well. Moving to Vienna with her husband, she began to preside over a distinguished literary salon.

Her sons, Philipp and Jonas Veit, both became painters of the Nazarene school, which devoted itself to religious Christian paintings in the early Italian manner. In 1830, Philipp, the more successful of the brothers, was appointed head of the Städel, the major museum of Frankfurt: by then, talented baptized Jews could hope for such careers. Now widowed—Schlegel had died in 1829—Dorothea came to live with Philipp and his family. Moritz Oppenheim, the painter of Jewish life par excellence, reports how troubled he was, as a good Jew, by his visit to this household. When her grandchildren came to say goodnight to her, Dorothea "gave them her blessing and made the sign of the cross in addition. This sign," he observes, "by the daughter of Moses Mendelssohn, always left me with a melancholy feeling." Her intense Catholic attachment was, he thought, rather "ostentatiously displayed." Steadfast in her new religiosity, however, she tried to convert her sisters as she had converted her sons. Oppenheim had every right to be troubled.

Still, what to Dorothea Schlegel and some of her friends seemed an inevitable progression—from legalism to faith, from interpretation to emotion, from Judaism to Christianity—proved far less inexorable than they believed. Despite the depth of feeling each of these women brought to her conversion, it could not obliterate their Jewish past. If anything, their baptisms made them more exotic than they had been as Jews, and they wrestled, openly and continually, with what their gentile friends took as given.

These three remarkable Jewish women— Henriette Herz, Rahel Varnhagen, and Dorothea Schlegel—came to symbolize the new aspirations of Jews in German society, but they represent the extreme, most visible end of the spectrum. Other salons led by Jewish hostesses ranged from the grand dinners given by Sara Levy, another of Daniel Itzig's nine daughters, to the musical soirées of Amalie Beer, the mother of Giacomo Meyerbeer, to the less notable gatherings of more conventional Jewish families. But in their ardent struggles, these three called urgent attention to fundamental questions confronting German Jews in their time: social organization, the nature of marriage, and the place of orthodox religion—indeed, any religion—in the modern world.

Philipp Veit (1793–1877), son of Dorothea von Schlegel and painter of the Nazarene school. Painting by Josef Binder.

From a letter by Simon Veit to his son Philipp Veit on October 28, 1810 shortly after Philipp Veit's conversion to Catholicism.

Let us draw a veil over the event that has gone on between us; give it over to forgetfulness. I will not stop loving the two of you and will do whatever is possible even though we are of different opinions from the standpoint of religion. . . . If religion is illuminated by tolerance, if it should and can go hand in hand with morality, then we not only do one another no harm, but come closer to one another, until our religions run practically side by side. Therefore, my beloved son, as long as we differ in religion but are united in our fundamental moral principles, then there will never be separation between us. Only don't believe, because you have gone over to another religion, that the millions of people who have other religious principles are poor sinners and are people hated by God, who have no part in eternal bliss. This belief has already too frequently separated friend from friend, father from child, the happy husband from his beloved wife and has brought nothing but disaster.

J. M. Raich, ed., Dorothea v. Schlegel . . . Briefwechsel im Auftrage der Familie Veit . . . *Mainz, 1881.*

Dorothea von Schlegel, in an engraving by her son Philipp Veit.

As Simon Veit lay on his deathbed in 1819, Dorothea von Schlegel wrote to him reflecting on their past life and absolving him of all blame in their separation.

I know that you are guilty of nothing. I know only too well that my stubbornness, my selfishness, my impetuosity, my vehemence, my unhappy recklessness and dissatisfaction and vagaries and a certain sickly drive toward something strange, unknown drove me on. And I alone am guilty of our separation; and for all that may God forgive me, as you have forgiven me. . . .

And at that time, if my struggles had been toward a true enlightenment instead of towards a false one, if I had had at that time the light of the true faith, if I had then recognized the only soul-saving direction toward the Grace of eternal life, then things would have taken another and better direction. God's mercy and the Grace of the Father spared me, and I have found the way toward eternal life, a way on which so many have lost their way, and I have been kept from frightful detours. I will praise God for it forever and beg him to bless you for your great benevolence, because you blessed where others would have cursed, and pray that he reward you with eternal Grace and give you the peace of God as he has given it to me so that we may live united at some future time in his eternal Clarity.

J. M. Raich, ed., Dorothea v. Schlegel . . . Briefwechsel im Auftrage der Familie Veit . . . *Mainz, 1881.*

Chapter Five

The Struggle for Emancipation

Decades of Ferment

For many centuries, the Jews in Germany, as elsewhere, had been the victims of history. Now, in the early nineteenth century, they became its beneficiaries. Everything pointed toward liberation and integration, exhilarating to free spirits and appalling to the orthodox. Communal organization, the ceremony of circumcision, secular education, the prevalence of Yiddish—indeed, the very survival of Judaism as a religion—were put into question.

This is not to say that Jewish acculturation was universal in these decades of ferment. In early nineteenth-century Nuremberg only a handful of Jews were permitted to live in the city, and it was not until 1857 that enough of them were in residence to form an organized community. And in Bavaria the old law limiting to one the number of children each Jewish family could settle remained in force until 1861.

But the winds of change were stronger than the forces of resistance. The secular schools founded in Berlin late in the eighteenth century became a model soon followed in Breslau, Dessau, Seesen, and Wolfenbüttel. A notable success was the Philanthropin in Frankfurt am Main.

Originally established in 1804 as a school for orphans, it quickly expanded and became almost a paradigm for the form that Jewish educational reform would take. From the beginning it enrolled both Jewish and non-Jewish pupils and employed both Jewish and non-Jewish teachers. In 1810, the Philanthropin established a sister school for girls, though with its own program emphasizing the "feminine arts of sewing, knitting, and embroidery." In both the boys' and the girls' Philanthropin, Hebrew and religion remained part of the curriculum. Even in the boys' school, though the range of its secular offerings increased, two hours a day were still given over to Jewish studies.

By the beginning of the nineteenth century, Jewish parents had a variety of alternatives. Some local governments invited or even required Jewish children to attend state schools. Church-sponsored and nondenominational schools also made room for Jewish children. Meanwhile the Jewish community itself had begun to introduce innovations into the millennia-old *heder* system.

Sulamith, the first Jewish magazine printed in German, had strong views on these matters. In 1807 its editor, David Fränkel, exhorted his co-

JAHRHUNDERTFEIER
des PHILANTHROPINS
14.-16. April 1904

Card printed to mark
the centenary of the
Philanthropin School,
1904.

Opening pages of *Me'assef,* which began publication in Königsberg in 1783 and appeared intermittently at various locations until 1811. Note the portrait of Moses Mendelssohn, the emblematic head of the movement.

religionists to action. "Awake, my brothers in belief, awake out of your long sleep and listen to the voice of reason. Nothing is more significant for the well-being of your children than the improvement of their schooling." If Jewish parents wanted to "guard them against irreligion and frivolity, then you must do away entirely with the old, inappropriate way of teaching that perhaps was good in the olden times but is now harmful. Instead build schools that are suitable to our times in which children can be taught the holy religion of their fathers with enthusiasm and warmth, a religion which, at the same time, has been brought down to a rational simplicity."

This was tantamount to asking the Jewish community to question its very traditions and to revise them where they were no longer pertinent. Not surprisingly, education became the central preoccupation of Germany's nineteenth-century Jews. It was no childish matter: it was a key to how Jews were to fit into what was clearly a new age.

From birth, a German Jew had three languages: Hebrew for prayer and erudition, Yiddish for daily speech and popular literature, and German (or a local dialect) for traffic with the surrounding world. But as Yiddish began to fade as the private language of Germany's Jews, Hebrew, the language of learning, underwent a brief renaissance with young Jews putting it to fresh secular uses. These *maskilim*—men of the Hebrew Enlightenment—were actually part of a movement that had spread to Eastern Europe, where it also attracted intellectuals who were trying to find some accommodation between the modern, secular world and Jewish religious culture.

In 1783, a group of young humanists in Königsberg had formed the Society for the Promotion of the Hebrew Language, which in the following year launched the magazine *Me'assef* (The Collector). Although *Me'assef* published papers on biblical and talmudic texts, its emphasis was not on hermeneutics but on the clear exposition of the text and on modern Hebrew poetry and prose. Its contributors wrote on literature, linguistics, and history and expanded the frontiers of Hebrew by including translations of world literature.

Inspired by Mendelssohn's translation of the Bible, they brought to their work a passionate insistence on creating a fresh understanding of Jewish sources while using the oldest Jewish language. Unfortunately, only a select few knew Hebrew well enough to qualify as readers of the magazine. The circle of *Me'assef* lasted until 1811 although the magazine never reached more than a few hundred souls. Yet it showed the new secular direction that was ahead for Jewish learning.

The great change in the nineteenth century was the separation of Jewish learning from the synagogue. Like their Christian counterparts, who were also casting analytic rather than devotional looks at the text of the Bible, the new university-trained scholars examined Jewish tradition and thought with modern, scientific (*wissenschaftlich*) tools. In Berlin in November 1819 seven young men founded the Society for the Culture and Science of the Jews (Verein für Cultur und Wissenschaft der Juden).

Just as important to this group as the reexamination of the Jewish past was the desire to make it both intelligible and desirable to a new generation. Dazzled by the richness of Western civilization and often only slightly acquainted with Jewish learning, young Jews had been turning away from Jewish life under the impression that they were exchanging an impoverished tradition for a rich one. The founders of the society attempted to counter this view. Judaism, they maintained, was not limited to religion as taught in the traditional schools but included philosophy, history, jurisprudence, literature, and moral and social teachings. Although the society's name became synonymous with a new approach to the study of Jewish texts, the group itself proved extremely unstable. Two of its leading members, Eduard Gans and Heinrich Heine, converted shortly after helping found the organization; only Leopold Zunz among the founders was enough of a scholar to make the purposes of the society his lifework.

Although he was never offered a post at a German university, Zunz nonetheless produced pathbreaking works analyzing Jewish liturgy

Title page of *Zeitschrift für die Wissenschaft des Judenthums* (Journal the science of Judaism), published in Berlin for only two years, 1822–23, under the editorship of Leopold Zunz.

and the literature and poetry of the synagogue. In seven decades of unremitting scholarship, he was able to demonstrate how in every place and in every epoch, Jews had been distinctly influenced by their surroundings. To traditional Jews, such historicism smacked of heresy, especially at a moment when the introduction of German-language sermons and prayers was being hotly debated. To others, Zunz's findings offered precedents for change.

At the same time, Yiddish was experiencing its own crisis. After a thousand-year career in the German lands, it was slipping into irreversible decline. By 1830 it was the poor, the artisans, and the rural Jews, especially in southwest Germany, who continued to speak Yiddish, as the more educated and urban Jews gave it up. In his memoir of his school days in Anhalt during the 1830s, Hermann Steinthal, later a prominent philologist and philosopher at the University of Berlin, describes the process by which Yiddish was gradually erased from the speech if not the memory of German Jews. He remembers how his teacher

> insisted that we speak proper German, but we only did it during the lessons. It seemed so strange and unnatural to say *nein*—no—instead of *nee*, or *gieb mir*—give me—instead of *jib mich*. In fact, we Jewish children had our own special dialect; in our little town, which at that time counted thirteen hundred souls, we did not speak like the Christian inhabitants, who retained a Middle German dialect. We spoke German substituting Yiddish for German vowels, with a Yiddish rather than German word order and often with a Yiddish inflection. But not in such an extreme fashion as our parents' generation when they were amongst themselves.

This candid recollection demonstrates how "unnatural" Jewish children attempting to speak High German sounded to themselves; yet once they had been taught literary German they could no longer return either to the Yiddish-German of their parents or to the dialect of their neighbors, especially as they moved on to the universities or the big city. The language lingered into the twentieth century, however, in the small Jewish communities of Posen and Silesia as well as along the Rhine. And as a permanent memento, it was embedded in German in

the speech of cattle dealers, in thieves' argot, and in common words such as *mies* (ugly) and *meschugge* (crazy), whose origins in Yiddish had long ago been forgotten.

As German Jews came to speak like Germans, they came to look like Germans. Yet in their appearance, as in their language, the old continued to coexist with the new for long stretches. Thus the Jewish hat had become so integral a part of Jewish life that Jews continued to wear it long after 1669, when the regulation making it compulsory was abolished (see plate 15). Still, liberation from degrading stigmas was naturally welcome; it was good news when in 1691 the Count Palatinate abolished the yellow badge for the Jews of Mannheim. It was a harbinger of the changes that would transform the Jewish world in the next century. By the early decades of the eighteenth century the old ways were fading. The beard, for example, which had been required by both biblical law and government decree was gradually disappearing among Jewish men. Court Jews such as Jud Süss, Jost Liebmann, and Daniel Itzig are all portrayed without beards. By the time Moses Mendelssohn had his portrait painted, around 1780 (see plate 13), there was plainly no longer any scandal in being clean-shaven.

Yet this gesture at emancipation was only partial. Where Jews had once been forced to wear beards, for example, they were now forced to be clean-shaven. The widespread discussion in the late eighteenth-century German states about the "improvement" of the Jews initiated by Christian Wilhelm Dohm included pressure to conform, to abandon idiosyncratic habits. In 1790, Jews in Prussia were required to stop wearing beards "in order to remove any outward signs of difference," and after the Prussian Edict of Emancipation, only those Jews who did not wear the Jewish badge could be admitted to the duchy of Posen. The integration of Jews into Western culture was not as easy as changing one's coat. New freedoms brought new compulsions, and the discovery of ever new layers of difference turned emancipation into a longer, more complex process than the original "improvers" had imagined.

Jewish thought also soared to heresies unthinkable in earlier days. In 1819, the Wissenschaft des Judentums even dared to question circumcision. Indeed, Abraham Geiger, a lead-

The Sabbath, in front of the synagogue at Furth, ca. 1800. The men and boys, as young as seven, are still wearing the medieval barrette first prescribed for south German Jews in the fifteenth century. Known irreverently as the *Shabbes deckel,* or Sabbath lid, it remained a staple of male dress. The men wear old-fashioned pleated collars and are bearded, while the older married woman has a headdress covering her hair, in accordance with Jewish custom. But the young women are fashionably dressed. (Color plate 15.)

A cooking pot of the kind used for schalet, Frankfurt, 1579/80. "The Hebrew inscription on this pot identifies its owner by association with a house sign. It reads . . . 'Hirtz Popet's s[pouse], daughter of Moses zur Leiter [ladder], in [the year] 5340 [1579/80]. To the left of the word *Leiter* is a schematic rendering of a ladder." *Treasures of the Jewish Museum,* New York, 1986.

ing Reform rabbi, called this oldest of Jewish rituals "a barbaric, bloody act, which fills the father with fear and casts the mother into transports of morbid anxiety." Some extreme elements within the Reform movement even advocated abandoning circumcision altogether.

True, the modernization of Jewish life in the nineteenth century broke with well-established beliefs and practices. But old pleasures kept their hold, even in the memory of those who had drifted far from their origins. In the last years of his life Heinrich Heine, for all his oft-proclaimed allegiance to Protestantism, called himself "an old Jew." And he wrote more than once, with enthusiasm, about the famous Sabbath dish called *Schalet* in Germany and *cholent* in Eastern Europe, a name derived from the French *chaud et lent,* hot and slow. A casserole made of meat, potatoes, beans, barley, and other vegetables and spices, the *Schalet* was set to bake on Friday afternoon so as to be ready and hot for the Sabbath dinner the next day. In 1851, Heine wrote a veritable hymn to the dish. Parodying Schiller's universally known "Ode to Joy," he wrote:

> "*Schalet,* beauteous spark immortal
> Daughter of Elysium,"
> Thus would Schiller have sung it
> Had he ever tasted *Schalet.*

> *Schalet* is the food of heaven
> Which the Lord himself taught Moses
> How to cook, when on that visit
> On the summit of Mount Sinai.

A half-century after Heine's culinary ode, when Jewish emancipation had further eroded the old enclosed life, many families continued to give the Sabbath a special place as the climax of the week. But the weekend festival did not accord with the rhythm of German life, in which Saturday was a regular school day. As early as 1815, David Friedländer suggested that the Sabbath be moved to Sunday, as did the radical rabbi Samuel Holdheim and the philosopher Hermann Cohen later in the century. In 1845, a Reform congregation in Berlin actually instituted Sunday services, but it remained alone in this experiment.

In the 1840s, in a series of rabbinical conferences on the Sabbath, progressive rabbis attempted to arrive at a resolution that would reflect the realities of the German-Jewish situation, particularly as it affected Jews who were government employees or who operated businesses that would be hurt if they had to close on the Sabbath. In an 1846 conference in Breslau they neither condoned nor condemned Sabbath work, throwing the whole question of Sabbath observance back to the local communities.

For most Jews, it was easiest to retain some remembrance of the traditional Sabbath at home. But the exigencies of daily existence and the modernization of German-Jewish life conflicted with the multitudinous Sabbath requirements. By the time Moritz Oppenheim painted his famous Sabbath Eve canvas (see p. 55), only a minority of German Jews observed the traditional ceremonials he depicted. The Sabbath was the first observance to suffer severe compromises as German Jews moved closer to acculturation.

Passover, too, felt the breath of modernity without losing its significant place in the Jewish year. As early as 1716–17, a drawing of a Seder table by Moses Leib ben Wolf of Trebitsch shows an elegant home complete with paintings, fine napery, and a spacious garden (see plate 17). The lady of the house, the children, and the guests are in sumptuous eighteenth-century dress, while the master of the house wears the *kittel* (burial shroud) customary among Jews in the German lands.

Throughout the nineteenth century, Passover retained its power. Moritz Oppenheim, who belonged to the generation that entered decisively into German life, writes movingly of the Seders he knew as a young child: "How exceedingly splendid this evening seemed to me," he recalled in his memoirs. For the ceremony, his father's chair was "transformed into a throne covered with red silk cushions richly brocaded in gold and silver," while his mother, "with the knowledge that she had happily accomplished the great labor for Passover, lovingly surveyed her table companions and sat during the ceremony at the side of her consort as his queen." Even on the eve of the community's extinction in the Nazi period, Seders continued to be celebrated. By 1937 the costumes had changed: the decor was modern, and so was the medium—the photograph—used to capture the scene. But the essential elements remained:

the Haggadah, the wine, the matzah, the family.

Such observances were islands in a world that was gradually becoming far more open. The Jews of Frankfurt were among the first to taste this modernity. When the French forces besieged Frankfurt in 1796, their artillery tore down more than the walls of the ghetto. Half its inhabitants—1,806 people—became homeless, and local Jews estimated their monetary losses at 2 million gulden. While many of them continued to live in the houses left standing after the bombardments, others had no intention of rebuilding their old dwellings or returning to their old ways. But the city council of Frankfurt, backed by merchants fearing Jewish competition, invoked the constitution of 1616 and proposed to rebuild not only the walls of the ghetto but the houses too.

The wars of the French Revolution and Napoleon, however, frustrated those intentions. The demise of the Holy Roman Empire, prudently decreed in 1806 by Francis II—now calling himself Francis I of Austria—brought to an end the status of the Jews as "serfs of the chamber." Napoleon promptly reorganized his newly conquered German principalities into the Confederation of the Rhine and named Karl von Dalberg as prince primate of Frankfurt. The descendant of an old German aristocratic family and the archbishop of nearby Mainz, Dalberg had declared himself in favor of equal rights for the Jews.

Still, between the physical fall of the ghetto walls and the fall of the legal barriers that segregated Frankfurt's Jews lay more than a decade. The city council was not to be hurried in its deliberations about the Jews, and it was only outside pressure that finally produced the Edict of Emancipation, proclaimed on February 8, 1811. Even Dalberg could not resist one last extortionate act: he set the price of freedom for Frankfurt's Jews at 440,000 gulden. It took them almost a year to raise even half that amount as a first installment. Hence the edict did not actually go into effect until December 28, 1811. However grudging this decree was in the making, its consequences were immense. The Jews now joined the larger culture as equals and were respectfully called "Israelites."

The Jews of Berlin also experienced this time of agitation to the full. By the early nineteenth century, when there were some 3,000 Jews in

Passover Seder,
Berlin, 1937.

Berlin (still less than 2 percent of the population), they were indistinguishable in speech, attire, and manners from other Berliners. They attended the newly established university in numbers far beyond their proportion in the population—in 1810, its first year, the University of Berlin took in 16 Jewish students in an entering class of 247, some 7 percent of the total. Admission to the university, however, was not yet a passport to academic or professional careers. Anticipating this silent segregation, Jewish students trained in medicine and law and then practiced largely among their fellow Jews. Similarly, Jewish opportunities for local government service or public office were severely limited. As in the past, a Jew's choice of profession was determined more by what Jews were permitted than by free selection. But whatever the constraints inherent in the Jewish situation, Berlin—by its very size, its sheer importance, and its proximity to the Prussian court—offered Jews opportunities far more abundant than in other cities.

The transition to modernity, which like all transitions was filled with confusion, reached its apogee in 1812, when for a few years the Jews of Prussia saw a glimpse of the Promised Land. Jews throughout their history in the Diaspora had sought legal guarantees, since their sole hope for equitable treatment lay in the self-regulation of the powers under which they lived. The edict of 1812 put the Jews of Berlin at last on an equal legal footing with their fellow citizens. Although the rights in this edict were withdrawn piecemeal and in the end not renewed until 1871, the Jews' attitude toward their new position in the world was changing. They no longer were willing to live on sufferance but fought for every social, economic, and cultural advance as a matter of right.

Napoleon and the Aftermath

Jewish emancipation, that elusive goal of modern times, was even more elusive in Germany than in other countries. In France, it had come at a single stroke in 1791 when the National Assembly declared the Jews to be free and equal citizens of the new republic. In the German lands, however, it became a process rather than an event. In part the difference lay with the crazy quilt of the many independent German states, each with its own laws. What later became Imperial Germany was, at the beginning of the nineteenth century, a conglomeration of some three hundred states of various sizes, with rulers of many philosophies and shades of political opinion. Changes in the status of the Jews in all these kingdoms, principalities, and dukedoms of necessity came piecemeal. But the bellwether for the century was Prussia, the largest of the German states, whose territory extended across Central Europe from the Rhine to the eastern reaches of the Baltic.

Even there, despite Prussia's eighteenth-century "philosopher-king," Frederick II, Jewish emancipation did not proceed as a steady upward trend. Privileges were granted and revoked. Anti-Semitic riots disputed in fact what had been declared in law, and the status of the Jews was one of the many pawns to be exchanged or moved in the aftermath of the wars and revolutions that punctuated the century. The "Jewish question"—a term coined in the 1830s—became a preoccupation of the German states, and even more, of the German Jews. Against this background of acceptance and withdrawal, the Jewish position in the German lands sustained its first substantive change in fifteen hundred years. The individual Jew emerged finally from the collectivity in which he had lived to become directly subject to the laws of the state rather than as mediated through the community.

The compartmentalized society, the *Kastenstaat*, which had determined every subject's destiny from birth, was gradually yielding to the pressures and opportunities of industrialization and the new technology. No longer content to negotiate tax privileges, the Jews wanted a new definition of their status. The peasants, too, sought freedom from their hereditary servitude, just as the individual in the family, in the workplace, and in the community more and more emerged from the corporate structure that had hitherto defined his life. As the revolutions of 1830 and 1848 later demonstrated, Europe had become a society in which many new voices demanded to be heard.

For the Jews, the first steps toward emancipation came in 1806 when Napoleon's forces conquered Prussia, occupied Berlin and organized the Confederation of the Rhine—an act that united thirty-eight states under a single legal code. Under its provisions, the Jews were granted the full equality their brethren already enjoyed in France. With this act Napoleon became the hero of the German Jews, while the French, too, perceived him as raising the Jews out of the mire of the past. In the Prussian province of Brandenburg, which had Berlin as its capital, the French troops settled in for a long occupation, which would be lifted only on the payment of a large war indemnity. How large may be judged by the levy for 1810, when the French demanded 14 million taler, 4 million more than Prussia's entire annual budget.

While the Jews on the Rhine achieved their freedom, Prussia's defeat had darker consequences for Jews elsewhere. In the rage and humiliation that followed the French victory, German intellectuals abandoned eighteenth-century ideas of the brotherhood of man for what was called, derisively, Teutomania. This new nationalist notion combined a mystique of the German folk and an idealization of the Middle Ages with a cult of physical training as propagated by Friedrich Ludwig Jahn, the father of German gymnastics. Born in 1778, "Turnvater" Jahn cultivated an eccentric style as well as eccentric ideas. Dressing in a romantic pastiche of garments that he called "old German style," he

"Napoleon the Great reestablishes the religion of the Israelites, May 30, 1806." Napoleon raises the Synagogue, once again depicted as a young woman. Ternisien d'Haudricourt, *Fastes de la Nation Française,* Paris, [18—].

developed a witches' brew glorifying the German peasant tradition while at the same time inveighing against the "mongrelization" of the German race. Four years after the Prussian defeat he published his ideas about *deutsches Volkstum*—German folkishness (a term of his own coinage)—and offered a defeated nation the balm of admiration. He dwelt on the purity and simplicity of the German character and castigated intermarriage with "outsiders," including Jews.

In 1811, Jahn founded the German Union for Liberation (Deutscher Bund zur Befreiung), which had a strong following among university students and combined for the first time an appeal to patriotism with the idealization of the *Volk*, the people. During the Wars of Liberation waged against Napoleon, he carried his admiration for the German medieval past to its logical conclusion when he ordered the unit under his command to engage only in hand-to-hand combat using axes. His passion for physical fitness developed into a body-building movement in the service of morality, fostering, according to Jahn, "a pure and chaste youth" as well as "an unshakable fidelity to king and fatherland."

The philosopher whose writings were seized upon by this generation was Johann Gottlieb Fichte. As early as 1793, Fichte had begun to raise doubts about the possibility of integrating Jews into German society. For him, they were actually a sinister force, spreading across Europe as "a mighty state with hostile intentions which is at war with every other existing state." Proud of their ancestry, he wrote, Jews form their own "state within a state," to which they owe their first loyalty. They can never be given civil rights, he concluded in a grisly and prophetic declaration, "unless in one night all their heads are cut off, and others are set in their place in which there is not one Jewish idea." The best solution, he continued, would be to "conquer their Promised Land and send them all there."

In 1807, in a series of *Addresses to the German Nation (Reden an die deutsche Nation)*, Fichte elevated the Germans to a model for all Europe as the one people whose purity had not been sullied by the Romans, an *Urvolk* with an ancient language whose philosophical leadership would produce the moral regeneration of Europe. This praise was accompanied by a hymn to German nationalism and patriotism, new

Friedrich Ludwig Jahn in "old German dress." His motto was, "Hatred of everything foreign is the German's duty." Frontispiece in Carl Euler, *Friedrich Ludwig Jahn: Sein Leben und Wirken,* Stuttgart, 1881.

First page of the Prussian edict of 1812 nullifying the existing discriminatory legislation against the Jews and listing their new privileges.

Letter sent on March 12, 1812, by the elders of the Berlin Jewish community to Chancellor Hardenberg on receiving the news of the Edict of Emancipation.

We have received with the profoundest rejoicing the gracious communication of your High Excellency of the eleventh of this month. The significant words which tell us that our express wishes concerning our civil position will be fulfilled by the constitution ratified by our benevolent ruler obliges us in advance to the deepest gratitude to the noble author for the most priceless benefaction. It also obliges us to the most intense effort to prove ourselves worthy of it through genuine loyalty and unconditional obedience.

May it please you, gracious Sir, graciously to receive this provisional assurance until we are able to render other proofs.

Ismar Freund, Die Emanzipation der Juden in Preussen, *Berlin, 1912.*

themes that became antecedents for the more malevolent anti-Semitism of the late nineteenth century.

The ideas developed by Fichte and Jahn, predicating nationality on a shared ancestry and a shared history, naturally excluded foreigners, Jews, and all others who did not fit into the national myth they had invented. Thus, the very beginning of the fateful century that was to bring Jewish liberation already harbored the contradictory forces at work in German society. By 1812, the political forces in Prussia were divided between the great noble landowners, together with other conservatives intent on maintaining the old structure, and the modernizing forces led by the chancellor, Karl von Hardenberg, who advocated opening up society, liberating the Jews, freeing the peasants from serfdom, offering the workers freedom of movement, and initiating a program of economic reform. A new class of politicians and administrators was attempting to modernize the state against what it saw as the stultifying hand of the feudal landowners. The proposals for change in the status of the Jews became part of what was called the revolution from above (*Revolution von Oben*) as Hardenberg pressed for their legal redefinition.

On March 11, 1812, the long-debated edict on the Jews was proclaimed, conferring on them the right to full citizenship, the right to settle wherever they chose, the right to buy land (if they took German names), the right to serve in the army, and the right to marry freely (including non-Jews). It also removed all discriminatory taxes. But while the edict opened the world to the Jews economically, it also set severe limits to their place in public life. Partly in response to an immutable prejudice of King Friedrich Wilhelm IV and partly in response to pressure from the aristocracy, all public offices with the exception of local ones were barred to Jews. Since the universities were also state-supported, this meant that Jews could not enter an academic career.

In 1815, three years after the promulgation of the edict, when Posen was added to Prussia following Napoleon's defeat, the 80,000 Jews of that province were excluded from the benefits of the act. Until the mid-nineteenth century, therefore, one-third of Prussia's Jews lived under the old restraints that limited their occupations,

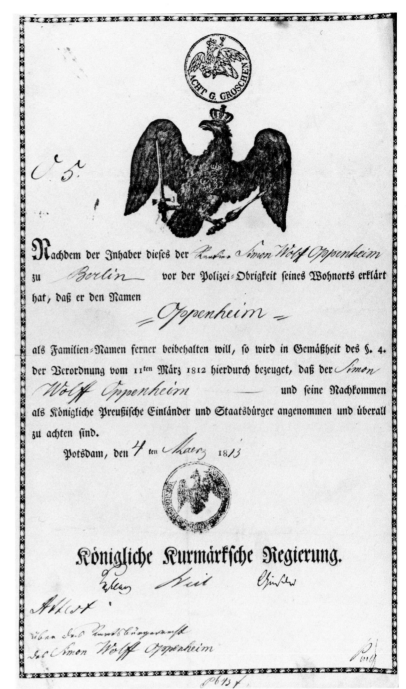

Government certificate declaring the banker Simon Wolf Oppenheim a citizen of Prussia, according to the decree of March 11, 1812. Dated March 4, 1813.

The departure of the East Prussian militia for the field in 1813, after their consecration in the church. Note the Jewish soldier at the right saying goodbye to his parents. Woodcut by L. Pietsch, after an oil painting by Oskar Graf, ca. 1860.

their right to own land, and their rights as citizens. Still, the Jews of Prussia greeted the edict as a tremendous step toward emancipation. In its comprehensiveness it gave them a sense of real progress in their struggle for recognition as equal partners in society.

When Prussia embarked on the Wars of Liberation in 1813, by joining the Russians against Napoleon, they hoped to expel the hated French occupier from their territory. With the addition of Austria and Great Britain, this partnership culminated in the Grand Alliance that ultimately defeated Napoleon at Waterloo in 1815. Although Jews had good reason to value Napoleon as an ally in their struggle for emancipation, when faced with the call to arms of Frederick William III of Prussia they enthusiastically volunteered for action. But the price to be paid for joining the secular world was the breakdown of customary Jewish life.

Meno Burg, the first Jew to become an officer in the Prussian army, was born in 1789, the year of the French Revolution, to a poor Jewish family in Berlin and was taken under the wing of an uncle who was a municipal building inspector with connections at court. Although Burg volunteered for service in the Wars of Liberation, he was never sent to the front but was employed by the artillery to teach geometry. A gifted instructor, he wrote two books on his subject and was eventually promoted to first lieutenant. This was not exactly the dashing life of an aristocratic officer, nor was it without its reminders of the prevailing anti-Semitism. Adamantly a Jew, although this often imperiled his further promotion, Burg candidly recalled in his memoirs how he coped with anti-Semitism. It is clear that the slights, the insulting jokes, and the social condescension that colored his life were part of the experience of all Jews at the time. Burg's strategy required above all a thick skin, a belief in the essential goodness of man, and a visionary hope that the gentile world could be taught to abjure anti-Semitism by contact with responsible and honorable Jews. But the burden, according to Burg, lay with the Jews, who were required to be paragons of virtue.

This was not exactly a heroic course, but for Burg, his advancement in the army was triumph enough. He was promoted to major only in 1847, thirty-four years after his enlistment, having been held back quite simply because he

Meno Burg (1787–1853). Frontispiece from his *Geschichte meines Dienstlebens* . . . Leipzig, 1916.

Meno Burg's account of his departure for the Wars of Liberation.

Then on February 9, 1813 the king issued his memorable call to arms. It is known all over the world how enthusiastically the Prussian youth responded to this call, and how it carried away with it the entire nation without distinction as to belief or class, and elicited a devotion and energy without example in history. We also know with what rare enthusiasm excited youths rushed to the appointed gathering places in order to join the army and struggle for Prussia's freedom and rebirth. Naturally, I did not remain behind and volunteered on the fourteenth of February. . . .

It was magnificent and gripped one's heart to see how the youths . . . tore themselves from the arms of their weeping loved ones and climbed onto the open wagons, and how, as the long column began to move, they swung their caps high in the air to shout a hurrah for Prussia, their beloved fatherland, and a meaningful "farewell" to those left behind, and how we were released from them with their blessing.

Meno Burg, Geschichte meines Dienstlebens *. . . Leipzig, 1916.*

The Return of the Jewish Volunteer, by Moritz Oppenheimer, 1882. The volunteer who has returned to his family lounges at his ease, bareheaded, while his father stares in consternation at the cross on his chest, a military decoration but for an Orthodox Jew a symbol of oppression. The father wears the cap of the religious Jew, and over the table hangs the traditional Sabbath lamp. The younger brother of the volunteer examines the military gear in the corner.

would not submit to baptism. Indeed, it was only the intervention of Prussia's Prince August, Burg's constant protector, that brought him this rank a few years before his retirement. King Friedrich Wilhelm IV was intent on insuring that his officers, like his officials, were Christians. For Burg, this was part of the accepted system in an imperfect world. What gratified him was the esteem of his fellow artillery officers, his high rank, and the fact that he had secured both without bending on the issue of religion.

The aftermath of the Wars of Liberation was hardly what the enthusiastic Jewish public had hoped. In the peace settlement at the Congress of Vienna in 1815, the Jews saw the privileges of the Napoleonic occupation and the edict of 1812 taken away. According to the cleverly worded paragraph 16, each state was permitted to restore the position of its Jews to what it had been before the French victories. What followed was a period of retreat and uncertainty for the German Jews.

At the same time, popular anti-Semitism took on a new secular and self-satisfied tone. In 1815, a play by Karl Borromäus Alexander Sessa called *Unser Verkehr* (The company we keep) became

the rage both on the stage and as an illustrated book. Its plot purports to show how a young Jew makes his way in the world. Exploiting the innate prejudices of a public that regarded Yiddish-German with amusement, if not contempt, it drew on the stereotype of the Jew as interested only in money. At every dramatic climax of the play—in the hero's striving for education, in his hope for marriage—his fate turns on money. The play epitomizes the popular image of the Jew as uncouth, money-grubbing, laughable, and, above all, alien.

The laughter was not confined to the theater. As German Jews of the early nineteenth century attempted to participate in society, they found their efforts largely unrewarded. On the one hand they were urged to "improve," but when they did so, they were faced with a storm of caricature. Jews learning to dance or to ride or engaging in polite drawing-room conversation all became subjects of hilarity. It was a humor that could quickly turn venomous. For all its ancient malice, this was a new kind of anti-Semitism, fueled less by abhorrence of the Jew as Christ-killer than by contemporary conditions. (See plate 16.)

Etching by J. M. Voltz illustrating the departure of the hero from home. *Unser Verkehr* (The company we keep), 1819.

A scene from The Company We Keep (Unser Verkehr, *1819). The parents are made to speak in a "comical" Yiddish-German.*

Go, go. Let yourself be stepped on by people. Let yourself be thrown out of rooms; let yourself be denounced to the courts; let yourself be pushed into kennels; let yourself be bound with cords and chains; let yourself be martyred half to death. But you must become rich.

"Nu, Itzig, where are
you riding off to?"
"O, weh. Do *I* know?"

*Invitation to the
Dance*, by M. Banse.

A Jewish Dandy,
1804.

"The Jew in the fox trap. A true story which occurred in the year 1840." A Jewish peddler (to judge by his staff and bundle) is caught in a trap set for a fox at the inglorious moment when he has just pulled his trousers down. He is visited first by the fox, who "laughs at his misfortunes." When the hunter at last arrives, the Jew promises to give him all he has if the hunter will release him. This broadside, written in southwest German dialects, was very popular and widely distributed. (See also plate 16.)

Hepp ! Hepp !

Anti-Jewish riots in Frankfurt, 1819.

In 1819, ugly words were followed by uglier deeds as a wave of attacks on Jewish communities erupted across the country. Called the Hep-Hep Riots, presumably from the Latin acronym *Hierosolyma est perdita* (Jerusalem has fallen), they started in August in Munich and in the next two months spread to thirty other cities. Generally they were of short duration, but in Hamburg, where young Jews resisted, the violence lasted for six days. Unlike the Teutomania of a decade earlier, these riots were not motivated by medievalizing romanticism but were carried out by workers and merchants who saw their livelihood endangered by the admission of Jews into society. Although observers at the time tended to minimize the seriousness of the riots—and they did subside—they were a reminder of a latent brutality.

In a divided Germany, the way to Jewish emancipation was neither direct nor equal. Progress in one state might be matched by defeat in another, and there was no guarantee that privileges once granted were immutable. After the Congress of Vienna, the Jews of Germany rode a roller coaster as their future was hammered out in a volatile political atmosphere.

Solutions

Conversion

Conversion has always been an act with a double meaning. It can be seen as an expression of religious faith or as a rejection of such faith. But for Jews it meant a rejection of an entire earthly world as well, in the hope of gaining another. In nineteenth-century Germany the social consequences of conversion were immense, for it resolved—effortlessly, it seemed—the thorny question of how Jews were to live in a Christian state. At a single stroke, it seemed to make issues of marriage, residence, career opportunities, and social standing simply vanish. Considering these advantages, it is remarkable how few German Jews took that path.

In the entire nineteenth century only 22,520 Jews in Germany converted to Christianity, an average of 225 a year in a population numbering a half million by the end of the century. But the opening of the century brought what seemed like a wave of conversion (*eine Taufwelle*) as prominent Jews, particularly in Berlin, had themselves baptized. Rahel Varnhagen had the impression that half the Jews of Berlin were now Christians. David Friedländer compiled a list of fifty cases in 1811, some representing whole families rather than individuals in a community of only 405 families.

The list consists largely of young, well educated, and often prosperous people. It was those who lived on the edge between two worlds who were most tempted by conversion and had the most to gain from it. As one Jewish observer wrote rather sardonically in 1792, "They resemble moths, who flutter so long around the flame that they are finally engulfed by it." Converts of the late eighteenth and early nineteenth centuries, such as Rahel Varnhagen, Dorothea Schlegel, and Henriette Herz, were impelled by a religious fervor that seemed rarer later in the century. The motives of those who took an instrumental view of conversion, who saw no way to use their talents in the world without the baptismal certificate, were equally simple. And every generation had its apostates who converted and then became enemies to the Jews.

Three young men, Eduard Gans, Ludwig Börne, and Heinrich Heine, each prominent in Jewish life, are examples of those who turned Christian quite coolly. Gans, one of the founders

of the Society for the Culture and Science of the Jews, was a student at the university in Berlin. As we know, the university was a state institution, and Jews had no chance of appointment to the faculty. Gans converted in December 1825, was appointed to the law faculty in 1826, and was promoted to a full professorship (*Ordinarius*) in 1828, a position he filled with distinction until his sudden death in 1839. What had begun as an act of convenience ended in an earnest change of sides. In 1838, he joined other members of the law faculty in signing a petition to prevent the granting of law degrees to Jewish students. Word circulated that Gans no longer wished to associate with Jews.

Ludwig Börne, born Juda Loew Baruch in the old Frankfurt ghetto in 1786, had gone to Berlin as a youth of seventeen to study medicine with Marcus Herz and at once became a votary of Henriette Herz. In the cosmopolitan atmosphere of the Herz household, which took Christianity seriously and Judaism lightly, he found fresh ways of looking at the world. With the death of his teacher shortly after his arrival, Börne changed his field and went to Halle and then Heidelberg to study law, politics, and ad-

Eduard Gans (1798–1839).

ministration. In 1808 he took a doctorate in law at the university in Giessen and returned to Frankfurt, where he was appointed an actuary in the municipal government. In 1815, after the Wars of Liberation, the pre-Napoleonic restrictions were reimposed and Börne, as a Jew, was summarily dismissed from his post.

By this time his political passions had been aroused and he had also discovered his talent for writing. Very early he had decided that the liberation of the Jews was part of the larger struggle for human emancipation. Believing that he would be more useful to that cause as a Christian, in June 1818 he quietly had himself baptized in Roedelheim near Frankfurt and took the name Karl Ludwig Börne. His conversion remained a secret, even from his father, for several years.

This drastic step was bound up with his intention to start a periodical that would not be a Jewish magazine; he wanted to feel free of the parochial fetters of his origins. The first issue of the magazine *Die Waage* (The scales) appeared in July 1818. In 1821 Börne gave it up, frustrated by the political censorship. Ten years later he emigrated to Paris, where he wrote the political essays that made him a leading figure among German liberals both at home and abroad. Rational or logical as his conversion had been, he lived to regret it. In 1836, the year before his death, he wrote angrily about the unfailing stream of anti-Semitism directed at him. "Jew, Jew," he exclaimed, "that is the last red cent in the miserable bank of their wit. But after all this, I wish that I could have my three louis d'or back, those with which I honored the pastor for my Christianity. I have been baptized now for eighteen years and it doesn't help me. Three louis d'or for a little place in the German madhouse. It was pure waste!"

Börne, who committed his life to political polemics, is now largely forgotten, as are his essays. But he represents many Jews who believed that the adoption of Christianity erased memory. Baptized Jews soon found themselves in a no-man's-land, outside the Jewish community and yet never entirely members of the larger world. They remained Jewish Christians to the end of their days, forming almost a caste as they socialized and married among themselves.

Heinrich Heine was no less matter-of-fact than Börne when he underwent baptism, also se-

Ludwig Börne (1786–1837). Engraving by T. S. Englehurt after a painting by Moritz Oppenheim.

cretly, in June 1825, a month before his final examination for his degree in law at the University of Göttingen. In many Jewish families in the early nineteenth century, it was understood that sooner or later their sons would accept baptism. Yet Heine agonized most publicly over the step, and his description of conversion as the equivalent of buying "an entry ticket to European culture" transformed it from a religious into a secular act.

As Heine discovered, however, although the conversion might have made a difference in a university appointment (which he never seriously sought), to the world at large he remained a Jew. Six months after his baptism, he wrote to his friend the Berlin banker Moses Moser: "I am now hated by Christian and Jew alike. I much regret that I have had myself baptized; I don't perceive that things have gone better for me. On the contrary, I have since had nothing but misfortune." As with Börne, his enemies continued to taunt him with his origins, and he could not divorce himself from his profound sense of connection with Judaism. When his friend Eduard Gans converted several months after he did, he responded to the news with a violent poem, "To an Apostate." It was not published in his lifetime, but its passion suggests the turbulent emotion this event elicited in him:

> As for that holy youthful spirit:
> How quickly you've been suppressed
> And in cold blood
> You have reached an understanding with the
>   good lords
> And you have crawled to the cross,
> The cross that you despised
> That only a few weeks ago
> You had thought of treading into the dust.

His prose and poetry alike are sprinkled with Jewish allusions and Jewish characters. His one attempt at a novel, *The Rabbi of Bacherach*—which he began in 1824, the year before his conversion, and never completed—opens peacefully enough with a Passover Seder. But when the rabbi discovers the dead body of a child under the table and realizes that an accusation of ritual murder and a subsequent massacre are impending, he takes his wife and flees. Three decades later, in 1851, Heine published his *Hebrew Melodies,* a cycle of poems on Jewish themes. He perhaps described himself when he wrote that poets "take a secret and malicious pleasure in remodeling in whatever ways they see fit what the people's memory has preserved."

Conversion, even for the illustrious and even for the true believers, did not bring rest but doubt. Rahel Varnhagen wrestled with its meaning even on her deathbed. And Börne and Heine found in it neither relief nor honor. Yet these were the great and visible figures in the world who could give expression to what the less articulate might feel. Ordinary people who converted, married, had children, and lived in communities did not engage in public debate. It took a journalist and a poet to declaim in public what others were experiencing in private, to shout out loud what the ordinary only whispered. The ultimate reality was that for the first generation, at least, conversion changed very little.

The group of converts who turned on their former brothers and sisters did less damage in the nineteenth century than earlier, but when they were powerfully placed they could sow needless discord and set back the cause of Jewish emancipation. One such was Friedrich Julius Stahl, who converted to Lutheranism in 1819. He not only embraced Christianity but allied himself with that mythical entity, the German folk, and denounced the Jews as morally inferior to the Germans. Succeeding Gans as professor of law at the university in Berlin in 1840, he expounded his ideas in a book published in 1847 which argued against the possibility of the emancipation of the Jews in a Christian State. Although Stahl refrained from the call for physical violence that marked the work of earlier apostates, his position in the university and later in politics gave him the ear of policymakers and lawgivers, to the detriment of the Jews.

The old libels about the desecration of the Host and ritual murder had lost credibility in most of Western Europe by the nineteenth century. They were replaced by a growing sense of peoplehood that became a powerful political force and used the "foreignness" of the Jews as a dramatic counterpoise. Bavarians and Prussians in the nineteenth century might look at one another with disdain and hostility, but they were all ready to claim the same ancestors in the oak forests of what the Romans had called Germania. And as long as conservatives such as Stahl and, more significantly, Bismarck insisted that Ger-

Heinrich Heine. Engraving by Ludwig Grimm, 1827.

A letter from Heinrich Heine to his friend Immanuel Wohlwill, one of the founders of the Society for the Culture and Science of the Jews. This letter, written on April 1, 1823, two years before Heine's own conversion, is acidly scornful of Jews who compromise with Christianity.

We no longer have the strength to wear a beard, to fast, to hate and through that hatred to endure. That is the motive for our Reformation. Those who are receiving their cultivation and their enlightenment from comedians want to give Judaism new decorations and a new stage set, and the prompter is to wear the white bands [of a Protestant minister] instead of a beard. . . . Others want a little evangelical Christianity under a Jewish firm and are making a talles [prayer shawl] from the wool of the Lamb of God, their jacket from the feathers of the Holy Ghost-Dove, and their drawers from Christian love. And they'll go bankrupt, and their descendants will be calling themselves God, Christ & Co. With luck, such a firm won't last long.

Friedrich Hirth, ed., Heinrich Heine: Briefe, *Mainz, 1950.*

many could only be a Christian state, the Jews were automatically second-class citizens.

Jewish conversion was also slowed by the growing secularization that crossed all religious boundaries and the growing reservation among Christians as to whether mass conversion of the Jews was really what they wanted. Henriette Herz's friend and mentor, the theologian Friedrich Schleiermacher, worried lest a mass wave of conversion lead to a "Judaization" of the church. Another theologian was so distrustful of what he regarded as the inherent evil of Jewish character that he proposed a six-year probation period for applicants. "The main enemy," one missionary to the Jews wrote, "is Jewish unbelief." But what made Christianity especially unpalatable to a people notoriously resistant to conversion was emerging modern anti-Semitism—a new "scientific" anti-Semitism clothed in elaborate economic, national, and biological arguments. Conversion, then, proved as much a problem as a solution in a society unprepared and unwilling to meet the converts on new ground.

The Migration of Nations

Whether forced or voluntary, movement has been a constant in Jewish life. But in the nineteenth century the smoke of the steam engine became the flag of freedom under which thousands of Europe's Jews massed for voyages that took them further from home than ever before. The introduction of the railroad into Germany in 1835 and the expansion of the steamship companies geared to carrying emigrants across the Atlantic opened possibilities that attracted thousands of Jews disappointed in the hopes that had been raised in the first decades of the century. With the period of reaction heralded by the Hep Hep Riots of 1819, many young Jews despaired of the possibility of a reasonable future. The old restrictions preventing them from practicing a trade, taking up permanent residence, and even marrying remained stubbornly in place. Yet across the sea—now only a month's passage away—was the United States, offering unbounded opportunity and freedom.

It was not the Jews alone who were tempted to throw off the shackles of old Europe for the New World. Between 1820 and 1850 some 600,000 Germans emigrated, and in the second half of the century the emigration became a ver-itable exodus. By 1910, 5 million Germans had left their homeland, 90 percent of them for the United States. As one observer in Bremen put it, it was "a true migration of nations."

Many did not even travel in German ships but embarked from German ports for Liverpool, which specialized in dispatching immigrant ships that could accommodate as many as a thousand passengers. In major German ports like Bremen and Hamburg, the city fathers sought to help the emigrants awaiting their ships by offering information on how to manage in the city as well as advice on life in the new world. At the same time, the German shipowners sought to compete with the cheaper English ships by offering hot meals (so that the emigrants did not have to carry their own food) and assurances of higher standards as against "the filth, the dissoluteness," and, a special danger, "the Irish" on Liverpool ships.

Among the Jews, groups from a single town or neighborhood formed traveling companies and made arrangements for preparing kosher food on board ship, often carrying with them a Torah as well as a teacher, cantor, ritual slaughterer, and mohel—in effect, the tent of Jewish life. Yet the departures were also days of lamentation for those left behind. By the 1850s, whole villages in the south of Germany were denuded of their young. By the end of the nineteenth century, nearly 120,000 Jews had left Germany, mainly for the United States, where they hoped to earn the money to bring over the rest of their families.

Not all emigrants crossed the ocean. As industrialization began to set its mark on the society, it was a time, as Richard Hofstadter once wrote of America, when Germany, which had grown up in the country, moved to the city. The factories, while offering wide opportunities for venture capital, also had a voracious need for hands; the cities became magnets for the young, the ambitious, and those disaffected with rural life. And the new trains made the move easy and cheap.

The great lodestar was Berlin, which in 1871 became the capital of the new German Empire. Long before then its size and diversity had drawn Jews, particularly from the eastern provinces of Prussia—Pomerania, Posen, and Silesia—drastically changing the balance in Jewish popu-

"Between decks on an emigrant ship." *Illustrated London News,* April 17, 1850.

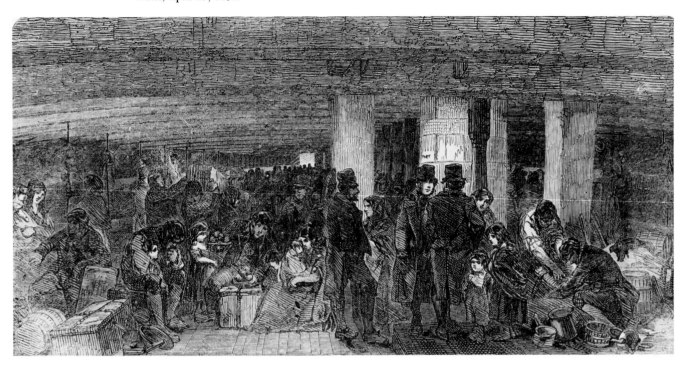

A *ship's doctor describes conditions on the emigrant ships.*

As a German I consider it my duty to warn Germans against the wild goose chase to Liverpool, since they can expect nothing pleasant aboard the English and American ships. . . . The large American ships take on at one time five hundred to six hundred, even seven hundred passengers, all in great confusion. Hence there is little decency aboard ship, much vermin, and also the dangerous ship's fever. The children and the aged suffer the most, and often thirty or forty, sometimes as many as a hundred will die during the voyage. (More than on the slave ships in the worst times!) Last spring the American ship Columbus *lost forty passengers between Liverpool and New York.*

Allgemeine Zeitung, Bremen, *March 13, 1852.*

"Announcement. An information bureau for the protection and care of emigrants is in operation in Bremen . . and distributes useful information as required for his plans to every immigrant." Poster, Bremen, February 1851.

Miniature prayer book printed for travelers to America. Fürth, 1842. Reproduced at actual size.

lation between country and city. In 1837, 100,000 Jews lived in the eastern provinces and 45,000 in the rest of Prussia, only 6,000 of them in Berlin. By 1871, all the large cities had dramatically increased their Jewish population—Berlin sixfold to 36,000, or counting all the suburbs, 48,000, making up nearly 10 percent of all the Jews in Germany. In Breslau, the number of Jews grew from 5,000 to 14,000; in Frankfurt, from 3,000 to 10,000; in Hamburg, from 7,000 to 13,000; and in Munich, from 650 to 3,000. Their concentration in the big cities and in highly visible occupations, such as retailing, made them far more visible than their small proportion of the population (1.25 percent) might suggest.

For all these migrants, whether Christians or Jews, the move to the city meant abandoning the tight organization of village life for the new rhythms and new ways of urban existence. These changes in structure reached deeply into the age-old practice of Judaism. In the contradictory economic scene, the Jew, who for centuries had lived on the margin, now moved closer to the center as his skills in marketing and banking became the hallmarks of the emerging industrial world. By the end of the century, then, the constellation of Jewish life in Germany was markedly different from what it had been at the beginning.

The Road to Politics

The inquiry into the "Jewish question" changed substantially in the four decades since Dohm first began to speculate about improving the condition of the Jews. Europe had experienced the French Revolution and was in the throes of the equally unsettling Industrial Revolution. In an atmosphere that had everywhere grown politically unstable, the Jewish question was no longer a matter of belief or good manners. In fact, it was no longer a question for the Jews alone but had become part of the political ferment that agitated Europe in the first decades of the nineteenth century.

For Jews who despaired of change in Germany, an alternative to conversion or emigration was political action. Some of those who stayed took the struggle for Jewish emancipation to higher ground, linking it to the emancipation of all German society. The German states in those years were emphatically not enjoying the first stages of industrialization, which had come late to Germany. The new technology brought unemployment and misery in its wake, disrupted centuries-old patterns of village life, and created a new class of urban poor. Meanwhile, the recurring revolutions in France served to admonish German rulers that changes were needed.

By the 1840s, the Jews had been transformed in public consciousness from a people to a problem as the term *Judenfrage*—the "Jewish question"—began to gain currency. In this new atmosphere Bruno Bauer, a theologian who taught at the university in Bonn, gave the question yet another twist in a series of essays first published in 1842 in the *Deutsche Jahrbücher für Wissenschaft und Kunst.* Bauer's essays, which held the Jews responsible for their disabilities, aroused a storm of protest in the Jewish community.

Bauer began by challenging not only the Jews' right to emancipation but even their claim to have been maltreated. If Jews were persecuted in the past, he maintained, they had only themselves to blame for persisting in practices that incited their attackers. If they wanted civil rights, they had to be prepared to give up the "privileges" of Jews. But if Jews wanted to live according to their own code in a Christian state, they must be prepared to live as a minority subordinate to majority rule. We are not yet emancipated, said Bauer, and Germany is not yet a state: how can the Jews ask for something the Germans do not have?

Bauer's essay aroused a young journalist named Karl Marx, who wrote an extensive review which appeared in 1844 under the title "On the Jewish Question." Marx, of Jewish birth but baptized at the age of six, was even more critical of the Jews than was Bauer, asserting that it was not the Jews who needed to be emancipated but society that needed to be emancipated from the Jews. The twenty-six-year-old Marx did not then attract much notice with his essay, but it was symptomatic of a new strain of thought as the Jewish question entered the modern era.

Whereas Bauer, a passionate atheist, wanted society to be emancipated from religion, for Marx it was the capitalist system that was the root of injustice and poverty in the world. And the Jews, according to Marx, were by nature and practice the archetypical capitalists. Both essays

Deutsche Jahrbücher

für

Wissenschaft und Kunst.

No **274.**   **17. November.**   **1842.**

Die Juden-Frage.

Von B. Bauer.

„Freiheit, Rechte der Menschheit, Emancipation und Vergütigung eines tausendjährigen Unrechts" sind so große Rechte und Pflichten, daß schon die bloße Appellation an dieselben in jedem Ehrenmanne einen Widerklang zu finden gewiß sein kann, ja die bloßen Worte schon oft hinreichen, die Sache, zu deren Vertheidigung sie gebraucht werden, populär zu machen.

Allein nur zu oft glaubt man eine Sache schon gewonnen zu haben, wenn man für sie nur Worte gebraucht, die gleichsam als ein heiliges Zeichen dienen, dem Niemand widersprechen darf, wer nicht für einen Unmenschen, Spötter oder Freund der Tyrannei gelten will. Man kann in dieser Weise augenblickliche Erfolge erreichen, aber die Sache nicht gewinnen, die wirklichen Schwierigkeiten nicht bezwingen.

In den jetzigen Verhandlungen über die Judenfrage sind die großen Worte „Freiheit, Menschen-Rechte, Emancipation" oft gehört und mit vielem Beifall aufgenommen worden; die Sache selbst aber haben sie nicht viel weiter gebracht und es wird vielleicht von Nutzen sein, sie einmal weniger oft zu gebrauchen und dafür ernstlicher an den Gegenstand zu denken, um den es sich handelt.

Wenn die Sache der Juden eine populäre geworden ist, so kann es nicht ein Verdienst ihrer Vertheidiger, sondern nur daraus zu erklären sein, daß das Volk den Zusammenhang ahnet, in welchem die Emancipation der Juden mit der Entwicklung unsrer gesammten Zustände steht.

Die Vertheidiger der Judenemancipation haben diesen Zusammenhang aufgesucht und wirklich dargestellt. In einer Zeit, in welcher die Kritik sich an Alles, was die Welt bisher beherrschte, gewagt hat, haben sie die Juden und das Judenthum kurz und gut das sein lassen, was sie sind, oder vielmehr man fragt nicht einmal, was sie sind, und ohne zu untersuchen, ob ihr Wesen mit der Freiheit verträglich ist, will man sie zur Freiheit erheben.

Man schreit sogar wie über einen Verrath an der Menschlichkeit, wenn die Kritik sich dazu anschickt, das Wesen, welches dem Juden als Juden eigen ist, zu untersuchen. Die-selben vielleicht, die mit Vergnügen zusehen, wenn die Kritik sich des Christenthums bemächtigt, oder diese Kritik für nothwendig halten und selbst verlangen, sind im Stande denjenigen zu verdammen, der nun auch das Judenthum der Kritik unterwirft.

Das Judenthum soll also ein Privilegium haben: jetzt, wo die Privilegien unter den Streichen der Kritik fallen, und auch später noch, wenn sie alle gefallen sind?

Die Vertheidiger der Judenemancipation haben sich daher die sonderbare Stellung gegeben, daß sie gegen die Privilegien kämpfen und in demselben Augenblick dem Judenthum das Privilegium der Unveränderlichkeit, Unverletzlichkeit und Unverantwortlichkeit geben. Sie kämpfen in der besten Meinung für die Juden, aber die wahre Begeisterung fehlt ihnen, da sie die Sache der Juden als eine ihnen fremde behandeln. Wenn sie für den Fortschritt, für die Fortbildung der Menschheit Partei genommen haben, so schließen sie die Juden von ihrer Partei aus. Von den Christen und von dem christlichen Staate verlangen sie, daß sie die Vorurtheile, die ihnen nicht nur ans Herz gewachsen sind, sondern ihr Herz und ihr Wesen bilden, aufgeben sollen, von den Juden aber nicht. Dem Judenthum soll man nicht ans Herz greifen.

Die christliche Welt muß die Geburt der neuen Zeit, die sich jetzt bildet, noch große Schmerzen kosten: sollen die Juden keine Schmerzen leiden, sollen sie mit denen, die für die neue Zeit gekämpft und gelitten haben, gleiche Rechte haben? Als ob sie es könnten! Als ob sie in einer Welt, die sie nicht gemacht haben, nicht machen halfen und der sie durch ihr unverändertes Wesen vielmehr widersprechen müssen, sich wohl und zu Hause fühlen könnten!

Diejenigen sind also die ärgsten Feinde der Juden, welche sie die Schmerzen der Kritik, die jetzt Alles ergriffen hat, nicht fühlen lassen wollen. Ohne durch das Feuer der Kritik gegangen zu sein, wird Nichts in die neue Welt, die nahe herbei gekommen ist, eingehen können.

Ihr habt die Sache der Juden auch noch nicht zu einer wirklich populären, zu einer allgemeinen Volkssache gemacht. Ihr habt über die Ungerechtigkeiten der christlichen Staaten gesprochen, aber noch nicht gefragt, ob diese Ungerechtigkeiten und Härten nicht im Wesen der bisherigen Staatsverfassungen begründet sind.

Title page of Bruno Bauer's essay, "The Jewish Question."

Karl Marx (1818–
1883).

had the effect of casting the Jews in an evil light, either as religiously obscurantist and separatist or as money-grubbing and exploitative. "What is the worldly religion of the Jew?" Marx asks in his essay. "Money. That is the jealous God of Israel before whom no other God can maintain his place."

In this hardening atmosphere, the Jewish community was discarding its mode of humbly asking for favors from the ruling powers. One of its most powerful spokesmen was Gabriel Riesser. Taking up where Ludwig Börne had left off, Riesser also saw the Jewish situation as bound up with the need for change in Germany. His feeling about his own Germanness, however, was not tinged with the irony and doubt that had embittered Börne's and Heine's love for German culture. "Whoever disputes my claim to my German fatherland disputes my right to my thoughts and feelings, to the language that I speak, to the air that I breathe, and therefore," concluded Riesser in a passionate outburst, "I must defend myself against him as I would against a murderer."

Born in 1806, the descendant of two notable rabbinical families, Riesser nonetheless chose a secular path, studying law at Kiel and Hamburg. Making a career, however, proved difficult. At neither university could he obtain a post as a lecturer, nor could he obtain permission to practice law in Hamburg. In 1838, when he applied to the state of Hesse for naturalization, hoping to enter on a political career, his application was turned down. When this last blow came, at the height of the emigration fever, he thought of leaving for the United States but decided in the end to remain. Finally, in 1840 he was permitted to settle in Hamburg as a notary, having already developed a reputation as a political journalist.

Riesser's boldness in political thinking showed itself as early as 1832, when he founded a magazine with the daring title *Der Jude*. At a point when Jews were attempting to substitute less pejorative terms such as *israelitisch* or *mosaisch,* Riesser's title elicited a flood of letters to the editor. He acknowledged the hatred that was bound up with the use of the name, but it was the anti-Semite, not the Jew, who needed to change. "Is it not the responsibility of those who hate," he asked, "to fight against the hatred and cast it off, if it is ever to end? Should we [Jews]

"Attention! Pull yourselves together, troops! We are marching to our commander's house. Regiment, beat your drums!" The banner reads, "Profit. Equal rights with Christians!" Bistre drawing, 1848.

Gabriel Riesser (1806–1863). Engraving after a painting by Moritz Oppenheim.

deny this ancient and honorable name in order to please those who hate it?" Freedom for all and the unification of the three hundred German states under one head became the keystones of his program, which he tirelessly pursued in addresses and publications.

The February 1848 revolution in France was the spark needed to set off the German revolution. The demands that propelled these forces in Germany in 1848 were for an end to censorship, the right to representation in government through political parties, the elimination of feudal rights, the abolition of serfdom, and, most revolutionary of all, the establishment of a constitutional monarchy over a united Germany.

In Berlin, where growing crowds demonstrated for a week, violence broke out on March 13, when the troops fired on masses gathered in front of the palace. In retaliation the demonstrators threw up barricades at various points in the city. In the fighting that ensued over the next six days, 230 people died, ten of them Jews. On March 19, King Friedrich Wilhelm IV withdrew his troops and consented to limit his powers in a constitutional monarchy.

In the countryside, the main impetus to the revolution came from the peasants demanding land and freedom from their feudal dues and their debts. Since the Jews were involved both as managers of estates and moneylenders, they became as important a target as the landowners; in many cases peasants destroyed or burned account books, leaving the Jews with serious financial losses even as they hoped for their own political and social liberation.

In the aftermath of the revolution, elections were held in many German states for a national parliament, which met in Frankfurt in July 1848. Among its 830 deputies were seven Jews, including Gabriel Riesser, and ten representatives of Jewish origin. Eduard Simson, a professor of law at the University of Königsberg who had been baptized at the age of thirteen, was elected president of the assembly in December 1848. In that same month, the work of the parliament culminated in a statement of basic rights (*Grundrechte*), which it hoped would serve as the foundation for the new German constitution. Article 5 guaranteed that the "enjoyment of civil and state rights would be neither conditional nor limited because of religious belief."

In the debate that preceded the adoption of

Dragoons charging the demonstrators before the Royal Palace in Berlin, March 18, 1848. *Illustrated London News,* April 1, 1848.

As the German public demonstrated before the Royal Palace in Berlin in March 1848, the Jewish residents of Dresden published the following appeal to their "Christian fellow-citizens and fellow-residents of Saxony."

The convulsion which has proceeded from the West to all parts of civilized Europe, calling us to freedom and an independent conditions, moves us, too, the Israelite citizens of Saxony. We, too, are taking part, active part, in the fight for the holiest possession of humanity, since we feel ourselves, with no less enthusiasm than our Christian brothers, to be Germans and Saxons. We are taking part in the peaceful struggle by legal means, just as innumerable Israelites risked their lives in 1813 for the liberation of Germany from the yoke of foreign rule. But we plead for and demand our proper rights, not only from the government, but also from you, our Christian brothers, from the Saxon people. You cannot be free from above, if you are not also free from below. Freedom is an unfreedom when it is not promulgated for all. . . .

The Israelite citizens and residents of Saxony feel themselves equal to all others through their intellectual and moral education, equal according to the eternal statutes of reason and humanity; we turn to you, our Christian brothers, and hope that you will no longer approve of those discriminatory laws that . . . set up a difference in the rights among citizens.

Allgemeine Zeitung des Judenthums, *March 20, 1848.*

the basic rights, the definition of the Jew took on more than theoretical significance. Riesser, with his accustomed eloquence, insisted that the Jews were a religious group and not a nation: "Where is that other state to which we owe loyalty? We have not emigrated to Germany; we have been born here, and either we are Germans or we are men without a country." Rabbi Leopold Stein echoed these sentiments in the Jewish press: "We are and want only to be Germans! We wish for no other fatherland than Germany! We are Israelites only by faith; in every other respect and in the deepest sense, we belong to the state in which we live."

In fact, the anticipation of becoming full-fledged citizens aroused great excitement in the Jewish community because it also freed Jews from what had become the tyranny of Jewish community rule. Treated as members of a state within a state in which taxation, legal decisions, and general control were in the hands of the community's officers, some Jews gave emancipation a double meaning. "Because the world shut us out, we are required to organize our own government. That was our situation before March," wrote a Hamburg reader to the Jewish paper *Orient.* "We were isolated; the community was by its nature a ghetto. Now it is different. We are citizens even though we are Jews." Religious Jews also welcomed this public recognition of their status since it would permit them to practice their religion more openly.

This period of jubilation and hope soon came to an inglorious end. In April 1849, acting on the instructions of the Frankfurt parliament, a delegation headed by Eduard Simson and including Gabriel Riesser appeared before the Prussian king, Friedrich Wilhelm IV, to offer him the crown of a united Germany. Unwilling to rule by the will of the people, Friedrich Wilhelm rejected the crown. As he wrote in a private letter to his friend Carl Josias von Bunsen, the German ambassador in London, "a legitimate king, by the Grace of God, could not pick up such a circlet [*Reif*] baked out of filth and dirt." Nor would he be "bound by a dog's collar to the revolution of 1848."

This rejection by the king once again threw the question of Jewish rights back to the individual states. Prussia, the state with the largest Jewish population (200,000 in 1848), did grant Jews legal equality in its constitution of 1850, but their status was hemmed in by the official declaration that Prussia was a Christian state, which effectively barred Jews from serving as government officials, university professors, and officers in the army. It took another two decades of stubborn struggle before that longed-for phantom of emancipation materialized.

New Ways and New Religions

The political and social changes of the early nineteenth century were not confined to the public arena; there were equally profound changes in Jewish belief and practice. A people intoxicated by the ideas of the Enlightenment thought that this was a time to take a new look at a religion founded in the sands of the Sinai and developed by the rivers of Babylon.

It was not only the scholars who were looking at Jewish tradition. As the Jewish communities grew more prosperous and assimilated, they grew impatient with the old ways in both content and form. Customary practices that were easy—indeed, inescapable—in a ghetto became difficult to maintain in a more cosmopolitan setting. And the noise and disorder of the synagogue, where people congregated but prayed individually—and aloud—also seemed questionable in a world that prized decorum and restraint.

These seemingly superficial matters of behavior propelled the first wave of change, in the form of the synagogue service. The reform of Judaism, as we shall see, owes as much to the need to bring religion into conformity with life as to any deep theological need. The first innovator, Israel Jacobson, a wealthy businessman, built his own temple in Seesen in 1810, installed an organ, arranged for prayers and the sermon in German, but continued the separation of the sexes by designing a balcony for women.

After Jacobson moved to Berlin in 1814, he continued to hold his innovative services in his home. When the congregation grew too large for him to accommodate it, services were transferred to the house of Jacob Herz Beer, a banker whose son was known in the world as Giacomo Meyerbeer. At the Beer house, which could seat more than four hundred people, the services consisted of a selection from the Sabbath prayers and a straightforward reading of the Torah portion in the Sephardic pronunciation rather than the customary Ashkenazic chanting.

A delegation led by
Eduard Simson offers
the crown to
Friedrich Wilhelm IV,
April 2, 1849.

An organ played by a gentile accompanied the hymns, which were sung in German. These services continued until 1823, attracting a substantial congregation and an equally substantial amount of controversy. In the Jewish community, the major effect of these services, as Leopold Zunz commented, was to draw people to worship "who for twenty years had no communion with Jews."

Objections from Orthodox Jews were to be expected, but the worshipers at the Beer temple were astonished in 1823 to find that their services were prohibited by royal decree. Jewish worship had always been a source of uneasiness for the ruling powers, and over the centuries certain prayers had been prohibited as objectionable to Christian believers; the noise of Jewish worship had often served as a pretext for interference, and the synagogue had also been used as the scene for forced attendance at conversion sermons. What made Friedrich Wilhelm III nervous about the new kind of services in Berlin was, paradoxically enough, that they seemed to be approximating the style of church worship. On the one hand he feared that as Jewish services became closer to the Christian form, they might lead Christians either to convert to Judaism or to intermarry. At the same time he was highly suspicious of any deviation from custom or ritual as an indicator of an unstable political climate. It was better, according to this reasoning, for the Jews to remain immured in their old practices and distinctly visible.

The private innovations introduced by Jews with the means to implement them were the first intimations of a movement waiting to be born. At about the same time, in 1818, a more formally organized temple in Hamburg began holding services. Although it retained the separation of men and women, it also printed what was tantamount to the first Reform prayer book in both Hebrew and German. The sermons were delivered in German, and the service included the use of an organ; the music was a curious mixture of Sephardic chant and specially commissioned hymns using traditional Hebrew texts set to music that could only be compared with contemporary German church music.

An extreme group in Frankfurt in 1842 calling themselves the Friends of Reform (*Reformfreunde*) rejected the authority of the Talmud, repudiated the traditional hope for the coming of the Messiah and the return to Palestine, and claimed as their fatherland the land of their birth. Furthermore, they raised questions about the practice of circumcision and the observance of the dietary laws. In other cities, the shape of the service and the languages to be used were steadily being altered. At the same time the role of the rabbi was undergoing a radical transformation—from ultimate authority, lawgiver, and judge to moral guide and educator. More and more communities demanded university-trained rabbis who could deliver sermons in German and take on responsibility for educating the next generation.

These innovations, which grew at first out of social rather than theological impulses, elicited a variety of responses from the German states. Uneasily aware of changes in the Jewish communities, each government attempted to steer them in the direction that seemed least dangerous, or most beneficial. While some, like Prussia, preferred Jews to retain their old separate ways, others, still hoping for their conversion, saw modernization as an opening wedge. In the grand duchy of Saxe-Weimar, the government hoped to foster integration and conversion by insisting that the service be conducted only in German and making attendance compulsory. Bavaria, with its 50,000 Jews, was less consistent, first proposing a Jewish theological faculty at the university, then forbidding all innovation and even preventing Bavarian rabbis from attending the three rabbinical conferences held between 1844 and 1846.

Despite these hindrances, within the Jewish communities congregations moved resolutely away from the customs and formulas of their fathers. But their destination was not yet clear, and it was surprising how long it took before the new practices were institutionalized. It was not until the second half of the century, in fact, that four coherent movements emerged from the experiments of the earlier decades, each with its own acknowledged spokesman.

At the extremes were Samson Raphael Hirsch, the originator of what was called Neo-Orthodoxy, and Samuel Holdheim, who stood for the most radical reform of Judaism. Hirsch came from a family of *maskilim* who had lived in Hamburg for ten generations. He had had the benefit of both a secular and a religious education, and while still a young man had rejected

Plate 1
The initial B from a commentary on the Psalms written in St. Denis in the ninth century. The head of a young Indian elephant holding a palmette in its trunk is remarkably lifelike, in contrast to the distorted animal heads usually found in illuminations, and suggests, according to the paleographer Bernhard Bischoff, that this head was drawn from direct observation of Charlemagne's elephant, Abulabaz.

Plate 2
An illumination from a Pentateuch dating from ca. 1300, showing how Jews saw the knights who figured in their ballads. The text, from Numbers 54, reads, "The Israelites shall camp each with his standard under the banners of their ancestral house."

Plate 3
A medieval town as depicted in a Passover Haggadah of 1428, showing the Jewish houses clustered near the wall. Although the figures in the foreground are supposed to represent the Jews as slaves in Egypt building the cities of Pithom and Rameses, the setting is local, including the figure of a Jew wearing a pointed hat and carrying a bundle and staff.

עָלֵינוּ וְעַל יִשְׂרָאֵל עַמָּךְ וְעַל יְרוּשָׁלַיִם
עִירָךְ וְעַל צִיּוֹן מִשְׁכַּן כְּבוֹדָךְ וְעַל מ
מִזְבְּחָךְ וְעַל הֵיכָלָךְ · וּבְנֵה יְרוּשָׁלַיִם
עִיר הַקֹּדֶשׁ בִּמְהֵרָה בְיָמֵינוּ וְהַעֲלֵנוּ
לְתוֹכָהּ וְשַׂמְּחֵנוּ בְּבִנְיָנָהּ וְנֹאכַל מ
מִפִּרְיָהּ וְנִשְׂבַּע מִטּוּבָהּ וּנְבָרֶכְךָ עָלֶיהָ

Plate 5
The blessing over
wine. In this mohel
book a Bacchus-like
figure sits astride a
cask of wine, holding
aloft a bunch of
grapes. The playful
incorporation of an
unmistakably pagan
motif shows that
Hamburg Jews shared
in the widespread
eighteenth-century in-
terest in pagan antiq-
uity.

Plate 4
Scene of a circumci-
sion. From an
eighteenth-century
mohel book.

כְּשֶׁהוּא חוֹתֵךְ הָעָרְלָה שֶׁהוּא חוֹתֵךְ הַדִּינִים וְהַנֶּאֱחָזִים בָּהּ · נִמְתָּק
בַּחִיתּוּךְ הַזֶּה הוּא מְסַלֵּק כמ"ל הָרוֹכֵב עַל הנ"חֵם וּמַמְתִּיק בְּשָׂרְתֵי
שְׁמוֹת הָרַחֲמִים שֶׁזְּכַרְנוּ בְּאָמְרוֹ בָּרוּךְ אַתָּה ה' שֶׁכְּתִיבָתוֹ הוי"ה
וּקְרִיאָתוֹ אֲדֹנָ"י כָּל הַדִּינִים הַכֹּל לִהְיוֹת רַחֲמִים גְּמוּרִים בְּסוֹד
הַמִּילָה שֶׁזָּכַרְנוּ וּלְפִיכָךְ יְבָרֵךְ בְּקוֹל רָס הַבְּרָכָה זוּ עִם
הַכַּוָּנָה :

בָּרוּךְ אַתָּה יְיָ אֱלֹהֵינוּ מֶלֶךְ הָעוֹלָם אֲשֶׁר
קִדְּשָׁנוּ בְּמִצְוֹתָיו וְצִוָּנוּ עַל הַמִּילָה :

Plate 6
Moritz Oppenheim,
The Wedding, 1861.
(See p. 52.)

Plate 7
Illustration from the
Darmstadt Haggadah.
Fifteenth century.

Plates 8 and 9
Views of the *sukkah* (booth) of the Deller family of Fischach, in Swabia, made in 1825.

Plate 10
A marriage contract
(*ketubah*) such as
would have been used
at the wedding of
Glückel's daughter
Zipporah in Cleves.
Amsterdam, 1718.

Plate 11
Between the last day of Passover and the first day of Shavuot (the Feast of Weeks) is a period of forty-nine days known as the *omer*, from the Hebrew word for the measure of barley that was brought as an offering to the Temple in Jerusalem on each of these days. Religious Jews count each day of the omer with a blessing after the conclusion of the regular evening service. This particularly graceful calendar, with the numbers running down the right-hand side, was a gift to Moses Mendelssohn.

Plate 14
Henriette Herz
(1764–1847) as
Hebe, the Greek god-
dess of spring. In a
painting by Anna Dor-
othea Therbusch,
1778.

Plate 12
Süsskind Stern
(1610–1686) was a
money changer and a
dealer in pearls in
Frankfurt. This por-
trait, said to be the
earliest painting of a
Jew in Germany, was
probably commis-
sioned by the sitter
on a visit to Amster-
dam in 1671. Origi-
nally the picture
showed his cloak with
the round yellow
badge Jews were re-
quired to wear; a ves-
tige of a badge is still
discernible in the up-
per left-hand corner.

Plate 13
Moses Mendelssohn,
painted by Johann
Christoph Frisch, ca.
1780. The only por-
trait of Mendelssohn
drawn from life.

Plate 15
The Sabbath, in front of the synagogue at Furth, ca. 1800.

Plate 16
"O God, thou giver of the good and true, / Save me from this very Jew." N.d., artist unknown.

O Gott, du Geber alles Guden
beschüze mich vor disen Juden.

Plate 17
Seder scene, 1716–17, from the Second Cincinnati Haggadah. The same artist duplicated this scene in the Van Geldern Haggadah, which belonged to a member of Heinrich Heine's family. It was the inspiration for the description of the Seder that opens his unfinished story *The Rabbi of Bacherach.*

Plate 18
Bethel Henry
Strousberg and his
family, as painted by
Ludwig Knaus, ca.
1870.

Plate 19
Walther Rathenau
(1867–1922),
painted by Lesser Ury,
1896.

Plate 20
Interior of the Liberal
synagogue in Berlin
on Oranienburger-
strasse, designed
by Edward Knoblauch
and consecrated on
September 5, 1866.
This watercolor by
Friedrich August
Stüler, who was re-
sponsible for the inte-
rior decoration,
shows the minute at-
tention to detail and
the reliance on
themes from Persian
carpets and Turkish
tiles. On the day after
the opening of the
synagogue a Berlin
newspaper reported,
"The light streams
through the multi-
colored panes mag-
ically softened and
transfigured. Ceiling,
walls, pillars, arches
and windows are dec-
orated with extrava-
gant magnificence
and create with their
gilding and ornamen-
tation a wonderful ar-
abesque wreath
interlaced into a har-
monious whole, con-
triving a fairylike,
ethereal effect."
Vossische Zeitung,
September 6, 1866.

Samson Raphael
Hirsch (1808–1888).

the liberal ideas with which he had started on his rabbinical career. In 1836 he published his *Nineteen Letters on Judaism,* a powerful polemical work in German cast as a dialogue between an Enlightened Jew and a faithful believer in Orthodoxy who triumphs as he demolishes the arguments of the Enlightenment. Hirsch regarded the Enlightenment's approach to religion as a fundamental error since it placed man at the center of moral and religious thought. For Hirsch and his Orthodox followers, God was irreplaceably central, and it was the duty—indeed, the mission—of Orthodox Jews to fulfill His 613 commandments. Hirsch's slogan put it succinctly: *Torah im derech eretz,* Torah in the way of the world. That is, Jews were to be both good Jews and good Germans.

Writing in impeccable German and thoroughly grounded in German culture, Hirsch became the ideal spokesman for those German Jews who wanted to preserve their religion from the process of integration that was transforming the other parts of their lives. Although the Orthodox gradually shrank to a minority among German Jews, they were tenacious in maintaining the old traditions and in 1876 were given legal permission to form a separate community with its own synagogues, burial grounds, and schools.

Samuel Holdheim, who grew up in an entirely traditional family in Posen, was at the opposite pole. Not only did he deny the authority of the talmudic dicta, the oral law, he also denied the divine origin of the Scriptures, maintaining that they were composed by men divinely inspired. His conclusion was that the contemporary practice of Judaism should be based on spiritual and ethical guidance from the Bible; the minutiae of customary observance were no longer applicable. Holdheim did not entirely reject the Mishnah and the Talmud, yet for him they were no longer repositories of binding legislation but simply storehouses of wisdom and ethical precepts.

What Holdheim was saying in a world where the Jews were being reidentified—and reidentifying themselves—was that they were not a nation, not a people, but a religion grounded in monotheism, governed by moral injunctions, and guided by ideas that were not very different from the beliefs and practices of their Christian neighbors. It followed, then, that Jews should adapt to the world in which they lived: he proposed, for example, that the Sabbath be celebrated on Sunday. He was ready to countenance mixed marriages on the ground that since the Jews did not constitute a nation and the laws of marriage and divorce were prerogatives of the state, Jews in Germany should abide by the law of the land. When he was called to head the Berlin Reform community in 1847, he also abolished observance of the second day of two-day holidays. His congregation, which survived into the twentieth century, remained at the extreme end of the Jewish religious spectrum although it never formalized to the point of establishing a seminary. (What is known as Reform Judaism in the United States was the equivalent of Liberal Judaism in Germany, whereas the Reform group in Berlin always remained a small minority.)

The two groups occupying the center—the Liberals and the Conservatives—commanded the greatest number of followers. Although we can now clearly mark them off from each other, each position evolved only after long years of thought and experimentation. The culmination for each group was the founding, under a strong leader, of a rabbinical seminary where its principal beliefs were codified and emissaries trained to go out into the world.

Breslau, long the site of a populous and active Jewish community, became the home of the first modern rabbinical seminary in Germany. Founded in 1854 with a bequest from the banker Jonas Fraenckel, its first director was Zacharias Frankel, who was called from his post as rabbi in Dresden. Frankel, born in Prague in 1801, received a thorough talmudic education and also took a degree in philosophy and the natural sciences at the university in Budapest. He soon became a significant figure at the rabbinical conferences of the 1840s causing consternation by leaving the conference of 1845 after it voted to replace Hebrew with German as the main language of prayer in the synagogue.

This act symbolized his position on the changing world around him. Frankel advocated what he called historical Judaism, which developed into a position comparable to what is called Conservative Judaism in the United States. In contrast to the founders of the Wissenschaft des Judentums (Science of Judaism), who used their research to cut away what they saw as superfluous outgrowths, Frankel wanted to use the new science as a way of justifying the integration of ancient Jewish institutions into contemporary life. Stimulated by the historicism of Leopold von Ranke, which saw cultural habits as as the continuing expression of the spiritual life of a people, Frankel proceeded down a different road from his predecessors. Recognizing the inevitable changes brought by time in the evolution of social forms, he also believed that the traditional rituals of Jewish life had deep meaning for contemporary Jews, and it was his goal to retain these forms, although with a better understanding of their origins and history. Hence he found the abandonment of Hebrew unthinkable.

Under Frankel's direction the Breslau seminary developed into the training ground for a rabbinate that would dominate Germany into the twentieth century. It became the model for similar institutions elsewhere in Western Europe, as well as the prototype for the Jewish Theological Seminary in the United States. The small but choice faculty at the beginning included, besides Frankel, the classicist Jacob Bernays and the historian Heinrich Graetz, who wrote a monumental eleven-volume history of the Jews while on the staff. Students embarked on a rigorous seven-year course during which they were also expected to take a secular degree at the University of Breslau. The subjects included rabbinical literature, Hebrew, Aramaic, and German literatures, Hebrew poetry, and the geography of the Holy Land. On the practical side were courses on homiletics and education. The intensive program of the Breslau seminary produced not only rabbis but also scholars who published extensively, bringing a secular perspective to ancient texts and writing a new kind of Jewish history. Among its stellar graduates were Moritz Güdemann, who doubled as rabbi and innovative social historian, Ismar Elbogen, the historian of German Jewry, and the talmudist Israel Lewy.

It took much longer for the liberal Jews to organize a rabbinical seminary, and it came at the end of the life of Abraham Geiger, the chief theoretician of the movement. Geiger was born in 1810, the youngest son of a cantor in Frankfurt, whose family had lived there since the sixteenth century. Although given a traditional education in preparation for the rabbinate, Geiger went off to the University of Heidelberg at the age of nineteen to study Oriental languages. He later moved to the University of Bonn, where he first encountered the ideas of the Wissenschaft des Judentums. In the summer of 1832 he read Leopold Zunz's newly published *Sermons of the Jews.* Under this rather dry title, Zunz was introducing the historical principle to Jewish learning as he traced the changing form of the sermon through two thousand years of Jewish life and analyzed the evolution of homiletical writings. For the young Geiger, it was a revelation, showing him a new way to look at Jewish sources by placing them in their historical context. Since so much of Jewish learning was anchored in a kind of timeless continuum in which sages addressed one another's arguments across the centuries, Zunz's historical approach was nothing less than revolutionary, and it deeply influenced Geiger's later work.

Committed to a rabbinical career, Geiger entered on it with great energy: while still at the university, he organized a group to discuss the art of preaching. During his long career as a rabbi, first in Wiesbaden, then in Breslau, Frankfurt, and Berlin, Geiger wrote prodigiously. He also founded and edited two scholarly journals. His crowning work, *The Original Text and Translations of the Bible,* published in 1857, was daring in its historical perspective, which implicitly denied Mosaic authorship of the sacred text.

Geiger's thought evolved steadily throughout his life, just as he believed that Jewish religious thought had evolved from the period of "revelation," when the Bible was created, through the period of "rigid legalism," which had ended in the eighteenth century, to his own era, the age of "liberation and criticism." Like Hirsch, he saw the Jews as endowed with a divine mission. For Geiger, however, it was not observance but the prophetic tradition of social justice that was the moving force in Judaism. With his tireless advocacy of the moral excellence of Judaism, he sought both in the pulpit and in his writings to show modern Jews how they could bring their old faith into accord with a new world. In 1854, while a rabbi at Breslau, he published a new prayer book that reflected how the service was changing. In a revised version published in 1870, he added explanations of the cuts and additions he had made.

Hoping "for the ultimate unification of all mankind," he had eliminated the prayers for the restoration of the Temple and of the Jewish state in Palestine, as well as for the "ingathering of the dispersed." On the ground that they offered no "religious edification," he also excised the passages relating to animal sacrifice. Despite these serious alterations in the content of the services, Geiger tampered little with the form. He kept the service in Hebrew because Hebrew was the classical language of Jewish prayer: although the members of his congregation no longer understood it, they nonetheless responded emotionally to the sounds and melodies that they carried in their memories. Geiger did not give up on intelligibility, however, and also printed paraphrases in German of the most important prayers, some of which were to be recited aloud.

Despite the widespread modifications in belief and practice, the Breslau seminary remained the only training ground for a modern rabbinate. Dissatisfied with its conservative point of view, scholars and rabbis of a more liberal persuasion

Zacharias Frankel (1801–1875). "Not he who fears but he who loves is the true believer."

Abraham Geiger (1810–1874). Frontispiece, Ludwig Geiger, *Abraham Geiger. Leben und Lebenswerk,* Berlin, 1910.

Abraham Geiger charted four stages in the development of Jewish thought: revelation, tradition, rigid legalism, and–the culminating stage–liberation. Here he contrasts the limitations of early Jewish study with his hopes for his own time.

The third is the laborious occupation with the received, the guarding of the spiritual inheritance, without feeling authorized to step outside the received boundaries, to reorganize it or to develop it further. This is the period of rigid legalism, *of casuistry, the gathering up of the tradition, which prevailed from the close of the Babylonian Talmud [ca. fifth century c.e.] until the middle of the previous century.*

The fourth is the time of liberation; the loosing of the bonds of the earlier period through the use of reason and historical research, without breaking the connection with the past, a period of experiments, to renew ourselves and to bring ourselves into consonance with the stream of history, the period of criticism, *the modern time.*

Abraham Geiger, "Allgemeine Einleitung in die Wissenschaft des Judenthums," in Nachgelassene Schriften, *Berlin, 1875.*

began to revive the idea of a scientific institute of Jewish learning dedicated primarily to scholarship and only secondarily to rabbinical training. In May 1872, the Hochschule für die Wissenschaft des Judentums (College for the Science of Judaism) opened for its first semester in a few rented rooms in Berlin. It was dedicated to the principle of nonpartisanship, including graduates of the Breslau seminary as well as Orthodox Jews among its teachers. Beginning with one full-time faculty member, Abraham Geiger, and twelve students, in time it became the standard-bearer of Liberal Judaism in Germany.

Some of the stellar names in modern Jewish scholarship were associated with the Hochschule, among them the historians Eugen Täubler and Ismar Elbogen, the linguist Franz Rosenthal, the sociologist Franz Oppenheimer, and the theologian Leo Baeck, who was its last director. Its ambitious curriculum included history, languages, the Talmud, Jewish theology, and ethics. Later there were courses in homiletics, methods of teaching, and comparative religion. In addition to foreign students, it drew Christian students of theology, who came to read Jewish law and literature under its hospitable roof. Always short of funds, the Hochschule nonetheless continued to grow in size, although it was not until 1907 that a donor provided it with the means to buy its own building in the center of Berlin.

To complete the triad, in October 1873 the Orthodox community founded its own rabbinical seminary in Berlin, under the dynamic leadership of Azriel Hildesheimer. Contrary to Orthodox custom, the new seminary required its students to have a thorough secular education in addition to traditional learning. While on the one hand the instructors wanted their students to be the equal of any talmudist in Eastern Europe, they also wanted them to be able to defend Jewish tradition against the onslaught of the higher criticism and Darwinian theory, as well as against the reformers of Jewish learning. Their strategy in this struggle was to broaden the base of learning instead of retreating to the narrower ground of the yeshivas. As a consequence, the seminary created a new figure for the Orthodox pulpit, the *Rabbiner Doktor,* who was prepared to lead a modern congregation.

Concerned about the modernization of the Orthodox community, Hildesheimer insisted on

Hochschule für die Wissenschaft des Judentums, founded in Berlin in 1872.

the systematic instruction of girls, whose education in Orthodox families had often been neglected. Graduates of the Berlin *Rabbinerseminar* carried their slogan, "Faith and Knowledge," to many parts of the world. Well-trained in the issues of modern scholarship, they were able to give assurance to congregations searching for ways to reconcile their beliefs with contemporary life. This immersion in the world also led Hildesheimer to cooperate with his liberal Jewish colleagues in the attempt to combat anti-Semitism, and this gave the seminary a worldly quality heretofore unknown in the Orthodox community.

By the end of the century, although Germany's three rabbinical seminaries were producing scholars and rabbis of marked talent, the great synagogues remained mostly empty as the appeals of secular life defeated the centuries-old commitment to observance. Organized Jewish life in the modern world began to take on new forms; charity, politics, Zionism, and other causes created new nodal points in Jewish life.

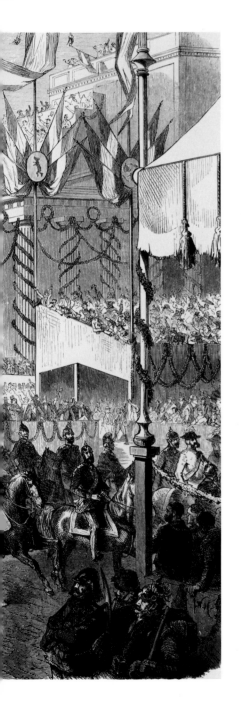

Chapter Six

In

the

Fifty-Year

Empire

Jewish Emancipation, 1871

The road to Jewish emancipation paralleled the road to the formation of the German Empire—a goal vigorously prosecuted by Prussia's chancellor, Otto von Bismarck. In achieving this aim, Bismarck united all Germany north of the Main River in the North German Confederation, and won two wars, against Austria in 1866 and against France in 1870–71.

In the Franco-Prussian War, 7,000 Jews served in the German army although they were still not full-fledged citizens. The edict proclaimed by the North German Confederation in 1869 abolishing "all remaining restrictions of civil and political rights derived from the difference in religious creed" was not extended to all parts of the new Empire until 1871, the culmination of a century of desire. But the national Jewish newspaper, the *Allgemeine Zeitung des Judenthums,* greeted the announcement coolly. The struggle had been too hard, too long, and too disappointing. In the lead article, "The Empire and the Jews," the editors congratulated the Jewish community on how far it had come. But "we are

The new emperor, Wilhelm I, and his troops pass through the Brandenburg Gate in Berlin on parade, June 16, 1871. The kaiser is greeted by one of the maids of honor. Max Ring, *Die deutsche Kaiserstadt Berlin und ihre Umgebung,* Leipzig, 1885.

The German Empire, 1874. *Appleton's Hand Atlas of Modern Geography*, New York, 1874.

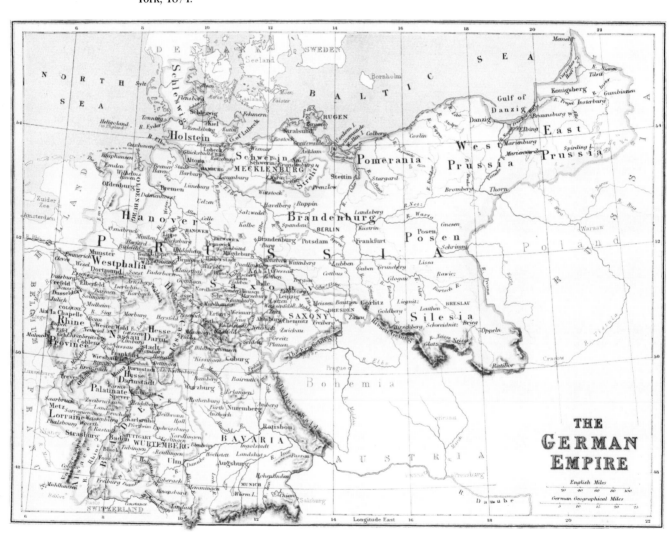

This engraving of the fictional Yom Kippur service before Metz, October 8, 1870, is widely known. Below a sergeant describes how he and his comrades actually observed the day.

Through an armywide order issued by His Excellency General von Manteuffel, the regiments and batallions were instructed to release from duty soldiers of the Mosaic faith for the afternoon of October 5 and the following day to celebrate the Day of Atonement, and to send them on leave to St. Barbe to the current headquarters of the army, provided that the troops were not put on battle alert.

Fortunately, this did not happen, and so we Jewish soldiers of the First Army Corps were granted our deeply desired wish! Our hearts were overjoyed that we could observe Yom Kippur in communal devotion, with services conducted in the manner of our fathers. None of us, not even in the most splendid temple that we knew at home, had ever prayed with such passionate devotion as we did in the little low room with a broken door, with windows lacking glass and with walls bored through by grenades. From time to time, a short distance from us, our cannons thundered toward Metz, and we felt the impermanence of our existence, and the need to reconcile ourselves with our God, since soon it might be too late. For many of us, for whom the meaning of Yom Kippur until this moment had been inwardly quite strange, it had now become unforgettably clear in the deepest depth of our hearts in a way never before suspected.

L. Hirschberg, *"Ein Jom Kippur im Kriegslager,"* Allgemeine Zeitung des Judenthums, *October 18, 1870.*

Representation of how a Jew takes an oath before the Christian authorities. Note that he is made to stand on a pigskin. The text of the oath reads, "I, [name], Jew, swear by the Almighty God Adonai who created the heavens and the earth and all that is in it, the Lord over all the angels, who gave his Chosen People the Holy Torah, which is also truly described in the book on which I have placed my right hand. I swear then that the matter is [here the matter is named] and that it is the truth and not otherwise, just as I have now pronounced it, and this do I attest by the Almighty God who brought Abraham, Isaac, and Jacob out of Egypt." Engraving, Breslau, ca. 1700.

still not at the goal," they insisted, pointing to the resistance of individual German states to the requirements of the new law. As they knew, old habits yielded only slowly to law and reason. The humiliating Jewish oath, which Jews were often required to take while standing on a bloody pigskin, was abolished piecemeal and very slowly, beginning with Hesse-Cassel in 1828, Saxony in 1839, and Anhalt-Bernburg in 1842. Prussia was last, in 1869. And as late as 1891 a Jew was prosecuted for ritual murder in Xanten on the Rhine.

Despite these areas of resistance, the new edict, enacted on April 16, 1871, ratified what had become a widespread reality. In the three generations since Moses Mendelssohn, the Jews had become Germans in speech, outlook, and culture, as well as in their patriotic feelings. Even the most Orthodox and tradition-bound affirmed their solidarity with the German nation. "We German Jews are Germans and nothing else," the religious newspaper *Israelit* proclaimed in 1870, and on Saturdays the Torah reading in Orthodox synagogues concluded with a Hebrew prayer for the fatherland.

Although the new law explicitly eliminated the last barriers to Jewish admission to government office, the social actuality of the Fifty-Year Empire proved otherwise. Jews were not admitted to the officer corps, were scarce in the teaching professions, and in public office were appointed only to positions of lesser influence or prestige. Jews might become judges, for example, but they were not appointed as public prosecutors, a post that had higher social rank and carried real authority.

How the Jews made their living by the time of the empire had been determined long before by a history of permissions and prohibitions. Their exclusion from landownership had made them traders rather than cultivators in rural districts, and their exclusion from the guilds had made them middlemen rather than craftsmen. Above all, Jews had been identified with the lending and exchange of money, as Hans Sachs showed in his *True Description of All the Classes on Earth,* published in 1568. It was a place in the world that had endured for a very long time. Even Moses Mendelssohn wrestled with these constraints as he confided to a friend about his son, Joseph. "He has no inclination for medicine," he wrote in 1785, "and as a Jew he must become a physician, a merchant, or a beggar."

"The German Reich and the Jews," a front-page article on Jewish emancipation in the leading Jewish newspaper, *Allgemeine Zeitung des Judenthums,* January 17, 1871.

Hans Sachs's *True Description of all the Classes on the Earth* (1568) shows where the Jew stood in sixteenth-century society. The ranking begins with the pope and descends through kings, emperors, princes, merchants, craftsmen, and agricultural laborers, ending with a representation of three fools. Somewhere near the end of this catalog we find "the Jew," who is depicted as a moneylender. Although he may have been regarded with scorn, the poem attributed to him reveals that he had his own low opinion of his clients.

It is not for nothing that I am called a Jew.

I lend only half the money against a pledge.

And if the pawner cannot redeem it in time

Then I get that as well.

In this way I ruin the loose-living mob

That wants only to feast, to gorge, and to
   drink.

Yet my trade does not diminish

Since I have many brothers like me.

Hans Sachs, Eygentliche Beschreibung aller Stände auf Erden . . . *Frankfurt am Main, 1568.*

A Jewish beggar from
Poland. Drawing by
H. Loewy, 1893.

Begging was, indeed, a fixture in Jewish life.
For centuries the Jewish condition had insured
that there were a very small number of rich Jews
and an overwhelming number of poor ones. The
beggars, in fact, formed a caste unto themselves
with carefully apportioned territories, rights,
and expectations. The *schnorrer,* as he was
called in Yiddish, who was the subject of endless
jokes and legends, was at once a beggar and
more than that. In his circuit of villages and
houses, he brought news of the world, gossip,
and commercial information. Some beggars
raised their table talk to such an art that they
became welcome guests, earning their night's
lodging and gift money as entertainers. As late as
the mid-nineteenth century, half the Jews of
Germany were either beggars or a step away
from it, without a permanent right of residence.

But by the end of the century, the economic
pyramid of Jewish life had been turned upside
down. These shifts were part of the economic
transformation of Western Europe and defini-
tively broke apart the system of estates and
classes so carefully delineated by Hans Sachs.

Miss Stern, of the
Jewish community in
Posen, waiting to
greet Wilhelm II on
his visit to that city in
1899. (She is in the
center of the first
row, holding a basket
of flowers.)

The Magnates

The new world opened up by the Industrial Revolution needed power and transportation, capital for new enterprises, and organizing ability. These opportunities gave Jews a new role. In the early decades of the nineteenth century, Jewish manufacturers produced a wide variety of goods, from metals to paper products and chemicals and, above all, textiles. The largest Jewish entrepreneurs were active in electricity, railways, newspapers, banking, and that new phenomenon, the department store. By their innovations they brought Jewish names into prominence on the national and international scene. Although many of these were substantial enterprises with five hundred or more employees, they were later dwarfed by the industrial giants Siemens, Krupp, Borsig, and Diesel. Nonetheless, the energy with which German Jews seized their opportunities is shown by the fact that by mid-century, although Jews made up less than 3 percent of Berlin's population, half of the new industrialists there were Jews. This impressive-sounding proportion for the early days of capitalism actually represents seventy-five Jewish entrepreneurs, only a minute if influential segment of the Jewish community, which numbered some ten thousand persons. Economic opportunity was not equally distributed or equally available.

For some Jews the way to industry led through the university, as a number of Jewish chemists used their scientific knowledge to create their own firms or become influential in existing firms. In 1866, Heinrich Caro, of a Sephardic Jewish family, was taken on as a chemist in a leading company in the growing aniline dye industry. On the strength of his discoveries, he advanced to the board of directors and eventually became one of the founders of I. G. Farben. Adolph Frank, also trained as a chemist, discovered the usefulness of a potash derivative as a fertilizer and by 1860 was exporting his product to America. In heavy industry, Ludwig Loewe began manufacturing sewing machines in Germany in 1869, a little more than a decade after their invention in America. Applying American production techniques, Loewe, with his brother Isidore, moved on to the production of rifles during the Franco-Prussian War and eventually merged his firm with Mauser, one of the largest German armament companies. He later went on to build streetcars, automobiles, and even airplanes.

What was distinctive about these modern Jewish entrepreneurs was not only their willingness to venture capital on new machines and new industrial processes but also their use of untried fiscal structures, such as issuing shares of the company to the public and trading them on the stock market. This readiness to experiment had unforeseen evil consequences for the Jews later in the century, when a modern anti-Semitic movement began to identify Jews with capitalism, a system the Jew-haters derided as the destroyer of an old and pure (if imaginary) German way of life.

Perhaps the premier example of the new entrepreneur was Emil Rathenau. Born in 1838 and trained as an engineer, Rathenau had watched Thomas Edison demonstrate the electric light bulb at a fair in Paris in 1881. Seeing the possibilities in this new device, he negotiated with Edison and two years later formed the German Edison Company for Applied Electricity, the beginning of a formidable enterprise. What was involved was more than the manufacture of light bulbs: the building of power stations, the laying of electric cables, in fact the introduction of electricity into German life. In 1887 his company was renamed the General Electric Company, and after two decades it was the largest electric enterprise in Germany. Rathenau's particular contribution was not just in the electrification of Germany but also in the export of installations to countries all over the world. When Emil Rathenau died in 1915 he left a world empire with 70,000 employees. As befitted a man whose life and work were one, his funeral was conducted from his home offices in Berlin.

The new industrial age also transformed the old function of the court Jew into that of the merchant banker; what had formerly been a servile relationship based on the grace of the sovereign now became a straightforward contractual arrangement between equals. The traditional Jewish prominence in the field of banking continued into the nineteenth century as Jewish banks underwrote the development of German industry. In Berlin in 1807, Jews owned 30 of the 52 banking houses, and as late as 1862, of the 642 banks in Prussia, 550 were Jewish, a proportion that did not drop in the period of the em-

Thomas Alva Edison (right) with Emil Rathenau on a festive visit to the Berlin electrical works in 1911.

pire. (Many baptized Jews were included in this number. Almost the entire Mendelssohn clan, for example, had long been Christians, but socially they were still regarded as Jews, and statisticians, too, have classified them as such. In these matters, perception often counts as much as reality.)

As industry and government required larger and larger amounts of capital, their demands brought about the consortiums that came to characterize the modern bank. The long-established Rothschilds in Frankfurt, the Mendelssohns in Berlin, the Oppenheims in Cologne, and the Warburgs in Hamburg continued to be closely held family businesses, but aspiring young Jews were not confined to these "Jewish banks." No matter how great the social distance outside the counting rooms, many of the new banks had complex directorates in which Jews and Christians joined together.

The Deutsche Bank, for example, began as a maritime bank aiming to broaden German operations to the Americas. When the non-Jewish industrialist Georg von Siemens and the banker Adalbert Delbrück, among others, organized it

Facade of the Mendelssohn bank, built in Berlin in 1885. In *Berlin und seine Bauten,* Berlin, 1877.

Last page of the original contract of association, still written in Hebrew, of the banking firm of M. M. Warburg in Hamburg, concluded between the brothers Moshe and Gershon Warburg on 20 Sivan, 5570 (June 22, 1810) before two officials of the Hamburg Jewish community, who signed as witnesses.

Ludwig Bamberger
(1823–1899). Fron-
tispiece from his
Erinnerungen,
Berlin, 1899.

in 1870, they invited Ludwig Bamberger, the son of a Jewish banking family, to join them as a founder and director. Bamberger was undoubtedly unique in his world by imperturbably combining the contradictory careers of revolutionary and financier. Exiled from Germany because of his activities in the revolution of 1848, he turned to banking, serving apprenticeships in London, Antwerp, Rotterdam, and finally Paris, where he took a post in his uncle's bank. Although immensely successful there, he returned to Germany in 1866 under a political amnesty and continued his dual career as banker and politician: in 1871, he was elected a deputy to the first German Reichstag. In Berlin, he put his fiscal experience to good use in organizing the national Reichsbank and establishing a single currency for the newly united German Empire based on gold reserves.

What became the second largest bank in Germany, the Dresdner Bank, was propelled into prominence by Eugen Gutmann, a Dresden Jew who saw a new field for investment banking when he took over in 1881. His first step was to break out of the provinces and open a branch in the capital. By courting industrial investment and establishing new offices in other cities, Gut-

mann transformed the Dresdener Bank in a single decade into a powerful nationwide institution.

The most famous of all the Jewish bankers in nineteenth-century Germany was Gerson Bleichröder, who was not only the banker but also the confidant of Otto von Bismarck. Bleichröder entered his family's banking business in Berlin in 1839 and upon his father's death in 1855 took over the firm. Four years later he was recommended to Bismarck, who was looking for a private banker to manage his estates and invest his money. It is reported that Bismarck particularly asked for a Jewish banker. This remarkable relationship was to endure for more than three decades, until Bismarck's dismissal from the chancellorship by Wilhelm II in 1890. But in 1862, upon Bismarck's advancement to the post of prime minister of Prussia, Bleichröder moved from being just a private banker to becoming an adviser to the government. At the end of the Franco-Prussian War in 1871, when Wilhelm, king of Prussia, became emperor of the new Germany, Bleichröder was invited to Versailles for the deliberations on the war indemnities that were to be levied on the French.

In the following year, at the age of fifty, he was ennobled, the first Jew to achieve this honor without first undergoing baptism. Although during Bismarck's career Bleichröder proved to be an indispensable figure whose advice and financial resources were sought in both governmental and private circles, the social barriers remained almost impermeable. Only through the most extraordinary intervention could he win an officer's commission in the army for his son. And despite his own title and the lavish balls he gave in his Berlin house, attended by members of the court and the foreign diplomatic corps, neither Bleichröder nor his wife was ever welcomed into the world of the aristocracy. Even Bismarck seems to have regarded Bleichröder as a shameful secret. Although they conferred almost daily for thirty years, both on matters of state and on Bismarck's private investments, in his massive memoirs Bismarck mentioned Bleichröder only once, and then in reference to his relationship with someone else.

At the same time that Bleichröder was courting admission to Prussian society, he continued to use his influence for Jewish rights in Germany

Gerson von Bleichröder (1822–1893), by Franz von Lenbach, the most fashionable painter of the period.

and abroad. He himself attended synagogue faithfully and attempted to counteract the anti-Semitic diatribes of the court preacher Adolf Stoecker by appealing to Bismarck. He also carried on an international campaign on behalf of civil rights for Romanian Jews and for the protection of Jews in the repressive Russia of Nicholas II. In this way, Bleichröder, along with other Jewish bankers, continued to shoulder some of the traditional responsibilities of the court Jew as intercessor with the state and as benefactor to the poor.

Bleichröder's story of accomplishment and exclusion was to be repeated many times and on many levels throughout the nineteenth and early twentieth centuries. Jews moved ahead in many new areas with an energy and prominence disproportionate to their numbers. Like their banking counterparts, the so-called Jewish press barons—Leopold Sonnemann, who founded the *Frankfurter Zeitung* in 1866, and Leopold Ullstein and Rudolf Mosse in Berlin—attracted attention and excited speculations about their power that far outran reality. Heinrich Mann, in his *Im Schlaraffenland,* a faintly disguised *roman à clef,* spoke of Mosse's newspaper empire as a "state within a state." These publishers were more than businessmen; all were deeply involved in the politics of the day and used their newspapers to further their ideas. Sonnemann, perhaps the most politically active of the three, served for eleven years in the Reichstag and stipulated in his will that his newspaper was to continue his liberal policies.

Rudolf Mosse, who founded the *Berliner Tageblatt* in 1871, was the first to turn to advertising as a source of newspaper revenue. Since newspapers were supported entirely by subscription, their cost was high, which naturally restricted circulation to the well-to-do. With Mosse's innovation of advertising supplements, the price of newspapers could be reduced and the audience widened. While the *Tageblatt* continued to address itself to the educated middle class, Mosse also introduced two additional papers, aimed at the working class: the *Volksblatt* and the *Morgen-Zeitung.* By 1914, the combined Mosse papers, all with an outspoken liberal stamp, had a circulation of 250,000 in a city of some 4 million inhabitants.

An even greater publishing baron was Leopold Ullstein, who began his career with the

The Mosse Publishing House, Berlin, 1916.

purchase of the *Neues Berliner Tageblatt* in 1877. His five sons, all of whom entered the firm, contributed to the innovative style of the house, which launched the *Berliner Morgenpost* in 1898 and built its circulation to 600,000. They also introduced the idea of selling newspapers on the streets instead of by subscription and added a string of other papers addressed to different markets. Later the firm expanded to publishing books and magazines, and with the advent of radio and the movies the sons moved into those fields as well.

With the Mosse, Ullstein, and Sonnemann houses all representing the liberal position in their publications and achieving ever-growing popularity, it was not long before there was anti-Semitic talk of a "Jewish press" unfairly dominating the scene. In the book industry, although Jewish publishers like Samuel Fischer and Kurt Wolff directed important houses with authors like Thomas Mann, Hugo von Hofmannsthal, and Franz Kafka, the Jewish presence was less significant. Yet that industry did not escape the same insinuations. The tremendous expansion that made newspapers and books available to a mass market was due to the introduction in 1897 of the linotype machine which replaced the old method of hand-setting type letter by letter. Ullstein boasted that his new machines enabled him to produce "the fastest newspaper in the world," with a lapse of only eight minutes betwee the reception of a news item and its appearance on the streets.

No Jews were involved in railroad building in the United States and England, but in Germany and in other parts of Europe they played an important role both in the financing of new lines and in the actual construction. It was not as if in the 1830s the railroad was universally welcomed. Medical authorities expressed concern over the possible damage to the human organism as a consequence of traveling at the speed of forty miles an hour, and King Friedrich Wilhelm III wondered what "great happiness could be derived from arriving at Potsdam a few hours earlier than otherwise." Undeterred by these doubts was Abraham Oppenheim of Cologne, managing director and later vice-president of the Rhenish Railway Company. In 1835 the company built one of the first railways in Germany, connecting Cologne and Antwerp, and then continued with branch lines that became the main network for the coal and steel industry in Westphalia.

The railways, with their need for immense capital, were harbingers of the interlocking arrangements between industry and finance that would characterize the modern era and brought old Jewish banking houses like the Rothschilds, Goldschmidts, and Bischoffsheims out of their counting houses and into the industrial world. Of the many Jewish bankers, financiers, and industrialists who played an active part in developing the railroad, two are remarkable for the international scale of their operations and for their contrasting histories—one a respected international financier and devoted defender of Jewish causes, the other a bankrupt and a convert.

Baron Maurice de Hirsch, known as *Türkenhirsch* because his railway line extended into Turkey, came of a wealthy, already ennobled family whose seat was in Planegg, outside Munich. In 1855 he married Clara Bischoffsheim, daughter of an old banking family, who brought a dowry worth $4 million. The young couple moved to Belgium, where Moritz von Hirsch took Belgian citizenship and became Maurice de Hirsch. With their combined fortunes at his disposal, the young baron was equipped for ambitious ventures.

In 1869 he obtained the right from the Turkish government to build and operate a railway

The first poster for
B. Z. am Mittag, by
Edmund Edel, 1904.
In *50 Jahre Ullstein,*
Berlin, 1927.

Caricature of Baron Maurice de Hirsch, *Vanity Fair* (London), July 26, 1890. An editor, John Junior, wrote, "He is a hard looking, elderly man who knows his way about. He is full of fellow feeling and he once offered the Czar a trifle of a million or so to endow an institution for the benefit of the Jews in Russia; which offer was declined with thanks. He has been blackballed by the French Jockey Club, but he has the entrée to St. James Palace."

line from Vienna to Constantinople, connecting Turkey with Western Europe. The line, which covered twenty-five hundred kilometers, took nearly twenty years to build; the first train of the famous Orient Express did not leave Vienna until August 12, 1888. In the same year, Hirsch retired from active business and devoted himself to the pleasures of entertaining the great of Europe and running a racing stable in England.

Despite their luxurious life, with houses in four countries, Hirsch and his wife were intensely interested in the plight of less fortunate Jews, particularly those in Russia and the Near East. Hirsch wanted to rescue the Russian Jews by bringing them out and settling them on land where they could lead independent and productive lives. But where? In a famous interview with Theodor Herzl in June 1895, he rejected the nascent Zionist movement as not yet offering a practical solution. When he died in the following year at the age of sixty-five, leaving a fortune estimated at $100–150 million, he had already given away hundreds of millions in charity, and he bequeathed $45 million to the Jewish Colonization Association, his most cherished enterprise, best known for establishing agricultural colonies for Russian Jews in Argentina.

Bethel Henry Strousberg (see plate 18) was no less ambitious, and although his origins were considerably more clouded than Maurice de Hirsch's, for one heady decade he also had his place in the sun. He was born in Prussia in 1823 into a family of protected Jews (*Schutzjuden*) and named Baruch Hirsch. But when his father died in 1835, he went to London to work in his uncle's import-export business. There he changed his name to Bethel Henry and converted to Christianity. In 1845 he married an Englishwoman, Mary Swan. After a sojourn in America, where he tried his hand at various enterprises, he returned to Germany. Around 1865 he became the agent for a group of English financiers who were building a railroad in East Prussia. From there he branched out to become an independent entrepreneur and successfully built railway lines in Germany, Russia, and Hungary; by 1870 they totaled some three thousand kilometers. His great innovation lay in developing a vertical industrial empire beginning with the acquisition of iron mines, then rolling mills for finishing the rails, and onward to a factory that built cars and locomotives. He saw himself

Bethel Henry Strousberg in his memoirs attributes the abandonment of Judaism among his contemporaries to a growing secularism and to the ambition of Jewish families for their children.

Millennia of repression have not persuaded Jewry to convert; but decades of considerate equality will be enough, at least in Germany, to bring Jewry in essence to an end, not by conversion, but because of the unfortunately prevailing lack of belief. The modern Jew, if he is not provoked by persecution, ceases to observe his religion and, as for his children, if they do not immediately convert to Christianity, their defection from Judaism is almost a matter of course, and further developments proceed quite naturally. The children and children's children of such Jews who have themselves baptized, who forget their origins or at least pay no attention to it, are a living example of the capacity of the Jew to develop in the best sense of the word. Among the judges and officials in Prussia, there are many of Jewish descent and who in point of honor, unselfishness, love of country and devotion to their profession, can be placed side by side with the best exemplars.

Dr. Strousberg und sein Wirken, von ihm selbst geschildert, *Berlin, 1876.*

After Strousberg's bankruptcy, Great Britain acquired his house to use as its embassy. Sir Edward Malet, who was appointed the British ambassador in 1885, gives his views on the house.

The British Embassy, a handsome building with Greek columns on the facade . . . is a good house, with many points to commend it, first among which is that the numerous reception rooms are all on the ground floor. . . . The size of the rooms at the British embassy at Berlin is their redeeming point. They have no pretension to good taste. The house was built by a banker of vast wealth, named Strousberg, who for a time blazed like a comet in the financial world, and at his zenith built this fine home in the most aristocratic street in Berlin. He was not destined to enjoy it.

Sir Edward Malet, Shifting scenes, or memories of many men in many lands, *London, 1901.*

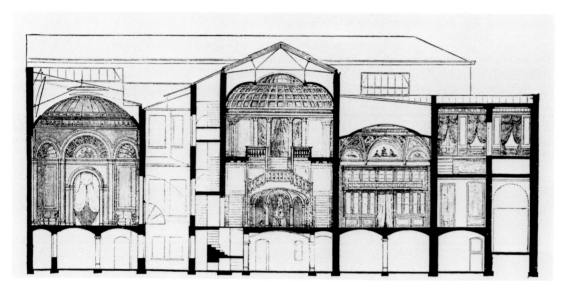

Cross-section of the "Palais of Dr. Strousberg," as it was known when it was built in Berlin in 1868. Shown are the ballroom, the grand staircase, and the library. *Berlin und seine Bauten,* Berlin, 1877.

not only as a technological innovator but also as the benevolent protector of his workers. And in the neighborhood of his factories in Hanover, Dortmund, and Zbirow, he took pains to build hundreds of houses for his employees.

At the height of his fortune in 1870, Strousberg owned ten estates in Germany and Bohemia as well as an entire county in Russian Poland. His palace in Berlin, for example, cost 900,000 marks to build in 1868 and included a conservatory, a picture gallery, a library, and a ballroom that could be converted into a theater. Gas lighting and central heating, as well as steam power for the kitchen and laundry, were part of the modern installation.

But his pyramid collapsed when the government of Romania defaulted on payments for a railway that he had been invited to build there. This crisis, combined with the crash of 1873, led to the unraveling of his various schemes. In 1875 he was arrested in Moscow on charges of fraud and imprisoned for two years; he was declared bankrupt in Germany and his remaining property confiscated. Upon his release, he and his family went to London, where they lived on his meager wages as a journalist until his death in 1887.

These life histories reveal the great volatility of early venture capitalism, especially in such complex schemes as railroads, where success or failure was often subject to elements outside the control of the entrepreneurs. Yet after long centuries as the shadowy financiers of magnates and rulers, Jewish entrepreneurs were emerging, for better or worse, into the light.

In shipbuilding, there was one outstanding Jewish name. Albert Ballin, at once one of the grandest and most tragic figures among the magnates, made a brilliant career as head of the Hamburg-Amerika line, generally known by the acronym HAPAG. Advancing from the post of chief of the passenger department in 1886, he brought immense originality to the task of transporting the millions of immigrants who were streaming across Germany from Eastern Europe on their way to the United States. Whereas earlier in the century, the Germans had largely transshipped immigrants to England who then crossed the Atlantic in English ships, Ballin built up a fleet of HAPAG ships that could accommodate immigrants more humanely than under the stifling between-decks conditions that prevailed

Albert Ballin (1857–1918), director of HAPAG-Lloyd.

Jews on their way to America praying in the synagogue established in the dock area of the Hamburg-Amerika Line in Hamburg.

in most steerage quarters. At the same time, he improved the condition of the hostels in which immigrants waited for their ships, setting up miniature villages with churches and a synagogue. In the process, he turned HAPAG into a major international carrier. Ballin also invented the idea of the pleasure cruise to the Mediterranean in order to utilize his ships during the stormy winter months when they did not cross the Atlantic, setting a new fashion for well-to-do Europeans.

More important than HAPAG was Ballin's later friendship with Kaiser Wilhelm II and his unofficial diplomacy before the First World War, in which he sought on the emperor's behalf to bring some moderation to the naval rivalry between Great Britain and Germany. Ballin could not, of course, prevent the onset of the war and saw first his own shipping empire and then the German Empire collapse. In the end, it was he who had to tell the kaiser that the war was lost. And when it was all over, despite plans for the rebuilding of his fleet, he resigned from the task and from a world that he no longer knew by taking an overdose of sleeping pills.

The magnates were exceptional men in their time, changing the face of German economic life; but their numbers were small, and they re-

main outsize figures. It is in the safer and larger world of the middle class that we can begin to outline the taxonomy of the modern German Jew.

The Middle Classes

Although the magnates, with their great wealth and often flamboyant lives, were highly visible and exercised a proportionately high degree of influence, they made up only a tiny part of the Jews in Germany. The rest made their living in far less spectacular ways. In an increasingly urban and industrialized world, German Jews found unprecedented opportunities in business and the professions; by 1871, some 60 percent could be counted as members of the upper middle class—a minute number in the German population but overwhelming in shaping the profile of the Jewish community. Of the formerly sizable class of beggars and marginally employed, only 5 percent remained. The others had either emigrated or, as the old laws limiting Jewish settlement were repealed, exchanged their vagrant status for that of the settled citizen. By the end of the century, the Jews in Germany formed one of the wealthiest Jewish communities in Europe.

In the way they made their living after emancipation, the Jews remained quite different from

Bird's-eye view of the
grounds of the
Hamburg-Amerika
Line in Hamburg.

the general population. Throughout the period of the empire, one third of the German population was on the land and another third in industry or in crafts; only 10 percent were in trade. Among the Jews, by contrast, 50 percent were in trade, with a small number also in various branches of transportation—moving companies, coach service, ship travel, and the hotel and restaurant business. These businesses were vital to Jewish travelers, particularly the many commercial travelers, who observed dietary laws. And as the fashion for taking the baths increased, Jewish-owned hotels at spas were doubly welcome to families who wanted to be sure of kosher meals and did not want to risk a possible rebuff from anti-Semitic innkeepers.

The category *trade,* used in compiling these statistics, was a catchall that included retail and wholesale, and everything from the grandest department store to the elegant specialty shop and the corner grocery. However broad the term, it did define the place of many Jews in German society as the middlemen moving the goods that poured from the new factories at home and abroad and offering them for sale. In the empire, Jews became the shopkeepers par excellence, particularly in the textile and clothing trades. In small towns, they were often highly visible mer-

chants among the few shopkeepers on the main street. An additional 20 percent were in industry and crafts, again a broad category that included everyone from Emil Rathenau of General Electric to the solitary tailor in his workshop. Professionals made up another 6 percent, those holding posts as government employees or working as lawyers and doctors.

The nineteenth century saw not only a redistribution of Jewish occupations but also a complete regrouping of their place on the map of Germany. In the course of a millennium and a half in the German lands, small Jewish communities had spread from the Rhine to the border provinces of Posen and Silesia in the east. But the general move to the cities in the nineteenth century eroded small-town Jewish life. In 1870 only 20 percent of Germany's Jewish population lived in large cities; by 1910 that percentage had trebled. Despite this concentration, the 600,000 Jews in Germany made up slightly less than 1 percent of the total population of 60 million. Even in Berlin, which by 1910 was home to 142,000 Jews, they accounted for only 4 percent of the population.

But while their numbers concentrated and their prosperity increased, the indigenous German Jewish population was actually declining,

Israelit.

Hôtel Schwed in Bad Kissingen,

seit mehr als 40 Jahre bestehend und vergrößert, streng religiös und curgemäße table d'hôte. Pension für ganze Familien im und außer dem Hause zu ermäßigten Preisen.

Es empfiehlt sich geneigtem Wohlwollen

Hochachtungsvoll **David Schwed.**

Jüdisch Coscher Restauration

der

Geschwister Goldacker

in Braunschweig, Damm Nr. 1.

Zum 1. Juli d. J. eröffnen wir am hiesigen Platz, Damm Nr. 1 (beste Meßlage), eine jüdische Restauration, und bitten ein geehrtes reisendes Publicum um geneigten Zuspruch. Es wird unser eifrigstes Bestreben sein, unseren werthen Gästen mit schmackhaften Speisen und Getränken bestens bedienen zu können und möglichst billige Preise zu stellen.

Geschwister Goldacker.

Advertisements for a kosher hotel in Braunschweig addressed especially to travelers, and for a "strictly religious" hotel in Bad Kissingen. *Allgemeine Zeitung des Judenthums,* June 20, 1871.

owing to late marriages, a dramatically low birth rate, and an inexorable rise in intermarriage over the decades. In 1910–11, 13 percent of Jewish men and 10 percent of Jewish women married non-Jews, nearly double the percentages of a decade earlier; by the 1920s, one Jew in five married a gentile. In fact an analysis published in 1911 predicted the dissolution of the entire community. "The German Jews are a declining people," wrote the ethnologist Felix Theilhaber, "who have bought their emancipation and their acceptance as German citizens dearly through the sacrifice of their religious and national impulses. . . . Mixed marriages, baptism, abandonment of the community, diminution of the people through fewer births, physical and mental defects, increase of the mentally ill, suicide in an alarmingly increasing degree, and from nowhere is there any substitution or compensation."

In actuality, what was transforming the picture of the Jewish population in Germany was immigration from Eastern Europe, which had begun in the 1880s. By the 1920s, these new immigrants made up a fifth of the Jewish population in Germany, although, as Theilhaber had correctly predicted, even with this fresh blood the total Jewish population had begun to fall and never again reached the high of 1910.

Bildung

The Jewish communities of Germany were living in a state of contradiction. In an era of diminishing faith, they built splendid synagogues; as their Jewish heritage dropped away, they became the carriers of German culture; in a nation riven by local rivalries, they were the pure patriots. They had converted trade from a despised to a respectable and even glamorous profession, and wherever they emerged in the arts and sciences, they added a new pungency to their chosen fields.

No one took German culture more seriously than did the Jews. They sent their sons to the university in numbers far outweighing their proportion in the German population. The universities in Berlin and Breslau were particularly popular among Jewish students, and in 1886, Jews made up nearly 10 percent of the students in Berlin although they accounted for only 1 percent of the general population. Few Jews rose to the top of the academic world, however,

Kaiser Wilhelm II, saluting, leaving the stationery store of the "court purveyor" A. Liebmann in Berlin.

Gustav Abraham and his assistant, Julius Wolfskehl, in front of their shoemaking shop in Musikantenweg, Frankfurt am Main.

without undergoing baptism. As of 1909, only twenty-five Jews in Germany had advanced to the rank of full professor, and by 1917 the number had dropped to thirteen.

Jews persevered in the "free professions," though, as independent doctors and lawyers, or entered publishing, journalism, or the theater, which were less constrained by social convention. Above all, German Jews were consumers of high culture—subscribers to the opera and concerts, omnivorous readers of contemporary literature, patrons of the arts. In their private lives they honored German culture as the highest of ornaments, as their ancestors had once honored a command of Hebrew and the sacred literature.

No home was complete without a piano, and children were set to learn instruments just as they were taught to read. Home concerts were as prized among educated German Jews as they were among their gentile compatriots.

All these cultural activities were subsumed under the German word *Bildung,* or cultivation. To the German Jews *Bildung* represented a new kind of intellectual and emotional home after the physical confines of the ghetto and the closed scholarly world of Jewish learning. It led to what the philosopher Gershom Scholem later wickedly called the "one-sided love affair" between the Jews and the Germans, which nonetheless determined the values and direction of German Jewish life. *Bildung* implied more than a static body of knowledge; it also incorporated those ideals of the Enlightenment that Jews had seized upon as offering so much promise for them in the modern world. For nineteenth-century German Jews, then, culture had an almost redemptive quality, fulfilling the promise of the Enlightenment by making Jews like other people and an integral part of the society in which they lived. With its universal nature, high culture did not require any particular pedigree of its practitioners, and through this free universe the Jew could join Western civilization. When there was a new edition of Goethe to be planned, an anniversary of Schiller to be celebrated, emancipated German Jews were of the party.

Indeed, even for gentiles, the Jews became the carriers of German culture, to whom quoting from the German classics was as natural as breathing. Siegfried became one of the most popular names among Jewish boys, and among

Helga and Alfred Kohnke of Breslau, 1909.

Although a successful novelist, Jakob Wassermann agonized all his life over the question of Jewish assimilation. He abhorred Jewish nationalism and praised the fruitful effects of the German-Jewish symbiosis. His death in 1933 spared him bitter disappointment and worse.

When I was born, two years after the Franco-Prussian War [1870–71], the day of civic rights had long since dawned for the German Jews. . . . I remember that on various occasions my father would say with happy satisfaction, "We live in the age of tolerance!" . . . In dress, speech and style of life, the acculturation [of the Jews] was in every way complete. The school I attended was state-supported and public. We lived among Christians, socialized with Christians and for progressive Jews, such as my father, there was a Jewish community only in the sense of religious ceremonies and traditions. And these ceremonies shrank back more and more, because of the temptations and the powerful forces of modernity, into secretive, alienated and desperate sects. Traditions became matters of legend, finally only words and an empty shell.

Jakob Wassermann, "Das Los der Juden," in Deutscher und Jude. Reden und Schriften, 1904–1933, *Heidelberg, 1984.*

Frack- und Smoking-Anzüge

Am beſten iſt's auch hier, wenn ihr nur einen hört.
[Fauſt. I. Teil]

Bamberger & Hertz
Leipzig

SMOKING-ANZÜGE, nach Maß angefertigt:
Preiſe M. 95.— 105.— 115.— 125.—
FRACK-ANZÜGE, nach Maß angefertigt:
Preiſe M. 110.— 120.— 130.— 140.—

To a people reverent of culture, Goethe was not inappropriate for selling men's clothing. In a pre–World War I catalog by the custom tailors Bamberger & Hertz of Leipzig, each display page carried a quotation from *Faust*. Here the lion sings, "Even here it's best if you listen to only one voice."

girls Hedwig and Helga were far more common than the biblical or Yiddish names of the previous century. Even in business, culture was not far away. Just before the outbreak of the First World War, the firm of Bamberger & Hertz in Leipzig put out an amusing catalog for men's custom-made clothing using quotations from Goethe's *Faust* with contemporary cartoons to point up their wares.

Yet deeply satisfying and absorbing as this immersion in German culture was to German Jews, it did not protect them from anti-Semites, who saw them as eternally alien. Quite apart from the anti-Semitism that limited Jewish participation in certain parts of German life, social segregation remained particularly stubborn, so that the Jews built up and occupied their own social sphere, continuing to live a double life. Here, of course, is the kernel of the problem. Although German Jews were steeped in German culture and conducted their lives as any German middle-class family would—cherishing the same values, reading the same books, enjoying the same entertainments—on the whole they were separated from gentiles by what the Zionist Richard Lichtheim called a "glass wall."

Ironically, one of the charges that anti-Semites

leveled against German Jews enjoying and displaying *Bildung* was that they knew it too well and had acquired it too greedily. Whereas in earlier centuries Jews had had to endure the complaint that they were clinging too obstinately to their exotic ways, they were now exposed to the opposite complaint, that they were camouflaging their "real" nature with sizable dashes of Kantian philosophy, Schiller's cosmopolitanism, and Beethoven sonatas. The implication was one that acculturated German Jews indignantly denied: that German *Bildung* was somehow not natural to them and must remain a superficial possession or convenient mask.

As though to substantiate this slander, denigrators of German Jews liked to see them as having played a prominent role in the invasion of "decadent" modernism. From the 1890s on, largely in the wake of French, English, and Scandinavian innovators, German high culture began to absorb the unconventional productions of naturalist novelists and playwrights, impressionist painters, and, after 1900, expressionists in poetry and painting alike. Emperor Wilhelm II spoke for dominant strands of opinion among Germans when he called these works the art of the gutter. He caught conservative accents, too,

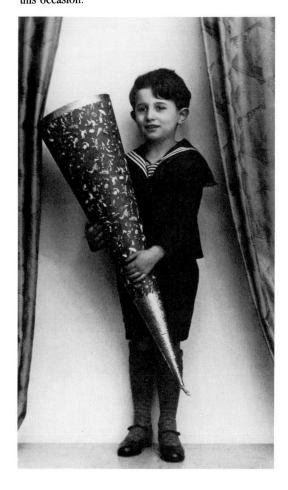

Jakob Katz of Zwickau on his first day of school. He carries a cone filled with sweets, customarily given to children on this occasion.

when in the early 1890s he told his chancellor, Leo Graf von Caprivi, that Paris, headquarters and leading exporter of much that was subversive in the arts and literature, was the "great whorehouse of the world." His fear, and that of many Germans like him, was that shocking writers like Zola and shocking artists like Van Gogh would undermine all that good Germans must prize: religion, patriotism, decency,. and the family.

It is certainly true that German Jews were among those who embraced the fresh breath of modernism. But whatever hostile observers might say, by no means all Jews were modernists, and—even more significant—by no means all modernists were Jews. German Jews were to be found, precisely like their gentile counter-parts, all over the cultural map. The tone-setting "revolutionaries" in the German culture of the empire—naturalistic playwrights like Gerhart Hauptmann, ironic novelists like Thomas Mann, expressionist painters like Emil Nolde, influential museum directors like Hugo von Tschudi, experimental architects like Walter Gropius—were all gentiles.

There were, of course, Jews in this country of modernists, many of them in the business of culture. They edited periodicals, reviewed novels and plays, dealt in art, produced dramas, published books, and owned cabarets that welcomed the new. They staged the unsettling plays of Ibsen and Strindberg, and exhibited the startling canvases of Cezanne. Among them were performers—gifted violinists, conductors, actors. Some of them made a lively presence in the Bohemian coffee houses of Munich or Berlin, where they wrote and recited their world-weary expressionist verses.

There was no shortage of talented Jewish artists and writers. But two names would stand out in any company: the painter Max Liebermann and the poet Else Lasker-Schüler. Liebermann became Germany's most famous and most controversial painter during the Wilhelminian years. Born in 1847 into an affluent family that had moved to Berlin a quarter century earlier, he studied the Dutch and French painters on his trips to the Netherlands and to Paris. A realist whose canvases glowed with an impressionist light, he never changed his way of painting. This made him a radical in his early years, when he specialized in what academic critics called "ugly" subjects like peasant women plucking geese, and a conservative in his later career. He collected Manet and loved the French impressionists, but the expressionists, let alone the abstract artists who increasingly dominated modern painting from 1910 on, left him cold.

It was as a rebel that he championed such disturbing innovators as the Norwegian expressionist Edvard Munch, in the early 1890s, and founded the famous breakaway group of artists, the Berlin Secession, in 1898, scandalizing aesthetic conservatives with his tastes. He produced major canvases, among them an anything but idealized portrait of Hamburg's mayor, Carl Friedrich Petersen, which caused a storm of troversy. As time went by, he often painted, etched, and lithographed his own eminently

Max Liebermann
(1847–1935). Self-
portrait, 1906.

Else Lasker-Schüler
(1869–1945), in a
photograph made
around 1900.

handsome face. For him, until the Nazis came to power, the double life of the German Jew raised no particular problems. He was a good Berliner, speaking with the unmistakable accents of the capital, proud to be a Prussian and a German— and a Jew. His painting was in no way confessional. "What does painting have to do with Judaism?" he asked.

For the lyrical poet Else Lasker-Schüler, the answer to that question was far more problematic. Her poetry and her Jewishness were mysteriously intertwined. Born into a devout Jewish family in Wuppertal-Elberfeld in 1869, she could boast a great-grandfather who had been chief rabbi of the Rhineland and Westphalia. She was an impassioned writer, a born poet who needed only the stimulus of modern poetry and painting to realize her vocation. Yet it took her years to find it. She married a physician in 1894 and after her divorce in 1900 moved to the city that was rapidly outdistancing Munich as the heart of the avant-garde maelstrom: Berlin. There she married again, not for long, but advantageously: her second husband, the publisher, composer, and writer Georg Lewin, whom she renamed Herwarth Walden, threw her into the dizzying world of Germany's leading experimental poets and painters. And the periodical *Der Sturm,* which Walden founded not long before their divorce in 1910, printed many of her best early lyrics. Short, erotic, expressionist, highly figurative, and lovely to recite, these poems won her an admiring audience among advanced spirits.

As early as 1902, the Roman Catholic poet Peter Hille had called her "the Jewish poet." A decade later, in her book *Hebrew Ballads,* she drew on themes from the Old Testament. Her verse was no less intimate, erotic, or playful than before, but the feelings it expressed (and, some readers thought, her luxuriant images) were explicitly Jewish. Although her verse is in German, late in life she said, poetically, that she had always written in Hebrew. When one reads her work or her autobiographical statements and compares them to Liebermann's witty, commonsensical pronouncements, one must conclude that there were many ways in which Jews during the empire experienced and expressed their Jewishness.

Department Stores

The institution of modern life in which the Jews succeeded most naturally was the department store. Although it began in France and the United States in the 1830s and 1840s as an outgrowth of dry-goods stores, the German variants did not lag far behind. As more and more people moved to the cities, the terms of country trading—barter, credit, and customer loyalty—became irrelevant in the impersonal, urban world. The new department stores grew on the basis of three main principles, all of which ran counter to the stereotype of the haggling Jew. Prices were fixed; customers were encouraged to browse without being pressured to buy; and goods could be returned. Another inducement was the low prices, since the owner could take a smaller profit on the expectation of a large turnover.

The department stores also established a new style of shopping, enticing their customers by luxury and flattery, so that countrywomen who came into the city to shop dressed for the event in their best Sunday clothes. The stores offered elegant surroundings, attentive service, free delivery, places to dine, lounges for resting, reading rooms, and music rooms, all in a festive atmosphere in which the purchase was the climactic moment.

The progenitor of the department store in Berlin was Herrmann Gerson, who came to the capital from Königsberg in 1835 as a young man of twenty-two. Gerson moved quickly from dry goods to the manufacture of ready-made clothes, then still a novelty. By 1848, when he opened his department store, which sold varieties of textiles ranging from piece goods to carpets, he was employing fifteen hundred tailors off the premises. In that year, he was also appointed an official purveyor of linens to the court, an honor he hastened to paint on his walls.

Another pioneer was Falk Valentine Grünfeld, a linen manufacturer in Landshut, Silesia, who like Gerson expanded his dry-goods business to include ready-made clothes, household linens, and complete trousseaus for brides. When he enlarged his store in 1869, he placed at the entrance a marble table with a huge bowl that contained a cold raspberry drink in the summer and hot punch in the winter, dispensed free to arriving customers. This practice was so successful that when he opened branches in sophisticated Berlin later in the century, the punch bowl remained the store's signature and became an emblem of a new style of customer service. In Berlin, Grünfeld's leadership was recognized by his colleagues, who elected him to head the trade association he founded and later named him a vice-president of the Berlin Chamber of Commerce.

Not all the department stores were born in Berlin. Tietz, which by 1907 had become one of the giants, with thirty-six affiliates, started in the town of Gera in Thuringia. Schocken, which eventually had eight branches, began in Zwickau in Saxony. Arthur Wertheim opened his first store, a modest dry-goods shop, in 1876 in Stralsund, but his three sons branched out, moving to Berlin in 1885.

Berlin, as the capital of the empire and its largest city, was naturally the home of the flagship stores of the major department chains. Here no expense was spared in employing eminent architects and seeking out sumptuous materials for the selling floors and lounge areas. Jewish-owned department stores built in Berlin at the end of the century were pioneering works of architecture, solving problems of multiple use that had not previously existed in the retail business.

One of the most admired buildings was erected by the Wertheim family to a design by Alfred Messel. When it opened in December 1897, huge crowds came to Leipzigerstrasse to marvel at what one contemporary called a "new cathedral."

The largest department store in Berlin was owned by the firm of N. Israel and was built over a fifteen-year period, from 1899 to 1914. Strongly indebted in its design to Messel, it took up an entire square block and was located at the city's center, directly across from the Red Town Hall, so called because of its color. Although the store bore the name of its original founder, Nathan Israel, who had opened his first shop in Berlin in 1815, the actual builder was his grandson, Berthold Israel, who lived until 1935 and saw the first inroads of the Nazi regime on the firm's management.

In the Wilhelminian age, the department store was a glamorous, highly visible feature of the urban landscape. Often carefully placed at the center of traffic, it became a magnetic focus

The Herrmann Gerson department store, opened in 1849, was the first building in Berlin designed for that specific purpose. The skylight that topped the central area allowed the maximum amount of daylight into the building; it soon became a standard element in department store design. The architect also provided an apartment for the owner on the third floor and workrooms for forty seamstresses.

of activity, a place of recreation as well as of business. The stores early became centers of controversy, too, as small merchants complained that their businesses were being undermined by these irresistible and unfairly competitive giants. Although the families whose histories are related here were all Jewish, a number of major department stores, such as Karstadt and Kaufhof, were owned by non-Jews. But the prominence of Jews in this area identified this new colossus with Jews, in the popular mind at least, and even led to a special tax in Prussia, levied beginning in 1900, designed to curb the size of the stores.

Despite the widespread view that the department store was driving out the small store owners, the old way of doing business, predicated on offering credit along with higher prices, did not vanish. In 1907, eight out of ten people, especially blue-collar workers, were still buying regularly in small stores that offered credit. And unlike the United States, where in the 1930s the department stores were responsible for 9 percent of all retail business, in Germany at the same time the department stores accounted for only 4–5 percent of the retail trade. Nonetheless, they had created an irreversible revolution in retailing that affected the way small stores did business, making fixed prices, attractive environments, and an emphasis on service new touchstones in retail trade. Shopping had become an entertainment, and a new word, "window shopping"—the *Stadtbummel*—had entered the language.

The Cologne branch
of the Tietz depart-
ment store, 1896.

"I've come to tell you
that your infamous
cut-throat competition
has totally ruined me.
There is nothing left
for me to do but to
put a bullet through
my head." "May I
suggest that the fire-
arms department is to
be found on the first
floor?" *Sim-
plicissimus*, 1898.

Georg Tietz, who headed the Tietz department store chain until he was expelled by the Nazis in 1934, reveals how the firm introduced a new institution around 1905.

The white sale, which so enlivened the usually quiet month of February, became a second Christmas month for us. The whole building was transformed into a melody in white; all the windows were decorated with linens, and in the open galleries there were splendid constructions of underclothes, handkerchiefs, and other textiles. At one time they represented an Indian temple, another time a Roman triumphal arch, or ships at dock or waterfalls and cascades. The facades of the buildings were covered with special advertising lights during this week. . . . Although our competitors copied our white sale, it always remained a special Tietz affair.

Georg Tietz, Hermann Tietz: Geschichte einer Familie, *Stuttgart, 1965.*

The Hermann Tietz department store on Alexanderplatz in Berlin around 1930, showing the elaborate night illumination during the white sale.

Interior of the Tietz
department store in
Berlin, ca. 1926,
showing the display of
linens during the
white sale.

The Wertheim department store in the Leipzigerstrasse, Berlin, ca. 1910. Its most daring architectural feature was that it had no display windows, a sign of the house's confidence in its reputation.

The innovations of Jewish department store owners did not stop at merchandizing. They were also responsible for pioneering architecture, such as the landmark Wertheim building opened in Berlin in 1897. Here is a contemporary architectural review.

Silent amidst the loud uproar, proud and confident as the giant trees that had gone before it, majestically, almost ceremoniously, the corner building rises above us. A department store? But there is no sign, no flag, nothing colorful displayed during the day, and no light show at night to disclose its purpose. There is nothing about it that suggests advertising. . . . The building beckons to us from across the plaza, not at all as if it were a department store, but rather as a part of an old gothic cathedral, without frivolity, or like one of the noblest, sweetly earnest chapels of an Oxford college.

Paul Göhre, Das Warenhaus, *Frankfurt am Main, 1907.*

In the Community

The Family

Despite the dissension that characterized the internal politics of the Jewish communities, they continued to carry on their many functions. In their long history in Germany, these communities had grown accustomed to caring for their poor and providing a range of social services that in other groups usually fell to local government. By the end of the nineteenth century, these long-standing institutions were gradually consolidated and professionalized as trained social workers, educators, doctors, and other specialists took their place among the officials and volunteers who were the backbone of the system.

The sheer number of these organizations displays the remarkable self-sufficiency of German Jews. The census of 1909 showed that for the 1,014 Jewish communities in Germany, there were 3,010 welfare societies. Although their programs still included some of the traditional pious functions, like providing dowries for poor brides, they also maintained schools, hospitals, vocational training institutes, homes for apprentices, counseling bureaus for criminals, and homes for the aged. The proliferation of these enterprises and the energy they attracted led the historian Ismar Elbogen to comment, "Charity seemed to many to serve as a substitute for religion."

These institutions served yet another function: they provided an opportunity for middle-class women to move beyond their domestic sphere. Often undereducated in view of their capacities and without any opportunity for real work except in charitable organizations, many intelligent Jewish women felt themselves, as the historian Marion Kaplan has put it, in a situation of double jeopardy, discriminated against both as Jews and as women. The importance of these organizations, then, was not only in the good they did but also in serving as an outlet for women who had no other place to exercise their talents.

Probably the most prominent of these organizations was the Jüdische Frauenbund (League of Jewish Women), founded in 1904 by Bertha Pappenheim and run by women for women. Pappenheim, a descendant of Glückel of Hameln, was born into a well-to-do family in Vienna in

1859. Markedly intelligent and active, as a young woman she fell victim to a serious hysterical episode after the death of her father in 1880 and was treated by Josef Breuer, Sigmund Freud's older, paternal friend. In 1895 her history, disguised under the name of Anna O, was published in a joint study by Breuer and Freud and became one of the founding cases for the new science of psychoanalysis. Following her recovery, Pappenheim moved to Frankfurt in 1889, where she published an article reproaching middle-class parents for keeping their daughters in ignorance of the real world. Although she wrote prolifically—poetry, religious meditations, and many translations from the Yiddish—her main reputation rests on her work with the Frauenbund.

Like many other Jewish women, Pappenheim had started her charitable work by helping in a soup kitchen for Jews traveling across Germany from Eastern Europe. Then, in 1895, she became the director of an orphanage in Frankfurt. As her attention more and more centered on the special needs of women and children, she finally came to focus on the serious problem of the white slave trade, in which Jewish traffickers lured young Jewish girls from Eastern Europe into a life of vice, often shipping them to brothels in Buenos Aires.

In 1904 Pappenheim, with a group of other women activists meeting in Berlin for an international women's congress, formed the Jüdische Frauenbund. Its purpose was to work for poor women and for the rehabilitation of prostitutes and women criminals. Although it began with the special mission of preventing white slavery, the organization soon expanded its work to provide lodging houses for single working girls as well as clubs for working women who lived independently. Most of those who attended were young women from Eastern Europe who, without family or social contacts in Germany, were subject to being preyed upon. Most ambitious was the home for unwed mothers established in 1907 at Neu Isenburg near Frankfurt. Here the women were sheltered while they learned to care for themselves and their children and were eventually placed in jobs that would allow them to be self-supporting.

Bertha Pappenheim served as director of this home from its inception until 1936, the year of her death. During that time, some fifteen hun-

Bertha Pappenheim
(1859–1936),
painted when she was
about twenty-five.

This passage, from a speech by Bertha Pappenheim at a meeting of the Frauenbund in 1932, reveals both the spiritual and the practical sides of her character. On the one hand there is her idealization of the high moral standards of Judaism. Yet as she discovers the existence of serious social problems in the community—unwed mothers, the white slave trade—she also discovers that her fellow Jews would rather deny them than deal with them.

Whoever ventures to become a leader of youth must follow a strict path for herself while remaining indulgent toward others. These days, it is terribly hard to kindle in others the ner tomid, *the Eternal Light, but that is our duty. Today Jews believe that they have the right to find their own way and need not, as in earlier days, submit themselves to moral prescriptions. For someone such as me, who forty years ago, innocent, bathed in the spirit of my parents' house, protected by my* jichus *[illustrious lineage], began my social work, it has been a frightful shock to the soul to discover that Jews, too, in the last decades have strayed from the line laid down for them, also in sexual matters. . . . People have denied that there are unmarried mothers and children even in the Jewish community. It meant a lot in those days to say it out loud, and it was difficult to organize women to abolish these things. Today these ways of thinking are alive in the entire civilized world; they are common to all mankind. But we must never forget that bringing these ideas and the demand for the strictest morality to the world was Jewish.*

Bertha Pappenheim, "Einführung in den Arbeitskreis für Gefährdeten-Fürsorge," in Blätter des jüdischen Frauenbundes für Frauenarbeit und Frauenbewegung, *Berlin, 1932.*

Sabbath dinner at the
Neu Isenburg home
for unwed mothers.

dred women and their children passed through its doors. Just as exceptional as the work of the Frauenbund was the response of women in the Jewish community. By 1917, it had 44,000 members in 215 branches, eventually counting 20 percent of all Jewish women in Germany in its ranks.

Outside of the welfare organizations, the main arena where women exerted a certain power was the family, which in the Wilhelminian era controlled the destinies of the young more firmly than ever again. In Jewish families, appropriate partners were a source of deep concern in a time marked by conversions and mixed mar-

riages. Most families engaged in some form of arranged alliances as they sent their children on long visits to relatives elsewhere or brought them to spas where they might meet eligible mates under supervision. In some cases, anxious parents even engaged the services of a professional marriage broker, although they generally concealed this unromantic fact from the principals.

Instances of moneyed Jewish parents searching for noblemen to marry their daughters, while documented in the 1870s, rapidly fell off with increasing anti-Semitism. But it is true that until the First World War, except among liber-

Chalizah-Brief.

Ich Unterzeichneter *Salaman Elias* erkläre hiemit, daß ich, wenn mein Bruder *Dr. David Elias*, was Gott verhüthe, mit Tode abgehen sollte, ohne einen Leibeserben zu hinterlassen, und die Vorschriften wegen Vornahme der Chalizah nach jüdischem Gesetze und Gebrauche in Kraft treten sollten, ohne Widerspruch und Widerrede bereit bin, mich diesem Akte zu unterziehen, ohne an meine Schwägerin, Frau *Rosa Elias* irgend einen darauf bezüglichen Anspruch an Geld oder Geldeswerth zu erheben, wann und wo sie es für nöthig finden sollte; und verpflichte ich mich, dieser Verbindlichkeit als Schwager vorschriftsmäßig und gewissenhaft nachzukommen.

Wien, am *26. October 1862.*

Elias Salomon

In this document Salamon Elias declares that he is ready to fulfill the halizah requirements in case his brother dies without leaving children and that he will not claim any money from the widow. Vienna, October 26, 1862.

ated Jewish university students, the dowry was the determining factor in establishing the basis for a match in Jewish and non-Jewish families alike. In many peasant villages, the bride traveled to her new home in an open wagon piled with her *Aussteuer*—furniture, linens, and household goods—to display the wealth she was bringing with her. Prenuptial contracts were less visible but no less fundamental to the conclusion of marriages. In those hardheaded, unromantic moments when the contracts were drawn up, nineteenth-century Orthodox families also considered the consequences of death and the still-prevailing Jewish law requiring the deceased husband's brother to marry the widow. Prudent families drew up a *Chalizah brief*, a letter certifying that in such an event the brother would release the widow without demanding payment. That this was a common practice is attested by the availability of a printed form with spaces for filling in only the names and date.

Mixed marriages were far less likely to be initiated by parents marrying off their daughters to satisfy their own social ambitions than by men marrying out of independent choice. The patterns were again strongly affected by where people lived: in Hamburg, in 1906, 26 percent of Jewish men and 22 percent of Jewish women married non-Jews, while in Bavaria only 4 percent of Jewish men and women married out. But in both the rural neighborhoods and the big cities the percentages continued to rise from decade to decade. Although there was some conversion to Judaism as a result of intermarriage, the stream tended to run in the other direction.

Conversion also nibbled away at the Jewish population. Early in the century, baptism had been a source of religious turmoil and anguish, but by the time of the empire it took on a more considered character. It was no longer what Heine had called the "entry ticket to European culture." The Jews had long since become not only acculturated but also important contributors to that culture. Baptism remained, however, the entry ticket to professional advancement. It was not unusual for parents who themselves remained Jewish to have their children baptized in the hope of rescuing them from bigotry.

Jewish self-mockery was unsparing on both conversion and mixed marriage. However

Five generations of the Kalischer family, photographed in Berlin in 1889 on the occasion of the ninetieth birthday of Lobl Kalischer. The portrait in an oval frame is that of his deceased wife, Charlotte. In the seventeenth century, in the wake of the Chmielnicki massacres, the family fled from Kremnitz to Lissa in Posen, where they produced several well-known talmudists. Mendel, founder of the Berlin line, arrived in 1832. He was one of the last to encompass both talmudic and university learning as a matter of course. Later generations became lawyers, doctors, bankers and rabbis. There was also an actor and a writer, the Parisian correspondent for the *Gartenlaube.* Although Yiddish rapidly fell away, the family remained faithful to Judaism with the exception of Dr. Alfred Kalischer, a composer who converted in the mid-nineteenth century and took the name Christlieb.

This cartoon, from *Simplicissimus* (1897–98), is titled *The White Raven:* "And you, Lieutenant, who have always been against marriages for money, is it true that you've become engaged to the daughter of Commercial Counsellor Baruch?" "Well, it can sometimes happen that one falls in love with a rich girl."

(Zeichnung von E. Thöny)

„Warum haben Se sich denn katholisch taufen lassen?" — „Ach wissen Se, bei den Protestanten sind mir zu viel Juden."

"How is it that you've been baptized a Catholic?" "Well, you know, there are just too many Jews for me among the Protestants." *Simplicissimus,* 1898.

"How can you condemn mixed marriages? If Esther hadn't entered into one, we wouldn't have a Purim Ball." *Schlemiel,* February 25, 1920.

„Wie können Sie die Mischehe verurteilen? Wäre Esther keine eingegangen, so hätten wir keinen Purimball."

coolly the step may have been taken, conversion cast a long shadow in both Jewish and non-Jewish communities, so that the high visibility and awkward social position of the converts far outweighed the actual numbers. The chart of Jewish conversions in Germany can in fact be read as a barometer of the level of anti-Semitism in the country, which reached a low point at mid-century and then rose again in the 1880s. Between 1880 and 1910, 12,000 Jews converted to Protestantism, an average of 400 a year. These relatively small numbers did not stanch the sense that the community was thinning out, in part because of the prominence of those who had left. Since a third of the converts were government officials or professionals, their actions were far more visible than if they had been businessmen. And as women began to enter the work force, they too increased the number of converts.

The real source of danger in the decline of the Jewish community, though, as the demographers pointed out, came not from the movement outward but from within. The Jewish birth rate, which had always been lower than that of the surrounding population, also fell more rapidly in the century of industrialization as the birth rate fell everywhere. Whereas at the beginning of the century Jews in Prussia had produced 35 children per thousand annually, by 1900 the number had dropped to 19; it would be only 11 in 1927. This was even lower than the French birth rate, notoriously among the lowest in Europe, which stood at 19 per thousand in 1924.

In the meantime, intermarriage and conversion were creating a new caste of Jewish Christians and Christian Jews whose very presence confused the old categories. How Jewish was Bethel Henry Strousberg, the converted Jew, or Edith Stein, the philosophy student, born in 1891, who became a Catholic nun but always said "we" when she spoke of Jewish philosophers? Or Paul Wallich, the son of a Jewish banking family, who was baptized as an infant in 1882 in accordance with his parents' wishes?

Judaism could not lay claim to souls; it continued to build its institutions representing an ever-widening spectrum of Jewish activity. In the Wilhelminian epoch, many Jews confessed themselves to be no more than "three-day Jews" who attended the synagogue only on the high holy days. But Jewish membership in the B'nai Brith lodges, in defense and Zionist organizations, as well as Jewish support and activity in welfare organizations, showed that the community was still there. Its center, however, had shifted.

The Centralverein

The acculturation that characterized Jewish life in Western Europe and the United States was put under the magnifying glass in Germany. As long as the status of the Jews was not legally settled, arduous philosophical and political questions over defining Jews and their place in society continued to be open. Yet as one of the many contradictions in the history of the German Jews, everyday life did not wait for the law. By 1871, Jewish integration into society had far outrun the legal boundaries that still pinched in so many areas.

Did German Jews assimilate? This question, which often became an accusation on the part of Eastern European Jews, remained acute for a long time among German Jews themselves. There is a difference, of course, between assimilation and acculturation. Assimilation implies a total merging into the majority culture so that all distinctions of religion, language, and custom are eliminated. Acculturation, which is really what happened all across Western Europe, is a process in which Jews took on the language, culture, and social conventions of the majority while retaining their own religion and a profound sense of their separate past.

The family and the community became the twin foci of Jewish life. Yet however much they mirrored their parallel German social class, they kept a flavor and style of their own, with both the self-mockery and special binocular vision that characterize people who live in two cultures. One of the recurrent themes in Jewish life and humor was exactly this question of acculturation and how far it could go. Christmas, as a universally celebrated Christian holiday, awakened a particular self-consciousness among the German Jews who joined in the celebration.

Although the forms of their lives may have seemed indistinguishable from those of their neighbors, the German Jews moved to a different rhythm. Questions of marriage, principles of child care, the tribulations of Jews abroad, and a heightened awareness of themselves and their fellow Jews at home all gave a coloring to Jewish lives that was absent from their neighbors'. The most telling index of where they stood was that by and large Jews lived almost entirely among other Jews. Inevitably this affected their politics. Movements such as Teutomania early in the nineteenth century and Jahn's *völkisch* enthusiasms, like later German racism, sent up immediate warning signals in the Jewish community.

Yet their way of living in two worlds was no longer recessive but affirmative. In an unprecedented wave of synagogue building in the second half of the nineteenth century, Jewish communities demonstrated both their prosperity and a new sense of confidence by erecting grand, indeed grandiose, structures. These buildings were not, as in the past, hidden in back courtyards or discreetly nondescript. A wildly eclectic style of architecture emerged for these synagogues with vaguely Moorish elements meant not only to evoke the golden age of the Jews in twelfth-century Spain but also to allude to their distant Near Eastern origins. They featured the bulbous onion domes, intricate geometric ornamentation, and brilliant coloring that Europeans associated with Levantine architecture. Placed prominently in the center of towns and cities, they were unmistakable demonstrations of the solidity of the Jewish presence. (See plate 20.)

By the beginning of the twentieth century, another style had emerged as the Jewish communities cast off the exotic cloak they had accepted in the nineteenth century. The last synagogue built in Berlin before the outbreak of the First World War was the liberal synagogue in Levetzowstrasse, which could seat more than two thousand people and was opened on April 7, 1914. With its imposing entrance marked by four massive pillars, it showed a return to classical architecture in its facade without sacrificing any of the monumentality so prized by the community.

Their burial places were no less splendid. In 1880, the Berlin community laid out a new cemetery in the suburb of Weissensee, which eventually became the largest Jewish cemetery in Europe, with 115,000 graves. Here the world of Berlin Jewry was replicated in death as it had been in life: the modest tombstones of the Orthodox, densely engraved in Hebrew characters;

Zeichnung von Fritz Julian Leo

,Und Dir als Blau-Weißem hat der Weihnachtsmann eine Menorah gebracht.,

"And because you're a member of the Blau-Weiss [a Zionist youth group], Father Christmas has brought you a menorah." *Schlemiel,* 1904.

Heilbronn.

Breslau.

Leipzig.

Königsberg.

Kaiserslautern.

Munich.

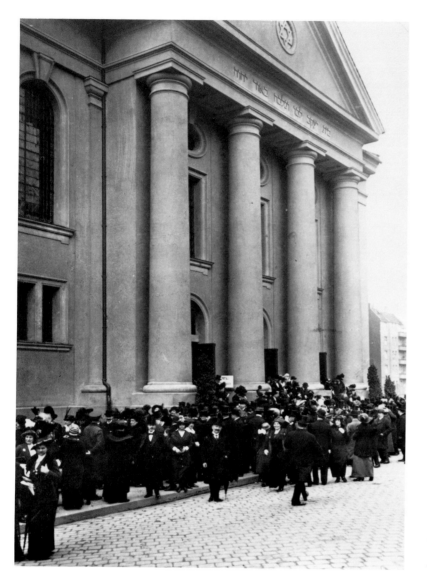

Levetzowstrasse syn-
agogue, Berlin. This
photograph was taken
on April 7, 1914, the
day the synagogue
was consecrated, only
a few months before
the start of World
War I. With seats for
two thousand wor-
shipers, it was one of
the largest synagogues
in Berlin. In 1941 it
became an assembly
point for Jews being
deported to the
camps.

The middle classes in Berlin were buried no less splendidly than they had lived. Mausoleum of the Michaelis family, built in 1890, in the Weissensee cemetery.

the sober rows of low markers for the Jewish soldiers killed in World War I; the Avenue of Honor for the Jewish notables, lined with somber man-high black tombstones. In the great mausoleums of the rich, decorum gave way to imagination in the elaborate funerary architecture, realized in sumptuous marble and colored stone.

Within the Jewish communities that erected these monuments, however, all was not peace and harmony. The elections for community office, which carried considerable power and prestige, were often stormy affairs. There were religious differences ranging from Orthodox to the most extreme Reform. There were profound secular political differences—those who saw themselves as German citizens of the Jewish faith and those who advocated Zionism as the solution to the Jewish question. In 1876, one element of strife was eliminated when the ultra-Orthodox Jews were permitted to secede from the official Jewish community and form an *Austrittsgemeinde* (secession community) tailored to their own needs and beliefs.

By the end of the century, the sense of accomplishment that had accompanied the emancipation of 1871 was tempered by the realization

that the struggle was not yet over. Although most Jews believed that in time the evils of anti-Semitism could be eliminated, they also saw that there was work to do. They launched a variety of self-defense organizations, both to combat anti-Semitic propaganda and to support Jewish self-esteem. The most significant of these associations defined its credo in its name: Centralverein deutscher Staatsbürger jüdischen Glaubens, (Central Union of German Citizens of the Jewish Faith). Their unwavering insistence on their German nationality sometimes aroused their opponents to refer to them mockingly as Jewish citizens of the German faith.

By 1916, the Centralverein claimed a membership of 70,000 individuals plus 200,000 others who belonged through affiliated organizations—a total that accounted for half the Jews in Germany! The Centralverein pursued a number of paths to achieve its goals. It took legal action to seek redress for Jews who had been defamed either privately or in the press. It was alert to anti-Semitic legislation, and its local branches campaigned against anti-Semitic candidates.

Although the Centralverein remained ardently nationalist throughout its history, it modified its original expectation that Jews would achieve equality as a right simply by waiting. By the 1900s, it was actively supporting candidates of the Progressive party, which never commanded more than about 10 percent of the seats in the Reichstag but whose representatives were willing to raise uncomfortable questions. Why were Jews not given reserve officer commissions? Why were Jewish law clerks not promoted to higher positions in the judiciary, or Jewish doctors in hospitals?

At the same time, the Centralverein turned its attention to the attrition within the Jewish community as a result of widespread conversion and intermarriage. The movement began to take a new direction, no longer urging Jews to become better Germans but instead insisting on their right to be Jews. The Centralverein abandoned the narrow definition of Judaism as a religion for one that better reflected the lives of the many secular Jews in Germany who nonetheless cherished their historical and cultural heritage. In 1912 Eugen Fuchs, a leading ideologist and later president of the organization, set forth in the Centralverein's newspaper, *Im deutschen Reich,* the new credo of the organization.

Ten years ago I had already indicated that it was not the shape of the beard, the color of hair, the curve of the nose, or the size of the body that was decisive, but the energetic dedicated will to be a German. . . . We are born into a German fatherland and on German soil . . . and that gives us the right to call ourselves Germans, without baptism and the so-called assimilation. . . . "Proud and faithful in their individuality" was how our King spoke only recently of our various German tribes [*Stämme*]. We would apply that phrase also to our own tribe.

Watchfulness, legal action, protests through channels, and alliances with Christian groups were all part of the strategy of the Centralverein, which in its hopes and program represented the solid majority of the Jewish middle classes. Jews chafed under persistent disabilities and were made uneasy by recurring anti-Semitism. But as long as they continued to prosper, as long as their world flourished, they continued to hope that the system would eventually, if with agonizing slowness, fulfill the promise implicit in the emancipation decree.

Sample issue of *Im deutschen Reich,* national monthly magazine of the Centralverein.

Zionism

Theodor Herzl in 1897, on the eve of the First Zionist Congress, in Basel.

Zionism in Germany appealed to the impatient. In the last decade of the nineteenth century, a generation gap opened between those who had celebrated the granting of emancipation and those who had grown up in the empire. For the young generation, the triumph of emancipation had long faded, and their field of vision was not dominated by the comfort and freedom their parents had achieved. For them, what chafed was the undying anti-Semitism, the checks on their careers, the humiliation of being treated as outsiders, and their sense of permanent exclusion from society. Zionism was a movement born in part out of disappointment, but it was also propelled by a powerful need for Jewish self-realization, whether in a Jewish state or in the Diaspora.

Since the mid-nineteenth century, nationalism had been a significant force in Europe, bringing about the first steps toward Hungarian autonomy in 1848, the unification of Italy in 1861, and that of Germany in 1871. It had inspired Moses Hess in 1862 to write *Rome and Jerusalem,* with its assertion of Jewish nationality as the key to Jewish self-respect in a modern Europe. The cultivated Austrian journalist Theodor Herzl, who published his pamphlet *The Jewish State* in 1896, gave these feelings a political focus that culminated in the modern Zionist organization.

In 1897, four years after the founding of the Centralverein, the German Zionist Federation (Zionistische Vereinigung für Deutschland) was formed just as the nascent Zionist movement prepared to hold its first world congress in Basel. Answering the implicit criticism from the rest of the German Jewish community, the first program of the German Zionists stated firmly, "Our Zionist beliefs do not prevent us from fulfilling our obligations to the fatherland, nor from fulfilling our civic obligations to the state." In its early years, German Zionism was sometimes decried as "third-party Zionism": one party (the German Jews) contributes to a second party (the Zionist organization) so that a third party (the East European Jews) could go to Palestine. Yet German Jews were hardly as detached as this caricature implies. On the contrary, in the first generation of the Zionist movement, the German-speaking world provided much of the leadership, including its founder, Theodor Herzl.

While Zionism in Eastern Europe was a kind of secular messianic movement with a broad popular base, in Germany its membership before World War I never totaled more than 9,000 in any year. It was not until 1920 that it reached 20,000. Yet the Zionists were a source of concern for the Centralverein because they undermined its attempt to show primary Jewish loyalty to Germany. The Zionist view that there was a separate Jewish nationality, with its own history and culture, only confirmed the long-standing anti-semitic accusations that the Jews were not and could not become part of the German people.

Judging by membership alone, the Centralverein certainly represented the majority of the German Jews. But in the first decades of the twentieth century, the Zionists attracted an active and outspoken leadership, among them a number of brilliant and eloquent young men such as Kurt Blumenfeld, who in 1909 became first secretary of the German Zionist organization, and Richard Lichtheim, a writer, editor, and later emissary of the Zionist movement. The sociologists Arthur Ruppin, who emigrated to Palestine in 1908, and Franz Oppenheimer were also drawn to the movement, as were the philosophers Martin Buber and Gershom Scholem, both of whom explored and interpreted traditional Judaism with the tools of Western philosophy.

Although their numbers were small, their fervor was high, for the movement offered not just a program but a cause and a source of support for much-battered Jewish self-esteem. Among the indigenous German Jews, the appeal was largely to the young and well-to-do, who joined during their university years and later occupied leadership positions. The other major component in the movement was the East European Jews who had migrated to Germany but once there found themselves excluded from the official Jewish communities. Where these two ill-assorted partners could agree was on the need to develop Jewish culture in the Diaspora. By 1902, the Zionists in Germany had established a Jewish publishing house. Then in 1916, Martin Buber began publication of the magazine *Der Jude*, whose title had lost none of its force since

Kurt Blumenfeld, president of the German Zionist Federation, 1923–33. He emigrated to Palestine in 1933, where he was one of the founders of the Keren Hayesod.

Richard Lichtheim describes how he became a Zionist in 1904.

Here were the answers to all the questions that I had been asking my-self and my circle for years: not through assimilation or baptism, but through one's own action in one's own land would the relations be-tween Jews and other peoples be normalized. . . . Not the imitation of strange manners, . . . of the English gentiles, the Prussian junker or other European social types, could produce the solution to the per-sonal problems that every Jew carried around with himself. . . . This solution must come from within, from one's own nature. Here, fi-nally, and only here, in Zionism, could the Jewish personality unfold free and unbroken. . . . The acceptance of Zionism was thus the ac-ceptance of myself.

Richard Lichtheim, Rückkehr. Lebenserinnerungen aus der Frühzeit des deutschen Zionismus, *Stuttgart, 1970.*

Richard Lichtheim, editor of the Zionist periodical *Die Welt,* 1911–13. He emigrated to Palestine in 1934 and continued to work for the Zionist organization, officially and unofficially, throughout his life.

Martin Buber, in a
photograph taken in
1916.

The first issue of *Der
Jude*, 1916–17.

Der Jude

EINE MONATSSCHRIFT

ERSTER JAHRGANG
1916 * 1917

R. LÖWIT VERLAG
BERLIN * WIEN

Riesser's publication of the same name nearly a century earlier.

By 1912, the radical faction led by Kurt Blumenfeld was ready to push the German Zionist movement to its logical extreme. At the organization's convention in Posen, members of the faction proposed and won passage of a resolution that made it the duty of every member "to incorporate emigration to Palestine in his life program. In any case, every Zionist should establish for himself a personal [presumably economic] interest in Palestine." The resolution created a storm of discussion in the Jewish community, and the controversy brought to the fore what Blumenfeld called the post-assimilatory position of the Zionist movement as it attempted to chart Jewish life in the Diaspora.

What emerged was the personal quality of German Zionism and its difference from the movement in Eastern Europe. There the Jews lived in homogeneous communities but under the constant threat of persecution. As a consequence, they looked to large political answers such as socialism or Zionism. Their German counterparts, by contrast, were living comfortably but seeking solutions to their private dilemmas; in the memoirs of the period Zionism takes on an almost religious meaning. One of the leaders of the youth movement, Siegfried Kanowitz, described its effect on his generation: "Our essential nature was not changed; we did not emigrate to Palestine, but we found a new strength in ourselves, we found a new meaning for our lives. . . . It brought about the miracle of rebirth." Lichtheim, too, used the religious term *Bekenntnis* (confession), and even the usually logical Kurt Blumenfeld could only speak of "revelation" to describe what had brought him into the Zionist fold.

The divisions in the adult community were reflected in the universities, where Jewish students were exposed more steadily than their elders to the frankest anti-Semitism, ranging from social slights to academic quotas and exclusions. Jewish self-defense took a particularly physical turn there in order to cope with the aristocratic student organizations whose members were unabashedly open in their disdain. In 1886, a group of Jewish students in Breslau organized a fencing club whose main purpose was to defend Jewish honor by challenging offenders

to duels. Its very existence was problematic, for the gentile clubs at first questioned whether Jews were even permissible as dueling partners. Nonetheless, the idea was immensely appealing to young Jews incensed by the insults for which they had no other ready form of response, and it spread rapidly to other universities. Modeling themselves on existing student corporations, they adopted uniforms, caps, and colors as the others did and also engaged in regular physical training so that their challenges were no empty threats.

Claiming its place in the university, the Breslau group called itself Viadrina, from the Latin name of the university, Leopoldina Viadrina. The mixture of bellicosity and hope that had propelled them to form the Viadrina was displayed in their banner, which incorporated the symbols of their ideas, among them three intertwined rings, a reference to the parable of the rings in Lessing's *Nathan the Wise*. Their motto was *nemo me impune lacessit,* "no one injures me with impunity."

Much of the same spirit moved the Jewish students in Berlin to form the dueling fraternity Sprevia in 1894. The name was taken from the river Spree, which flows through the city, but their colors—yellow, white, and black—were grounded in Jewish history. In one of their songs they explain the yellow: "What was once a mark of shame became a mark of honor and a memorial to the guilt of our enemies."

In 1896, there were five color fraternities in Germany, which formed a federation called Kartell-Convent der Verbindung deutscher Studenten jüdischen Glaubens (Convention of Fraternities of German Students of the Jewish Faith), known as the K-C. In their constitution, adopted in 1908, they affirmed that their purpose was both "the fight against anti-Semitism among German students and the education of their members as self-confident Jews," who were, nonetheless, "inextricably bound to the German fatherland by history, culture and a community of law."

Choosing words rather than sabers as their weapons, the Zionist youth also organized at the universities. Although a number of Jewish organizations had existed from as early as 1882, the first committed to Zionist principles was the Hasmonea, founded in Berlin in 1902. In the

next few years, Jordania was established at Munich and Ivrai at Freiburg. Just as the Jewish dueling fraternities took Latin names based on their university or locality, the Zionist groups also took Latin names but with Hebrew associations. They too adopted colors, sashes, and caps, held weekly drinking parties, wrote songbooks, and used the same hierarchical structure as other student corporations. In form, at least, they mirrored the university world.

In 1906, three of these groups met and formed a federation, the Kartell Zionistischer Verbindungen. Then, after an intense campaign spearheaded by Kurt Blumenfeld, it won over a less ideological group, the Bund Jüdischer Corporationen, to the banner of Zionism. In 1914, the two united, vowing to educate their members to a consciousness of Jewish unity and to defend the renewal of the land of Israel.

Whereas the K-C was directed outward, priding itself on the pugnacity by which it hoped to intimidate or suppress expressions of anti-Semitism, the Zionists were more inward, study-

Maccabaea, the Zionist student organization at the university in Berlin, 1906–07. Note that the officers are dressed in the same style as the members of the K-C. The central figure, in uniform, is Felix Rosenblüth, who changed his name to Pinhas Rosen when he emigrated to Palestine in 1923. After independence he served as minister of justice from 1948 to 1962. The bearded alumnus in the front row is Arthur Biram, principal of the Reali High School in Haifa from 1920 to 1948.

Members of the Bund
Jüdischer Corpora-
tionen in 1907.

ing the Jewish past and Jewish culture while affirming the Jewish position in the contemporary world. This high self-consciousness extended beyond the university to include a variety of youth groups whose politics ranged from German nationalist to labor Zionist positions. Emancipation, as it turned out, had not been the final answer to the Jewish question, and in Germany there were many solutions as to how Jews were to live. Jews had won their legal rights, but, as Ludwig Holländer, the leader of the Centralverein, often pointed out, they were still stepchildren. Whether they were to be "doubly good" (as Holländer recommended) or challenge the place that had been assigned to them was the stuff of controversy in the community during the empire.

Modern Anti-Semitism

In the nineteenth century, political philosophers, economists, and eventually politicians discovered that the idea of race could move men and win allegiances and votes. One of the first to test this premise was Adolf Stoecker, the court preacher at the Berlin church attended by the Imperial household. Stoecker's ambitions, however, extended beyond these aristocratic circles; in 1878 he launched the Christian Social Workers party, whose purpose was to draw the working poor back to Christianity. More concretely, it was to win them from the Social Democratic party, which they had embraced as representing their interests.

Troubled by the social changes that industrialization brought in its wake, conservatives denounced those very symbols of modernity—capitalism and urbanism—that had freed the worker from a condition little better than serfdom. In their place Stoecker offered appeals to folk memory, loyalty to the monarchy, and the consolations of religion.

In March 1879, Wilhelm Marr, a disappointed revolutionary and unsuccessful journalist, further muddied the political waters by publishing a pamphlet, *The Victory of Judaism over Germanism*. Marr maintained that in winning emancipation for themselves, the Jews had come to control the German economy. "In all branches of life," he wrote, "the way to success proceeds through Jewish mediation. The very struggle for existence is no longer possible without Jewry taking its commission." Until the "indolent" German bear roused itself in some great upheaval, however, Marr could only predict *finis Germaniae* as the fate of his nation.

By September 1879, the *Allgemeine Zeitung des Judenthums,* which had reviewed Marr's pamphlet severely when it appeared, grew concerned by the direction of public opinion. To characterize Marr and his supporters, it introduced the word *Antisemiten*—anti-Semites. This was a term whose time had come, for shortly thereafter the formation of the Anti-Semitic League was announced.

In the same month, Stoecker decided to change the target of his ambitions; addressing himself to small shopkeepers, clerks, and artisans, he delivered his first anti-Semitic sermon. With his new message and in these circles he

Adolf Stoecker (1835–1909) was a court preacher and politician, member of the Prussian Legislative Assembly and of the Reichstag, and founder of the Christian Social Party. This photograph was taken in 1902.

"Greeting from Borkum." This postcard from Borkum, a popular resort on the North Sea, shows a Jewish family being refused admission to a hotel. The "Borkum Song" printed below the drawing of the rejoicing diners concludes with the verse, "Whoever approaches with flat feet, / With crooked nose and kinky hair . . .; / He must be sent away, sent away [*hinaus*]." The verse is echoed in the handwritten message, "Hurrah hinaus!"

was a success, so much so that he renamed his party the Christian Social party, dropping the word *worker.*

The battlefield moved to the university in November when Heinrich von Treitschke, a prominent professor of history in Berlin, published the first of a series of articles on the "Jewish question." Treitschke, a passionate German nationalist and monarchist, feared the rise of a democratic pluralistic state that labor and minorities might dominate. If Jews would abandon their religion and their Jewish ways, he argued, if they would intermarry and so vanish as a separate entity, the Jewish question would be solved. But in the meantime, he denounced the "trouser-selling" Jews from Eastern Europe and then, as if only reporting what was being said in well-bred circles, introduced the fateful phrase, "The Jews are our misfortune." The phrase would reverberate into the twentieth century, when it was adopted by the Nazis.

The agitation reached a popular climax in June 1880 when a high-school teacher and an army lieutenant circulated what was popularly called "The Anti-Semites' Petition" and gathered the signatures of 250,000 citizens. Addressed to the German chancellor, it asked that Jews be limited to subordinate positions in the state, that they be prevented from teaching German children, and that the number of Jewish immigrants be limited. Although the petition represented many voices, it also aroused wide protest, not only from Jews.

In November 1880, Theodor Mommsen, the distinguished professor of Roman history at the University of Berlin joined with other notables in decrying the inflaming of public sentiment against the Jews—the *Judenhetze*—likening it to a contagious disease. Even more significant was his pamphlet *Another Word about Our Jewry,* clearly intended as a reply to Treitschke. His concern, he wrote, was not only to combat Treitschke's argument against the Jews but also to put forth his own observations about the fragmentation of German society since 1848 and the first attempt at unification. He defended the Jews' rights as citizens and as Germans, citing Heine as an illustrious example. Yet for him Europe was essentially a Christian civilization, and although Mommsen was opposed to religious domination of the state, he deplored Jewish particularism. Certainly, he thought, those Jews who were no longer observant should convert,

wir daher in keiner Weise verbürgen. Danach soll Marr's Pamphlet die zehnte Auflage erreicht haben — darauf käme es nun wenig an, vielmehr auf die Höhe der Auflagen — er will es als Tractätchen in 150,000 Exemplaren verbreiten — wir wollen abwarten, ob er dies ausführen könne – er habe Freunde gefunden und durch diese werde das „antisemitische Wochenblatt" zu Stande kommen — das wird die Welt auch nicht erschüttern — das erste Feldgeschrei, das er erheben wolle, werde sein: „Wählet keinen Juden!" Würde Marr hiermit Anklang und Erfolg finden, so würde dies nicht etwa ein Unglück für die Juden sein, deren Vertreter die Abgeordneten jüdischer Religion ja gar nicht sind, sondern nur ein schwerer Schaden für das deutsche Volk. Denn es könnte diesem vor dem Angesichte der ganzen civilisirten Welt nur zur Schande gereichen, sich vor dem Einflusse von fünf oder sechs Abgeordneten zu fürchten, und dann hat das deutsche Parlament durchaus keinen solchen Reichthum an bedeutenden Parlamentariern, daß es so leichthin eine Anzahl tüchtiger Männer, als solche bezeichnet sie ja eben das Benehmen der Gegner erst recht, entbehren könne. Daß aber ein solcher

The term *anti-Semitic,* used in quotation marks as a neologism, first appeared in a Jewish newspaper reporting on the activities of Wilhelm Marr: "He is supposed to have found friends and through them the 'anti-Semitic weekly' will be brought into being." *Allgemeine Zeitung des Judenthums,* September 2, 1879.

Heinrich von Treitschke (1834–1896).

Heinrich von Treitschke's tirade against the Jews in Germany, first published in 1879, encapsulated many of the standing prejudices and coined slogans that were used to great effect by the Nazis. Here are two of the best known passages from a pamphlet published in 1881 that reprinted the original articles.

The number of Jews in Western Europe is so small that they cannot exert any palpable influence over our national culture; but across our eastern border, out of the inexhaustible Polish cradle, there stream every year the ambitious trouser-selling youths whose children and children's children will one day dominate Germany's stock exchange and the press. . . .

When one reviews all these relationships [of the Jews in society] . . . then the noisy agitation of the moment appears as brutal and spiteful, but also a natural reaction of the Germanic folk-feeling against an alien element that has taken up much too large a space in our life. . . . It is indeed an advantage that an evil that everyone felt and no one wanted to touch can be discussed openly. Let us not deceive ourselves: the movement is very deep and strong; a few jokes about the slogans of Christian Social soap-box orators are not enough to suppress them. It reaches up into circles of highest cultivation, among men who would reject every thought of religious intolerance or national arrogance; it resounds today from every mouth: "The Jews are our misfortune!"

Heinrich von Treitschke, Ein Wort über unser Judentum, *Berlin, 1881.*

and in time, if they were not pressured, the others would too. The price for integration had to be allowing Judaism to lapse so that the Jews could coalesce into the German nation.

Such a view was of course deeply offensive to many Jews, however much they may have been aware of Mommsen's good intentions. It illustrates how little Jews and non-Jews sometimes understood about one another's aims. Mommsen continued as an active supporter of Jewish rights and became a member of one of the first defense organizations against anti-Semitism. In a famous interview in 1893, he spoke out fiercely: "Scum remains scum, and anti-Semitism is the sentiment of scum. It is like a horrible epidemic, like cholera, that one can neither explain nor heal." He urged his interviewer to write a statement of protest that would be signed by "all the most important men of Europe. . . . Then at least we could rescue our honor in the eyes of our grandchildren."

The seesaw of anti-Semitism began to rock. Stoecker was elected to the Reichstag on an anti-Semitic platform in 1881; this was also the year that saw the condemnation of the anti-Semitic outbursts by two quite different groups—2,500 electors of the Berlin provincial diet (Landtag) and 3,000 Berlin workers. As the decade went on, a rising number of anti-Semites were elected to the Reichstag—five in 1890 and sixteen in 1893. Then, in the mid-1890s, as general prosperity returned after some years of slow economic growth and real hardship, anti-Semitic politicians found their support shrinking, and after 1900, however many problems remained, Germans and Jews entered into a period called, perhaps a shade too cheerfully, the German-Jewish symbiosis.

Soon new and severe tests challenged that symbiosis: war, defeat, and revolution. The short-lived German Empire was brought down after the First World War, a conflict that started in a paroxysm of patriotism in which the Jews were caught up with the rest of the nation. On August 4, 1914, the day the war began, the kaiser received the principal officers of the political parties as well as representatives of the various religions in his palace in Berlin. In asking for their support, he pledged his own policy of unity: "I no longer recognize any parties," he said, "I recognize only Germans, and as a sign that you are firmly determined to stand together

"Germany at War,"
August 4, 1914.

Passover Seder of German-Jewish soldiers at Metz. 1917.

David Katz was born in Langen, Hesse, in 1898 and was drafted into the German army at the age of eighteen. He wrote these recollections of World War I in Jerusalem in 1944.

And so we sat hunched over on our blankets in this damp burrow, reciting the Haggadah by the light of a candle. The burrow rose and sank, the candle repeatedly threatened to go out because of the air pressure from the shells bursting around us, and rolling like continual thunder with ever-returning echoes. None of this disturbed us any longer. This night I asked myself honestly, Why is this night different from all other nights? and found the answer in the full bitterness of the hours that we were now experiencing and that made the symbol of the bitter herbs superfluous. A stream of hot tears delivered the salt water [used in the ceremony] which I suddenly could not hold back, even though as "tough soldiers" we felt ourselves hardened against any sentimentality. Schreyer [his superior officer] appeared to me now as a severe, merciless taskmaster who for months had not spared any means in order to destroy me. . . . I felt myself suddenly in the midst of the Egyptian tyranny and understood parts of the Haggadah that had, until now, seemed to me innocuous tales from Biblical times. . . . Now all distance had vanished and I cried out with our Fathers to God to free us from this oppressive yoke.

David Katz. *"Frontjahre im ersten Weltkrieg,"* Bulletin des Leo Baeck Instituts, *1988.*

with me through thick and thin, through danger and death, without distinction of party, without distinction of rank or religion, I ask that the leaders of the parties come forward and swear their solemn oath before me."

In a nation that entered the war with enthusiasm, the kaiser's ringing words, *Ich kenne keine Parteien mehr* (I no longer recognize any parties), were taken up as a symbol of a new spirit of unity and brotherhood. The slogan appeared everywhere—on banners, placards, even shaving mugs—and represented the first stages of goodwill in the war. But the bureaucracy moved in its familiar ways, and Jews soon found that their applications for advancement in the army or admission to the officer corps were treated with the old contempt. Among the rank-and-file, Jews who otherwise might not have thought about their religion were often brutally reminded of their origins by bigoted officers. As a consequence, at the Jewish holidays soldiers were drawn together in part through the heightened emotions of their wartime situation, in part in search of the brotherhood of a common past.

In the midst of the war, when many young Jewish lives had already been lost, the Jewish community was stunned by a new development. In June 1916, an anti-Semitic representative in the Reichstag addressed a question to the Minister of War: "How many Jews are serving at the front?" The intent of the question was clearly to provoke a reply that would show Jews as shirkers, an allegation widespread in anti-Semitic circles. Thus challenged, the War Ministry launched a full-fledged Jewish census (*Judenzählung*). The various Jewish organizations, after deciding against a public demonstration, sent vigorous protests to the ministry, only to receive the bland reply that "the gathering of material concerning the participation of German Jews in the field was permitted." Then, despite the inevitable rumors that surrounded the census, the ministry would not release the results, declaring that they "were intended only for the information of the War Ministry."

This last insult by the German Reich continued to gnaw away at Jews in Germany long after the war was over and long after the empire had been dissolved. Jews knew that they had served and suffered in the bitter and bloody struggle, and they were determined to prove it, although it was questionable whether anyone was listening.

Graves of Jewish soldiers killed in World War I, in the Jewish cemetery Weissensee in Berlin.

A rural Jewish family sitting near their tiled stove in Franconia. Etching by Johann Christoph Erhard, 1817.

Rural Jews

For all but the last hundred years of their existence in the German lands, the Jews were country dwellers living in small towns and rural villages, particularly in the Rhineland, the oldest area of Jewish settlement, and later in the provinces of Posen and Silesia. Even in the first decades of the nineteenth century, 90 percent of the Jews in Germany still lived in small villages, most of them in great poverty. After the middle of the century, the situation of the rural Jews substantially improved. Nearly 120,000 German Jews emigrated during the nineteenth century, particularly from such desperate areas as Bavaria, which allowed only one child in each family to settle where he was born. As the villages emptied of young Jews, there were mounting opportunities for those who were left. The wretched poor vanished, and the richest families also abandoned the villages for the towns, leaving the comfortable middle as the characteristic Jewish rural family by the end of the century.

The Jews in Posen and Silesia occupied a doubly marginal position. Silesia, which had been annexed by Prussia in 1742, and Posen, which was granted to Prussia in 1815 at the Congress of Vienna, contained large Polish-speaking populations. As the Prussian government took vigorous measures to introduce the German language and culture into these provinces, the Jews were among those who learned German; thus they stood as a third party, outside both the Polish and the German ethnic groups and yet allied culturally with the Germans in language and education. Their cultural role was particularly visible in the city of Posen, where the German officials were rotated for their term of service and the number of resident Christian German families was relatively small. "As a consequence," recounts Adolph Asch, a lawyer born in Posen in 1881, "the established Posen Jews, for whom German was their mother tongue, felt themselves to be the representative of the German middle class [*Bürgertum*] despite their second-class standing in society."

At one extreme were those Jews nourished by the talmudic traditions, whose premier exponents were perhaps exemplified by the Eger family. Rabbi Akiva Eger the Younger, born in 1761, the best-known member of the family, was a model of talmudic learning, the founder of a large yeshiva, and an outspoken opponent of secular education as well as of the new Jewish religious reform movement. His son Solomon continued the family opposition to reform, and his grandson Judah Loeb became a hasidic holy man (*zaddik*) presiding over a congregation in Lublin. At the same time, the region produced figures prominent in the secular world: the historian Heinrich Graetz, the politician Eduard Lasker, and the composer Louis Lewandowski. It is perhaps symbolic that the conservative rabbinical seminary under Zacharias Frankel was located in Breslau, the point of confluence between East and West.

In 1910, there were 40,000 Jews in Posen and 50,000 in Silesia, but their numbers steadily decreased as many emigrated to Berlin. Horse-trading was a principal activity for those who remained, but the Jews here as elsewhere were also manufacturers, merchants, artisans and laborers, ranging from well-to-do businessmen to poor peddlers on the land who bought and sold rabbit skins.

In southwest Germany, by contrast, cattle trading was the backbone of Jewish existence. In 1917, a survey counted 40,000 cattle dealers in

The Meyer family of Bardewisch (Oldenburg) at the turn of the century.

Market square in Breslau.

Germany, 25,000 of whom were Jews. In this as in their other functions in the countryside, the Jews were middlemen—peddlers, intermediaries between town and country, and, after emancipation, shopkeepers. In addition, significant numbers worked for the Jewish community as rabbis, teachers, cantors, and slaughterers. As middlemen they bought and carried the peasants' produce to market and returned with manufactured goods and cattle to sell in their villages. Many of these dealers also became moneylenders, either lending cash outright or selling cattle and other goods on credit according to established custom.

The usefulness of this classic social function, which for centuries had been condemned by the church as immoral, was not really appreciated until the latter part of the nineteenth century. Then local officials suddenly became aware, as they wrote in their reports, of how the Jews "were satisfying the economic needs of the widely scattered rural population," activities that were essential to the well-being of the neighborhood. More informally, the Jewish peddler also brought news of political and social events in the great world, market prices for produce and cattle, local gossip, and, inevitably, a breath of town life.

For these wanderers in the countryside or the cattle dealers who had a long way to travel between home and market, it was a hard and lonely

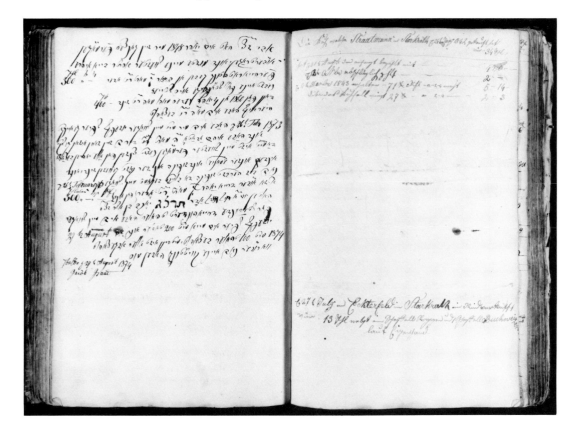

Pages from the record book of a cattle dealer. The left-hand page, which notes the transfer of property in 1848, is in German written in Hebrew script yet follows standard German spelling; note the umlaut in the last word of the first line, *vermögen*. The right-hand page, written in ordinary German, records the sale of a cow to Straatmann on June 24, 1824, for thirty-four thaler and lists the installment payments.

Jewish traders selling a cow to a gentile, Zizenhausen, Germany, ca. 1840. The inscription on the base reads, "As true as I live, she gives two bucketsful a day."

life. They were on the road for the whole week, returning to their villages late on Thursday or early Friday morning to be home for the Sabbath. Each peddler in fact had his own territory called the *medine,* the Yiddish-Hebrew word for a country, whose boundaries were strictly defined. Since most of these travelers were observant Jews, they suffered a further disadvantage because they could eat no cooked food while on the road. Instead, they lived on the bread and sausage they took with them and drank only black coffee without milk and sometimes a glass of the ritually permitted brandy.

Anti-Semitism in the country, simpler in content there than in the cities, was also steadier. Whereas in the towns visible anti-Semitism rose and fell with changing economic and political conditions, in rural neighborhoods the Jew remained always the Other. The fundamental divider was of course religion, with the Jew's position as the universal creditor a further source of alienation. If a peasant could not meet a payment due his landlord or another creditor, it was the Jew from whom he had borrowed who was the villain; as during the riots after the revolution of 1848, one of the first acts of violence was the destruction of the ledgers of Jewish moneylenders.

This left a residue of carefulness and watchfulness that Jews impressed on their children from their earliest days. Always lurking in the background was *risches,* a word whose literal Yiddish meaning—malice—had been extended by German Jews to mean anti-Semitism. "It was an unspoken duty," wrote Max Spangenthal, who grew up in a Hessian village, "to avoid everything that might provoke *risches* . . . rushing about, emphatic gesticulation, loud talking, careless dress." All these were considered the telltale characteristics of the Jew and were consciously suppressed. The same standards were applied to the synagogue, but "the noisy, loud prayer only gave way quite late to the 'orderly, correct' style of worship." For non-Jews, therefore, any noisy gathering was a "Jewish synagogue," a *Judenschul.* As Spangenthal remembered, "From the middle of the nineteenth century, the progressive-minded community officers, who paid attention above all to decorum, engaged in a long struggle and banned from our community unconstrained behavior during the

services. . . . Everything proceeded in the politest manner and in stiffly regulated order; on Saturday one appeared in a dark suit, and on holidays in a top hat. . . . The spontaneity and emotional gratification that was lost with the bourgeois respectability was probably regretted in the first generation after emancipation. In our time [the early twentieth century], its loss was no longer felt."

Severely divided though they were by religion, there were edges where the boundaries between the gentile and Jewish communities merged and local custom overtook religious belief. During the Hanukkah-Christmas season, Jewish women baked *Lebkuchen,* the traditional Christmas honey cakes, as part of their own festival. And at Passover, Christians expected a gift of matzah from their Jewish neighbors, which they carefully preserved in the house to ward off lightning. And in Catholic parts of the country, Jews adorned their houses with green branches for Corpus Christi as other villagers did.

The decoration of the synagogues also reflected local tastes as well as the generally modest resources of the communities: not for these rural houses of prayer the marble and gilt of the city synagogues. As in the neighboring country churches, Jewish communities contented themselves with wooden pillars painted to imitate marble and with carvings of emblematic lions that had their own charm even if not entirely accurate. Quite exceptional, however, were the four synagogues in southwest Germany decorated between 1733 and 1740 by an itinerant painter from Eastern Europe, Eliezer ben Solomon Sussman of Brody. Bringing country art to a new level, he covered walls and ceilings with a richly colored interlace of flowers, fruits, animals, religious symbols, and views of the heavenly Jerusalem. Depending on artistry instead of opulent materials, his style accorded well with the rural setting while providing a glowing, exuberant background for worship.

The Jews, then, who lived side by side with the peasants in the rural villages, spoke their language, attended the same schools, and shared much of their way of life, also lived as a community apart much more consciously than did their city brethren. Indeed, the Jewish communities in the rural areas retained Yiddish in

The synagogue in Kassel. Taking the scroll of the law out of the ark, 1898. Engraving by Wilhelm Thielmann.

Carved and painted Torah ark, Westheim bei Hassfurt, Bavaria, eighteenth century.

East wall of the synagogue at Blechhofen near Ansbach. Painted by Eliezer Sussmann in 1733.

their speech into the twentieth century, and Yiddish words permeated the local language. Rural Jewish communities also remained more observant than their city counterparts and had a much lower rate of intermarriage.

Whereas from the perspective of the town, rural Jews seemed most conservative in their habits, on the land they seemed like restless spirits, traveling from village to village, to cities and markets, buying and selling. This steady recourse to town and market, which the peasant might attend only once a year, inevitably gave the Jews a keener sense of the world as well as a broader outlook. It was often a Jew, therefore, who was the first in a village to try such innovations as the electric light, the telephone, even the automobile.

Just as the peddler who came to the farmsteads brought with him a touch of the outside world, that same aura clung to Jews in their villages. The ways of the city and the world beyond were part of his life, however long he or his family had been settled in the country. In their houses Jews lived differently from the rest of the neighborhood, often with a piano in the parlor, which was used regularly by the family and not reserved for ceremonial occasions. They ate differently and had a reputation for being kinder to their servants and workers than were the peasants. And friendly as the Jewish and gentile children may have been in their village schools, as they grew toward marriageable age their paths separated. The Jews were readier to send their children to another town for education or training. Their daughters, especially, often left their village permanently when they married. The double life was probably nowhere lived more visibly than in the village, which offered neither the anonymity nor the neutral zones of the city. Individuals were born to a people, to a class, to a station, and for all but the exceptional, that was how they lived out their days.

East European Jews in Germany

For Jews from Eastern Europe, Germany was both a place and a state of mind. Most who came were migrants fleeing pogroms and poverty, but a small number came in search of a life and ideas different from those they had inherited. A third group consisted of rabbis, teachers, cantors, and other religious functionaries, who had long

been imported by the German Jewish congregations and who represented the tradition that had united the Jews of the German lands and of Eastern Europe until the eighteenth century.

Two mass movements unleashed by violence at home sent East European Jews into Germany before World War I. The first, in the seventeenth century, came in the wake of pogroms initiated by the Cossack leader Bogdan Chmielnicki in the Ukraine in 1648; the Russo-Swedish war of 1655 only renewed the exodus. From the time of the refugees' arrival, the official German attitude toward them could be measured by the innumerable decrees prohibiting their settlement and severely defining the conditions of their passage. They were no less a problem for the established Jewish communities in Germany, which attempted to take in at least some of these wanderers by semilegal strategies—claiming them as household servants or apprentices in their workshops or as functionaries of the community. But a private attitude was reflected in a Hebrew verse that came into currency just before the first influx in 1648:

The first day he is a guest,
The second day he is a pest,
The third day is his last.

The first flight, inspired by terror, was extended by poverty, so that there was a continuing trickle of unwanted Jews across German borders. By the end of the eighteenth century, 10,000–15,000 had arrived, but since only a few were permitted to settle, they became a permanent wandering class of begging Jews, *Betteljuden.*

The second westward movement, which began in the 1880s in response to pogroms in Russia and continued into the twentieth century, brought the number of Eastern Jews in Germany before the First World War to 90,000. Repeated catastrophes in the East made them an ever-renewing population for the West. The refugees from the pogroms of the 1880s were succeeded by those who fled after the Kishinev massacre of 1903, a pogrom in which 49 Jews were killed and 2,000 families left homeless in the wake of mob fury. The revolution of 1905, together with a second pogrom, led many more to flee. Nor did it require violent events to propel the Jews westward: the unending want and the limited horizons of their lives sent many East European Jews out into the Western world.

Jewish beggar, early
nineteenth century.

Like immigrant groups everywhere, these Jews clustered together carrying on their autonomous life just as they had in the villages of Eastern Europe. Bringing the dress and language of the shtetl with them, they were living caricatures of everything the German Jews thought they had left behind. Yiddish, which had still been spoken in Germany half a century earlier, was now all but forgotten and fell strangely on German ears. Despite its German foundation, it no longer sounded like modern German although the occasional word or phrase was intelligible. Jews and non-Jews alike called it a jargon, as if it were somehow a debased form of German. This peculiar language, which became a tempting target for dialect jokes, made these odd-looking strangers seem all the more ludicrous.

Their agglomeration in the big cities, particularly Berlin, made the Eastern Jews a highly visible sector of the population. In 1910, some 21,000 Jews, nearly a quarter of the immigrant Jews in the empire, were concentrated there. In the famous Scheunenviertel in the center of the capital, which was home to about a quarter of the immigrants, the men continued to wear hasidic garb and the stores advertised their wares in Yiddish more often than in German. Naturally, these Jews founded their own synagogues where they could pray in the manner and with the cantillation they knew. The mixed choirs, the organ, and the music of German synagogues were as alien to the inhabitants of the Scheunenviertel as were the services in the nearby church.

In Munich, the 3,000 Jews from the East clustered around the Gärtner-Platz and established many little synagogues divided not by differences in ritual but by nationality. Galicians, Russians, and Lithuanians each had their own place of worship, some with fewer than fifty members. But these *shtiblach* (little rooms) satisfied the need for a familiar environment, for the company of countrymen, and for a place where the buffeted immigrant was master in his own house. Leipzig and Dresden in Saxony were such popular places of settlement for Eastern Jews that by 1910 they outnumbered the native Jewish population. Of the 9,000 Jews in Leipzig, 6,000 were immigrants, and they accounted for 2,000 of the 3,700 Jews in Dresden.

Unlike earlier generations of newcomers,

In the Jewish quarter
of Berlin, 1928.

**Alexander Granach, who arrived in Berlin from Galicia in
1905, became a prominent actor after studying at the Max
Reinhardt school.**

*People explained to me how to get to the Scheunenviertel, and sud-
denly I was in the midst of a neighborhood like Lemberg [Lvov]: Grenadierstrasse, Dragonerstrasse, Mulackstrasse, Ritterstrasse,
Schendelgasse. . . . Little narrow, dark alleys with fruit and vegetable
stands at the street corners. Women with painted faces, with great
keys in their hands loitered about, as in the Zosina-Wolja Gasse in
Stanislau or in the Spitalna in Lemberg. Many stores, restaurants,
dairies, bakeries with the sign "kosher" displayed in their windows. Jews
went about dressed as in Galicia, Romania, or Russia. Those who had
no businesses dealt in pictures or furniture which they sold on the installment plan. Others went peddling with tablecloths, towels, sus-
penders, shoe laces, collar buttons, stockings and ladies' underwear.
Others went from house to house buying old clothes, which were then
bought up by wholesalers who sold them in turn back to the old home
countries. Most of the men and women in this neighborhood, though,
were workers who had jobs in the cigarette factories of Manoli, Gar-
bati, or Muratti.*

Alexander Granach, Da geht ein Mensch. Autobiographischer Roman, *Berlin-Grunewald, n.d.*

who had been condemned to live as wandering beggars by exclusionary legislation, the Jews from Eastern Europe who settled in the German cities after the 1880s quickly took their place in the working class. They were artisans, tailors, furriers, shoemakers, and cigar makers; often they combined retail sales with their crafts and became proprietors of small shops. In 1914 in Leipzig, which had been the center of the fur trade since the seventeenth century, half the registered firms were in Jewish hands.

The concentration of Jews in small businesses and independent crafts was shaped as much by a policy of avoidance as by opportunity. Many of them were reluctant to work on the Sabbath, and the fear of anti-Semitism deterred some of the immigrants from applying for jobs with large firms. This led Jews to seek employment with other Jews or, after they had accumulated some capital, to establish their own workshops and retail stores. Unlike in the United States, where the clothing industry was the main employer of Jewish immigrants, in Germany the East European Jews scattered across a wide range of occupations. Although poorer on the whole than the settled German Jews, they followed the same pattern in their choice of work. Half were concentrated in commerce, with an additional 35–40 percent making their living as artisans and manual laborers. This was an intensely industrious immigrant group; as a count in 1925 showed, nine out of ten were employed.

Jewish immigrants to Germany, like their counterparts in the United States, sent their children to state schools for a secular education rather than to traditional religious schools; often they supported them through the university. The second generation, therefore, included professionals, businessmen, and a number of rabbis, cantors, and teachers who had been educated in the new rabbinical seminaries established in Germany instead of in the yeshivas of the East. This was a generation that moved quickly to take its place in the surrounding German world, although it did not produce the outstanding figures that emerged in America.

Those who came from the Austro-Hungarian Empire, where they had learned German as children, found it easier to make their way in Germany. The publisher Samuel Fischer, the violinists Joseph Joachim and Leopold von Auer, all from Hungary, as well as many opera singers and actors, were reminders of the East European Jewish presence.

Germany had a special fascination for Eastern Jewish intellectuals as the apotheosis of Western learning. Salomon Maimon was, as we have seen, perhaps the first to leave a record of what Germany meant to an East European Jew. After he had lived there for a number of years, he was pressed by his wife either to return to Poland or give her a divorce. Recounting the episode, he wrote that he "had happily emancipated myself from the fetters of superstition and prejudice, had abandoned the rude manner of life in which I had been brought up, and had extended my knowledge in many directions. I could not return to my former barbarous and wretched conditions, rob myself of all advantages I had gained and expose myself to rabbinical anger over the smallest deviation from rabbinical law and every free expression of thought." His wife returned to Poland with her divorce and her son; Maimon remained in Germany.

Germany appealed to young rebels who not only craved secular learning but at the same time rejected the world they knew. The words *barbarous* and *superstitious* recur in their memoirs too often for accident. Many of these young Jews arrived with only a sketchy knowledge of German, sometimes self-taught out of grammars so that they could decline weak verbs perfectly but could not put together a coherent sentence. In his memoirs, Jakob Fromer, born in Lodz in 1865, describes his secret struggle to learn German while a yeshiva student in Poland. To read, he had to use two dictionaries: first German-Russian and then Russian-Hebrew. Nor was he alone in his laborious efforts to penetrate another world. By the end of the nineteenth century, the yeshivas of Eastern Europe were honeycombed with skeptics. Books were passed from hand to hand, and groups sometimes met to read together in hidden places by moonlight. They read in a totally unsystematic and undiscriminating way, as excited by penny novels as by Schiller. They read philosophy and mathematics using the methods of studying talmudic texts, memorizing pages at a gulp. Nor did they shrink from learning Latin and Greek in order to read the classics.

Above all, they read surreptitiously because in the eyes of the community, trafficking in such knowledge was little short of heresy, and to be

Metamorphose

(Zeichnungen von Th. Th. Heine)

Moische Piſch handelte in Tarnopol mit abgelegten Kleidern,

als Moritz Waſſerſtrahl ſiedelte er nach Poſen über und handelte mit Pariſer Modewaren

jetzt lebt er als Maurice Lafontaine in Berlin, wo er eine neue Kunſtrichtung gegründet hat und mit abgelegter Pariſer Kunſtmode handelt.

discovered meant abuse and humiliation for the culprit. Their teachers were correct in principle, of course, if not in fact. Reading Schiller did not immediately lead to the baptismal font, but it did drive a wedge between the student and Jewish tradition. For many, it shook the foundations of their faith. And for the sake of this foreign yet liberating world of knowledge, they broke with their homes and families to attend universities abroad and steep themselves in Western learning. When the immigrants compared life in Germany to the poverty and degradation they knew, it seemed "a land blessed by God, a paradise."

The vision of Germany that drew them was of a world of plenty, of order, opportunity, and reasonable relationships between people. "People there," Jakob Fromer was told by a friend who had lived in Germany, "ate three or four times a day, and had meat at least once a day, dressed neatly and lived in a way that was worthy of the dignity of a human being. Everyone had his own recognized profession and did not need, as in the ghetto, to puzzle out every morning when he woke up how he would make his living that day." Even private life seemed to be conducted so as to guarantee happiness. "If he had a wife, he could go for a walk with her, and have a rational conversation," an invidious reference to the

"Metamorphosis: Moische Piss deals in used clothes in Tarnopol. As Moritz Waterjet he emigrates to Posen, where he deals in fashionable clothing from Paris. Now he lives as Maurice LaFontaine in Berlin, where he has established a new artistic fashion and deals in second-hand Parisian art." Drawing by Thomas Theodore Heine in *Simplicissimus*, June 2, 1903.

strict boundaries that separated men and women in the Orthodox Jewish world. "They were people who tasted their lives to the full, who were able to bring all their strengths and abilities into play and could use their intellectual gifts freely and rationally."

Not all these rebels were starry-eyed and poverty-stricken yeshiva students. A considerable number came from well-to-do families, who sent their children abroad for education but expected them to return to practice their profession at home. Some were socialists or revolutionaries in flight from their government; others were seeking the technical training in medicine and the sciences for which Germany was famous. The numbers were always modest, of course. In 1886, only 129 foreign Jewish students gained admittance to the universities in the empire. But by the academic year 1905–06, following the revolution in Russia, the number had grown to 483, making up more than a quarter of the Jewish student population in Germany. Once there, however, they had little contact with the German Jewish students, except for the Zionists. Excluded from the Jewish fencing societies, they formed their own organizations. Without the flash of sabers or the decoration of uniforms, these groups offered the fellowship of their shared past with the urgency of intellectual inquiry.

The separation of the East European Jewish students from their German Jewish fellow students was only a special case of a more general phenomenon. Socially at least, Eastern and German Jews led totally separate lives; where they were not divided by language, they were often divided by culture. The East European Jews who came as poor workers, inept in Western ways, speaking faulty German, felt accurately enough that the German Jews looked down on them as uncouth. What they valued and knew—Jewish learning and tradition—suddenly had no currency in their new world, while the term *Ostjude,* Eastern Jew, itself carried a pejorative overtone.

Antipathy to the Ostjuden went so far that many of the local Jewish communities refused to allow Eastern Jews to vote in the community elections on the grounds that they were not German nationals. It took an edict by the Prussian minister of the interior in 1914 to force the local communities to give the Eastern Jews equal voting rights. Parity in communal affairs, however, did not increase social intercourse, so that on the whole the Eastern Jews lived as a minority within a minority.

This situation, which had persisted for decades, underwent remarkable changes during World War I. The first shock on the outbreak of the war was the discovery that not all Ostjuden were alike. The government immediately divided them into friends and foes: the allies were from the Austro-Hungarian Empire, while Jews from Russia and its territories were enemy aliens. Strict German naturalization laws had kept immigrant Jews from acquiring citizenship, and even their children born in Germany rarely acquired it. As late as 1933, when nearly half the 99,000 Ostjuden were German-born, only 16,000 had qualified for citizenship.

The second change followed the German invasion and occupation of Russian territories. In the Jewish villages of Poland and Lithuania, the Jews at first regarded the Germans as their liberators from the hated czarist regime and as rescuers from the latest pogroms. As the Germans moved forward, the fury of the local population was vented on the Jews, who thus had as much to fear from their neighbors as from the advancing enemy.

Among these German troops were young Jewish soldiers swept by new emotions as they met their almost incomprehensible fellow Jews. As they reported in emotional letters and diaries, they felt they were back at the source. One soldier wrote from the front in 1916, "It took the war to bring us to them, and amazed we stand in their midst and cry: 'So, something like this really exists! . . . Only the Jewish masses in the East strike me as Jewish. The few members of the Jewish people in Western Europe possess no living Jewish actuality." Another stressed "how much more natural the social organization was than in Germany, where the Jewish world consisted only of intellectuals and the bourgeoisie; how much more Jewish and how much more connected they were to tradition."

In these poor Jewish towns, whose enduring poverty was made worse by the hardships of the war, the soldiers saw beyond the squalor to what seemed to them an enviable integrity and wholeness. The Jewish chaplains, too, found

Members of the organization of Russian-Jewish students in Germany, ca. 1890.

themselves not only attending to the needs of the soldiers but also taking responsibility for the suffering local Jewish population.

Although the young soldiers did not return home in caftan and earlocks as some prewar Jewish enthusiasts had done, many of them wondered about the bargain they had made in acculturating as they began to consider East European Jews in a more complex light. They were not just oddly dressed and oddly spoken: perhaps they carried the secret of survival.

Even the philosopher Hermann Cohen, whose sympathy for the Polish Jews was limited and who thought that their "theatricality, gestures of mourning, and open lamentations during prayer" needed to be replaced by more "present-minded ceremonies," recognized their "autonomy of spirit." While Cohen was not ready to give up the path of assimilation, he also remembered from his Orthodox childhood the poor but learned Polish Sabbath guests who crossed his father's threshold and taught him "that poverty was bound up with spiritual dignity." His resolution, then, was the "pairing" of

Army rabbi Dr. Sonderling talking with bare-footed Jewish children in Poland.

Leopold Rosenak was a rabbi from Bremen who served as chaplain in the German army from 1915 to 1918. Posted to the eastern front, he was overwhelmed by the desperate Jewish poverty and organized soup kitchens for needy Jews as well as shipments of food. First sent to Stryz in Galicia, he described in letters home how the Jews welcomed the German soldiers as their liberators from the Russian occupiers. In 1916 he was in Bialystok, where 60,000 Jews still remained. Following the Jewish New Year, he wrote to his wife about events there.

On Simchas Torah the poor [Jewish] women with their children and infants pressed forward into the synagogue in an unstoppable stream, pushing toward my place and calling out for bread. It was a deeply affecting moment which began to cause concern with all the crowding and screaming. I went to the lectern and . . . in front of the open ark of the Torah, I promised them to take the necessary steps immediately. . . . One woman told me that she had only two entreaties to God—either her children should die or she should die so that she would no longer have to see them starve. . . . Today I could fulfill my vow, since last night I was able to move the military authorities to provide bread, herring, and salt for five to six thousand people. . . . This morning an infant boy was found in front of the hospital with a note asking that he be brought up as a Jew. An unhappy mother had laid him there. . . . The Catholic dean wanted to claim him for his holy church, but he got nowhere with me. I reminded him that Russian arbitrariness was no longer in command, nor would Polish rapine be tolerated. What the Jews suffer at the hands of the Poles is still no small matter. . . . But I cannot remain here forever. My duty calls me to the front again.

Minnie Rosenak, *"Rabbiner Dr. Leopold Rosenak: Vom Feldrabbiner zum politischen Engagement,"* *in* Bulletin des Leo Baeck Instituts, *1988.*

A sympathetic, almost reverential image of the East European Jew by the Berlin-born artist Hermann Struck. During the war he made a series of fifty such drawings in Lithuania. These were published in Berlin in 1920 with a text by Arnold Zweig in a volume called *Das Ostjüdische Antlitz* (The Eastern Jewish countenance).

Arnold Zweig contrasts the Eastern Jews with their brothers in the West, much to the advantage of the former.

The aged Jew of the East preserves his face. We recognize it from the tales of Mendele, this face: naive and dreamy and of a purity that can be bought only at the price of great accomplishments. . . . To establish a little business, to eat bread and herring, to produce and educate children, to say the prayers for the day and for each meal, and to learn many pages of Gemara; from his little means to give a little to the poor, provide dowries for brides, visit the sick, bury the dead and comfort the mourners—that is the pattern of his chain of duties. And how lightly he carries it. All this because he is of a young and cheerful spirit, because he is not paralyzed by the race for earnings, a race only made possible when, by a turn of mind, money becomes the highest value—a turn to which he is unwilling to accede. Then with his young and cheerful spirit, the spirit of the eternal student, which knows of the imperfection of knowledge and the high peaceful joy that comes from honoring great teachers, there overflows from him the joy in his duties and their self-evident significance. The clear, quiet eyes and the mouth, which shyly and softly hides his great goodness behind his beard, attest that here the originality and the splendor of all these obligations are still on the watch.

Arnold Zweig, Das ostjüdische Antlitz, *zu 50 Steinzeichnungen von Hermann Struck, Berlin, 1920.*

the two cultures to restore to the West the "natural" and "primordial" strength still preserved in Eastern Jewish life.

By the end of the war, the number of East European Jews in Germany had grown to at least 150,000. In addition to the original 90,000 who were resident in 1914, there were 35,000 who had been brought to Germany as forced laborers and another 25,000 who were prisoners of war or civilian internees. Added to these were several thousand who were fleeing the pogroms of 1920–21 in Poland. In an unprecedented gesture of unity, German Jews rallied to ameliorate their desperate situation. In 1920, twelve Jewish organizations joined to form a single agency dedicated to helping the displaced East European Jews—the Workers' Welfare Bureau of the Jewish Organizations in Germany (Arbeiterfürsorgeamt der jüdischen Organisationen Deutschlands).

But Germany was not the land of first resort for Eastern Jews. The United States offered the prize of American citizenship to every immigrant within five years, whereas in Germany citizenship was elusive and the freedom of the immigrants to work and settle was hedged with administrative barriers. A native Jewish woman who married an immigrant Jew, for example, would instantly lose her citizenship. An immigrant businessman living in Königsberg and trading with Russia would be permitted residence but denied the right to bring in his family.

The movement westward, therefore, continued beyond Germany. In the 1920s, nearly 50,000 Jews left, 30,000 of them for the United States; 12,000 returned to Eastern Europe, and the rest settled in Western European countries. By the time of the Weimar Republic, one in five Jews in Germany was of East European origin. Their colorful centers of life in Munich and Berlin loomed disproportionately large, however, in creating the public image of the East European Jew in Germany. In actuality, they quickly took on German speech and culture, often reluctant to reveal their place of birth so as to blend all the more seamlessly into the local scene. But their existence in a civic no-man's-land proved to have dire consequences under the Nazis. The fate that awaited German Jewry also fell upon this marked segment of the population. For the Polish Jews, it fell even more swiftly and mercilessly.

"Grenadierstrasse, Berlin." *Simplicissimus,* August 3, 1921.

Chapter Seven

The End

The Weimar Republic

For the Jews of Germany, the short-lived Weimar Republic was a dream that turned into a nightmare. The end of the republic, put to death by Hitler's accession to power in January 1933, also marked the end of any hope for completing the process of Jewish integration into German society that had begun so promisingly nearly a century before.

The collapse of the German army, its surrender to the Allies, and the abdication of Emperor Wilhelm II on November 9, 1918, had unleashed passions on all sides. Extreme left-wing forces, the Spartakists, called for a republic of worker-peasant councils; unreconciled monarchists went into the streets to frustrate those reconciled to, or even enthusiastic about, the end of empire. Bloodshed became the food for daily headlines. On January 15, 1919, the astute and outspoken Jewish Spartakist leader Rosa Luxemburg was brutally assassinated in Berlin with her gentile colleague Karl Liebknecht. In the following month, in Bavaria, which was moving toward a republic of socialist councils, its premier, Kurt Eisner, an idealistic Jewish radical,

was murdered. This was not anti-Semitism but politics: Eisner's assassin, Count Arco, was himself half-Jewish. It looked for a time as though there would be no orderly government in beaten Germany.

This violence was all the more reason for the founders to choose Weimar, the city of Goethe, as the seat of the constituent assembly, thus underscoring German humanism, German cosmopolitanism, and German pacific intentions in place of German militarism and German imperialist adventures. The Weimar constitution, adopted on July 31, 1919, declared the country to be a democratic republic with universal suffrage, an administration responsible to the legislature, and a strong president entitled to act by decree in case of dire emergency. In its first five years the republic seemed an emergency incarnate, to German Jews no less than to everyone else.

Jews had actively participated in the revolution, and they participated no less actively in the making of the new republic. Indeed, the principal architect of the Weimar constitution, Hugo Preuss, a left-leaning, witty, and outspoken lawyer, was a Jew. Like other German Jews, he had

Kurt Eisner and his wife, shown during a demonstration in Munich, February 16, 1919. Eisner led the revolution in Bavaria and became prime minister of the new Bavarian republic on November 8, 1918. He was assassinated on February 21, 1919.

Friedrich Ebert
(1870–1925), the
first president of the
Weimar Republic, in
a drawing by George
Grosz. Ebert served
from 1919 until his
death.

found academic advancement painfully slow, but he had gained public prominence through a pamphlet, *The German People and Politics*, in which he had pitted the authoritarian state (*Obrigkeitsstaat*) against the people's state (*Volksstaat*). Now, with the empire in tatters, he had a splendid opportunity to help transform Germany from the former into the latter.

The Weimar constitution, with all its flaws, enshrined the high hopes that German Jews had treasured during the decades preceding the First World War, hopes that had been partly dashed by the notorious census of Jews in the armed forces during the war. Nor was that hope tied to laws alone: the new society would be purged of the remnants of aristocratic privilege and bigotry that had made German-Jewish life before the war an affair of great expectations and frequent rebuffs. There would be unquestioned civic equality, careers open to talent, unobstructed admission to all posts including the bureaucracy, and access even to kinds of enterprise that had hitherto kept Jews out.

Not all the Jews of Germany welcomed the new dispensation. Though in general clustering on the liberal side of the political spectrum, a few of them, in company with pugnacious antirepublicans of other religious persuasions, formed paramilitary Free Corps that dispensed justice, as *they* defined it, gun in hand. They could not swallow what they viscerally resented as the dishonor of their country, the pathetic exile of Wilhelm II and the humiliating peace the Allies were imposing on their country. And it *was* a humiliating peace, however deserved. It split East Prussia off from the rest of German territory, returned the provinces of Alsace and Lorraine to France, from which Prussia had wrested them in 1871, distributed Germany's overseas colonies among the victors, reduced the German army to 100,000 men, imposed a military occupation on the Rhineland, and demanded exorbitant reparations. Most intolerable of all to enraged patriots, the treaty declared Germany and its allies responsible for the loss and damage the Allied Powers had incurred during a terrible four-year war.

Although the word *guilt* did not appear in the Treaty of Versailles, the so-called war guilt clause became a gathering point for Germans panting after revenge—including, soon enough, the Nazis. Furious and frustrated, they stigmatized the German negotiators, who after much hesitation signed the treaty, as criminals and renegades. Germany, these fanatics insisted, had not lost the war fairly on the battlefield; rather, it had been stabbed in the back, at home. Nor did they have any trouble "proving," naturally without evidence, that those who had held the treacherous knife were Jews. It was during this anxious and angry time that the Munich chapter of the Centralverein published a poster in protest. "It is all supposed to be the Jews' fault," it read. "This is the message that resounds today in handbills surreptitiously distributed. . . . It is supposed to be the fault of us Jews that the war came, but there were no Jews either in the government or in the diplomatic corps, either in the armaments industry or on the general staff. . . . We refuse to be made into the scapegoats for all the evil of the world."

The message was strongly worded, well meant, and largely futile. Many in those desperate days were glad to resort to the traditional anti-Semitic explanation for the ills of the new republic. They found welcome fodder in the results of the wartime census of Jews in the armed forces, released in 1919 by an unofficial, pseudonymous, anti-Semitic author, "Otto Armin." The statistics he offered, presumably reflecting the official count, supported the slander that Jews had hung back behind the lines. His figures showed only 62,000 Jews in the German armed forces, of whom some 35,000 had served, he claimed, either behind the lines or as troops in the occupied zones, while only 27,000 ever got to the front lines.

Anticipating such slander, a special consortium of Jewish organizations had set up a Committee for War Statistics at the beginning of the war. It worked under the direction of two highly placed statisticians: Jacob Segall, head of the Berlin Bureau for Statistics on Jews, and Heinrich Silbergleit, director of the Office of Statistics for the city of Berlin between 1906 and 1923. They released their results in 1922, and the facts were very different from the story in the Otto Armin report: among the 550,000 Jews of German nationality, 100,000 had served in the war, 80,000 at the front. And 12,000 had died for Germany. What is more, 35,000 Jewish soldiers had received medals, and 23,000 had been promoted—2,000 of them, in fact, to officer's rank. The Reichsbund jüdischer Front-

Poster issued by the Jewish veterans' organization noting that 12,000 Jews had been killed in the war and calling upon German women to defend Jewish mothers from calumnies against their sons.

soldaten (National Organization of Jewish Front-line Soldiers) was founded in 1919 with the express purpose of documenting, and thus honoring, the Jewish war dead.

But the truth never quite caught up with the lies. And it was in this atmosphere of cold, irrational hatred that German right-wing extremists found their most conspicuous Jewish victim, Walther Rathenau (see plate 19). The son of the industrial magnate Emil Rathenau, he had made a reputation as an economist, industrialist, and utopian thinker before he became a public official. In January 1922, Chancellor Joseph Wirth, a Catholic Center party politician, appointed Rathenau foreign minister. Given the tough stance of the victors, any German diplomat had to face difficult negotiations, and Rathenau's being Jewish made him all the more vulnerable. Soon a piece of doggerel viciously attacking Chancellor Wirth and his foreign minister made the rounds of Free Corps meetings and right-wing students: *Knallt ab den Walther Rathenau / Die gottverfluchte Judensau.* This demand to "shoot down the god-damned Jew sow" was translated into action late in June 1922 when Rathenau was shot to death by young activists. "The enemy," Chancellor Wirth told a shocked Reichstag, "stands on the right." But the right seemed almost invulnerable; putschists and political murderers were let off easily by complaisant courts, which avenged left-wing violence, though far rarer, with draconian punishments.

To make life in the first five years of the Weimar Republic more precarious still, the country—burdened with vast reparations, foreign occupation, and political unrest—was haunted by harrowing inflation. In January 1921, the German mark had stood at 45 to the dollar, already a sign of decline in the currency. By the end of the year, more than 160 marks were needed to buy one dollar. When, early in 1923 the French reoccupied the Rhineland on the grounds that Germany had failed to pay the agreed-upon reparations, more violence erupted, productivity plunged, and tax payments virtually ceased. Under these circumstances, inflation began to gallop; by October, it took literally trillions of marks to buy a loaf of bread. There was hoarding, farmers withheld their products, and those on pensions or with bank accounts lost all their savings. It was not until November that the currency was abruptly stabilized. Amid such turmoil, Jew-hatred could only flourish.

For all these dismaying realities, German Jews tried to live in the fledgling republic in peace. The idealization of East European Jews that had begun during the war, as Jewish troops on the eastern front first encountered real Ostjuden, continued at the very time that thousands of new arrivals were arousing a certain hostility among their coreligionists. A number of educated German Jews read Martin Buber's monthly, *Der Jude,* a journal that acquainted its readers with the folklore, humor, and philosophical and religious traditions of their Eastern brethren. A few adopted Zionism, and a handful, like the eminent scholar Gerhard—he would call himself Gershom—Scholem, emigrated to Palestine. But most of Germany's Jews, even in the face of political violence and anti-Semitic libels, felt at home and wanted to stay.

The war had brought a new sobriety that undercut the optimism of the Wilhelminian years. Being a Jew in Germany needed to be reexamined yet again and fell under the keen scrutiny of a generation who wanted something different from the splintering that had marked Judaism in the nineteenth century. A new direction was charted by two remarkable men—Martin Buber and Franz Rosenzweig—who eventually collaborated on the translation of the Bible. Both were determined to wring a modern message from Judaism, not to reform its institutions but to find the truth they were seeking within its traditional boundaries.

Rosenzweig, from a well-to-do secular family in Kassel, returned to Judaism as a result of an old-fashioned disputation. In 1913, he had been challenged by the philosopher and theologian Eugen Rosenstock-Huessy, a distant relative, either to refute Christian beliefs or to accept Christianity. Bested in the discussion, Rosenzweig agreed to convert. But he wanted to build his Christianity on his Judaism and decided to attend high holy day services at an Orthodox synagogue in Berlin. Moved by the services, he realized that "closeness to God" did not depend on the mediation of Jesus but was accessible to any Jew who sought it. There was no need to find something else or something more; what he needed was to recapture the Judaism that he knew too little.

In December 1922, the Reichsbank was overprinting regular currency to keep up with inflation. Here is a thousand-mark note overprinted to read *Milliard*—that is, a thousand million marks. By 1923, the Reichsbank was printing thousand-milliard-mark notes.

From a letter of October 9, 1923, by Betty Scholem to her son Gerhard (Gershom) Scholem, who as a principled Zionist had emigrated to Palestine in the previous month over the objections of his family.

In any event, you can be happy that you are living abroad; it is simply terrible here. I can imagine that abroad people must have the strangest notions about Germany, but what is actually happening is even stranger. When you left, sausage, for example of the sort that I gave you to take along, cost 12 million a pound. Today it costs 240 million and the prices for everything have risen at this rate and even faster, the streetcar 10 million. One can only go shopping with billion-mark notes. The collapse of the economy is complete; no one can buy anything and with that, unemployment is rising.

Betty Scholem and Gershom Scholem, Mutter und Sohn im Briefwechsel, 1917–1946. *Munich, 1989.*

A crush of depositors, hoping to withdraw their money, in front of the Reichsbank at the height of the inflation of 1923.

In 1915, Rosenzweig joined the army and began to formulate what he called the "new thinking." His book, *The Star of Redemption,* which he wrote on postcards he sent home from the Balkan front starting in August 1918, acknowledges Judaism and Christianity as two branches of the truth. But Jews carry this truth as their birthright, whereas Christians are in effect pagans who need to be converted in each generation. Rosenzweig also attacked the reigning philosophy of German idealism, advocating a philosophy of "real life."

What Rosenzweig wanted was to educate Jews to their tradition, and when he returned from the war he moved to Frankfurt am Main, where he opened the Freie jüdische Lehrhaus (Free Jewish House of Learning). He hoped to reverse the flight from what he called the "center" of Jewish learning, which had been in progress now for more than a century. Without asking for religious commitment, the house opened its doors to all—Jews and gentiles alike—who wanted to study the Hebrew language, Jewish history, and the classic Jewish texts. In this enterprise he was surrounded by a brilliant group of like-minded men, among them Martin Buber,

Erich Fromm, Rudolf Hallo, Gershom Scholem, Nahum Glatzer, and a charismatic rabbi, Nehemia Anton Nobel, who died suddenly in 1921.

Catastrophic illness cut down Rosenzweig as well; in the same year, 1921, he discovered that he was suffering from a progressive paralysis, which killed him in 1929. Nevertheless, he continued to work, particularly on translations from the Hebrew. His major work was the translation of the Scriptures which he published, through the Book of Isaiah, in 1925. (The work was later completed by Martin Buber and published in Israel in the 1950s). Between 1925 and 1929, branches of the Lehrhaus were established in eight cities in Germany, but with Rosenzweig's death the movement withered away.

His collaborator, Martin Buber, was born in Lemberg, in the heart of East European hasidism, yet educated in the West, receiving a degree in philosophy from the University of Vienna. He was the ideal mediator between traditional Judaism and the new philosophical approach to Jewish ideas. Buber retold and published collections of hasidic tales and joined with Rosenzweig in pressing for the idea of a personal communion with God, which he called the I-Thou relationship. It echoed in modern language the ecstasy of hasidic prayer.

But in the years of the republic, most German Jews remained committed to the secular culture around them. They also found openings in cultural life that their fathers would have thought virtually unreachable, or at the least most unusual. Albert Einstein (who had returned to Germany in 1914 from self-imposed exile) received the Nobel Prize in physics in 1921. And the ablest and most enterprising among German Jews were soon occupying leading positions in the liberal professions and the arts. In the empire, 12 percent of all lecturers teaching in German universities—and waiting, normally without hope, for a professorship—were Jews; the proportion of Jews among full professors was a mere 3 percent. But if one adds the Jews who had in fact converted to Christianity, the numbers considerably improve: 19 percent among lecturers and 7 percent among professors.

All this now changed. In 1919, when he was forty-five, Ernst Cassirer, a prolific historian of culture and Kantian philosopher of Jewish background, was finally appointed to a chair in the new university in Hamburg. In 1924, Martin Buber was named to a chair for Jewish religion and ethics at the University of Frankfurt. And there were others like them. But some of the most rewarding scholarly work of the Weimar Republic went on outside the universities, especially in the privately endowed institutes, several of them financed by Jewish philanthropists and staffed by some of the finest intellects the country could muster.

One of these institutes, with which Cassirer would be intimately connected throughout the life of the republic, was the Cultural-Historical Library, named after its founder, Aby Warburg, the scion of a Jewish banking family. His institute was more than a library: such regular visitors as Cassirer delivered memorable lectures on cultural history. The great art historian Erwin Panofsky, like Cassirer a Jew and the holder of a university chair, taught and did much of his writing at the Warburg Library.

Other institutes were closer to contemporary political realities. The Frankfurt Institute for Social Research, also endowed by a wealthy Jewish donor, sought to marry Marxian social analysis and Freudian psychoanalysis into an amalgam at once politically radical and socially aristocratic. Its publications enjoyed considerable prestige— as long as the Weimar Republic lived. But after its demise, its leading minds, notably Theodor Adorno and Max Horkheimer, were to end up in the United States as Jewish refugees.

One other such institute, promptly co-opted and largely destroyed by Nazi Germany— certainly its Jewish members quickly found that emigration was the only solution to the German question as it presented itself from 1933 on— was the Berlin Psychoanalytic Institute. Its nucleus had been established before the war, by Karl Abraham, but it became an important psychoanalytic clinical training center in 1920, with a generous grant from a wealthy Russian immigrant Jew, one of Freud's closest disciples, Max Eitingon. In 1930, the institute celebrated its tenth anniversary with a little festschrift, edited by the young psychoanalyst Otto Fenichel, in which it recounted statistics: 1,955 consultations, 721 psychoanalyses, and—perhaps a little naively—111 complete cures. The Nazis were to call psychoanalysis a Jewish science. If one were to list the names of those associated with the Berlin institute, one would have to acknowl-

Reading room of the
Warburg Library,
Hamburg, 1926.

edge that the label, at least in one respect, made sense: virtually all of those who founded, taught at, and were trained in the institute were indeed Jewish.

Both the civilized Marxists of the Institute for Social Research and the hardworking Freudians of the Berlin Psychoanalytic Institute were caviar for the few. During the Weimar Republic, Jews also succeeded in entering areas of activity that placed them at the heart of German culture, such as music and theater. The great magician of the Weimar stage, the imaginative, extravagant Max Reinhardt, whose stagings of classical and modern, conventional as well as expressionist plays became legendary, had been a prominent producer before 1914, but the republic gave him ever-wider scope. His principal rival, a far more austere master of the stage, was Leopold Jessner, whom the Prussian minister of culture, the Social Democrat Konrad Hänisch, appointed to the powerful post of *Intendant* at the Staatliche Schauspielhaus in Berlin. Germany's favorite tenor was the flamboyant Richard Tauber, who sang Mozart arias with as much panache as the lead in Lehar operettas. Other men of the theater, Jews and gentiles alike, gave the German stage an electric vitality it had not had before and has not had since.

But the anti-Semites refused to accept Jews as genuine fellow citizens. In late 1919, a small nationalistic group calling itself the German Workers' party recruited an Austrian, Adolf Hitler, even in those early years a spellbinding orator. Intent on enlarging his tiny fringe party, he sought out like-minded Free Corps militants and other populist extremists, developed a grandiose twenty-five point program, and changed the name of the party to National Socialist German Workers' party, the NSDAP. At congresses and mass meetings, Hitler pronounced the new gospel: anticapitalist, anti-Bolshevik, anti-"November criminals," and, most emphatic of all, anti-Semitic. By November 1923, Hitler and his followers, who included General Ludendorff, felt ready to stage a putsch in Munich. It failed, and some of the conspirators were even convicted; in a characteristic bit of self-destructive leniency, the courts sentenced Hitler to five years in relatively comfortable confinement, of which he served only about eight months, writing *Mein Kampf*.

But then the changes in the fortunes of

Richard Tauber (1891–1948). He is shown here with his trademark monocle. In 1933 he emigrated to London and in 1940 became a British citizen.

Weimar Germany forced Hitler and the NSDAP into obscurity. The good days of the Weimar Republic, the somewhat misnamed Golden Twenties, date from early 1924, after the stabilization of the currency, the gradual readmission of Germany into the family of nations (in 1926 the country was admitted to the League of Nations), the calming of political storms, and the pleasures of prosperity.

Germany's Jews prospered with the rest of the citizenry, both economically and culturally. As they did so, legends formed, most of them hostile. It was widely believed that the ready-to-wear clothing industry—the *Konfektion*—was in the hands of the Jews. It never occurred to the mythmakers to explain in what way that industry, or for that matter any other, would have been different if it had been run by gentiles. But the truth, however earnestly preached by Jewish defense organizations, never caught up with the Nazi libels. The presence of Jews in general cannot be called a Jewish presence. No one, to take just one instance, would recognize the fascinating expressionist buildings designed by the Jewish architect Erich Mendelsohn as in any way characteristically different from the buildings he would have designed if he had been a gentile. What mattered was that he was responsible for some distinguished buildings, mainly erected during the more prosperous years, particularly the Universum movie theater in Berlin (1927) and the Schocken department store in Chemnitz (1928–29).

There was another famous design in which Mendelsohn had anticipated, as it were, the Golden Twenties: a radically new, sophisticated, rounded facade for the headquarters of the liberal Rudolf Mosse publishing house in Berlin, a design carried out between 1921 and 1923. It was testimony to success: by the mid-1920s, the principal Mosse newspaper, the *Berliner Tageblatt,* enjoyed a circulation of over 300,000. Mosse's great rival, the no less liberal Ullstein house, was if anything more successful. Nor did the Ullsteins insist on best-selling properties: since 1914 they had owned the venerable *Vossische Zeitung,* with a more limited circulation—in 1926 it sold 55,000 copies—and were pleased with the prestige this well written, if sober, daily gave them. They also published slick monthly journals, fashion magazines, and a line of reasonably priced books, mainly popular nov-els. The chief seller was a heavily illustrated weekly, the *Berliner Illustrirte,* with a regular circulation of 1.6 million copies. In 1928, the Ullstein house launched a new afternoon newspaper that paid tribute to, and was a characteristic expression of, the speed that so many observers connected with the intoxicating excitement of Weimar culture at its best. It was a racy tabloid, with large and striking photographs, and was called, intriguingly enough, *Tempo.* An unknown wag nicknamed it *die jüdische Hast*—Jewish haste, or perhaps more to the point, Jewish nervousness.

By 1929, the Jews had good reasons to be nervous. Early that year, a serious economic recession had begun to grip the country, imposing 2 million unemployed on the harassed German welfare system. In October, two disasters struck the republic: Gustav Stresemann, Germany's widely respected foreign minister, who after a militaristic youth had been converted to a moderate and pacific political stance, died. He proved irreplaceable. Then later that month the U.S. stock market crashed, and economic depression rapidly spread across the world. The German economy, vulnerable and precariously recovered, suffered quickly and catastrophically. As country after country pulled up the drawbridges of protective tariffs, German exports declined and foreign loans dwindled away. In the resulting political scramble, the Social Democrats demanded more generous unemployment compensation while the conservative parties vehemently resisted. As joblessness reached disastrous heights, sellers of nostrums—among them anti-Semitism—found ever-growing numbers of adherents. The old canard of Jewish shirking in the First World War, which had never quite disappeared, gained new circulation. Once again Jewish organizations responded: during 1928 and 1929, the Reichsbund jüdischer Frontsoldaten, relying as before on the material compiled by Jacob Segall during the war, sent questionnaires to Jewish community organizations, and launched appeals in its own newspaper, to compile a well-documented list of Jewish war dead. It was a refutation spoken into the wind.

Not surprisingly, there was much cynicism about the republic that all too few loved and increasing numbers were willing to exchange for an authoritarian regime. Not all this cynicism

was a response to the Great Depression; some of the sharpest, most amusing critics of the Weimar regime, like the prolific journalist Kurt Tucholsky, had busily caricatured burghers, military men—and Jews—during the prosperous mid-1920s. Ironically, the very freedom of Weimar culture had made room for the most unsparing, even irrational self-criticism.

Probably the most enduring product of this self-satire was Kurt Weill's and Bertolt Brecht's *Threepenny Opera* of 1928. It was to impress many thousands across the decades as the quintessential product of the Weimar republic, what with its memorable music and no less memorable lyrics. Weill, the Jewish partner of this team, had been born in Dessau, the son of a cantor, and had enjoyed a thorough musical training. The year before his greatest success, he and Brecht had put on *The Rise and Fall of the City of Mahagonny*, a merciless satire of American corruption and lawlessness. In the *Threepenny Opera*, they made cruel fun of bourgeois smugness and selfishness. Adapting the eighteenth-century *Beggar's Opera* by John Gay, they exercised their considerable gifts for sardonic commentary by presenting some of the most unsavory characters ever gathered on stage—thieves,

The Universum movie theater in Berlin, designed by Erich Mendelsohn as part of a larger complex of shops and apartments. Shown just before its opening in 1928.

Kurt Weill (1900–1950), ca. 1930.

This Passover wall hanging, spelling out the grace after meals, was commissioned in 1925 by Siegfried Guggenheim of Offenbach from the workshop of Rudolf Koch, a Christian book and textile designer who specialized in sacred texts. This commission seems to exemplify the German-Jewish symbiosis, since Koch used the talents of a Jewish student in the workshop, Berthold Wolpe, for the design of the Hebrew letters.

pimps, prostitutes, corrupt officials—with a melodic and poetic verve that made their odd production into a masterpiece.

Meanwhile, the republic deteriorated. In March 1930, the aged president Hindenburg asked Heinrich Brüning, a touted financial expert and conservative Catholic Center politician, to form a cabinet. After a few months in office, Brüning governed under emergency decrees, but the economic situation, far from improving, deteriorated. Extremists took to the streets in ever-larger numbers and fought with ever-greater ferocity.

The Reichstag elections of September 1930 offered brutal confirmation that the Weimar Republic was near death. Whereas the Social Democrats, the Catholic Center, and the Communists retained virtually all their votes and their seats, a number of smaller parties lost most of their support. The lion's share of that support, to which one must add many among the 5 million

new voters—mainly young people who had moved directly from school to the breadlines— went to the Nazis. In the previous elections of 1928, the NSDAP had garnered 800,000 votes and 12 seats in the Reichstag; now they leaped to 6.5 million votes and 107 seats. They did not yet have anything like a majority, but perceptive spirits saw in the gutter politicians of the Nazis the party of the future. Hitler was back.

The Jews of Germany did not sit by idly and passively. In November 1932, the Reichsbund jüdischer Frontsoldaten published a *Gedenkbuch,* a memorial volume, listing the Jews who had fallen in the war. The book, they hoped a little naively, would puncture once and for all the mendacious accusation that Jews had shirked dangerous duty during the war. To underscore the significance of the book, they arranged to present a prepublication copy to President Hindenburg on his eighty-fifth birthday on October 2, 1932. They were heartened to discover that

A scuffle with the police during a demonstration by SA men, the Brown Shirts, in Berlin in 1931.

the book was sold out within its first two weeks of publication, and a second edition, slightly enlarged, contained thirty-two new names. But by then, German politics was out of the hands of reason.

Yet most German Jews, solidly anchored in their country, settled in their trade and profession, innocent of foreign languages, with close gentile friends, and incredulous at developments, stayed on. Were they not integrating daily into gentile Germany? It has been estimated that around 1930, perhaps a quarter of all Jewish marriages were to a gentile partner. Only a handful of prescient German Jews decided to emigrate during Brüning's tenure. A very few, happening to be abroad, were encouraged to remain abroad. The art historian Erwin Panofsky, who held two professorships, one in Hamburg and the other at New York University, was teaching in New York in the spring of 1933. There he received a cable from Germany dismissing him, along with all other Jewish professors, from his post. The cable, he later recalled, was sealed with a strip of green paper which said, "Cordial Easter Greetings, Western Union." Very few of Germany's Jews were so well placed, and very few of those who survived Hitler could look back on their exile with such wry humor. On January 30, 1933, Hitler was appointed chancellor of the German Reich. The country's Jews, briefly insiders, were outsiders once again.

The Nazi Period

Developments after Hitler's appointment as chancellor followed so rapidly upon one another that within a few months the Nazis had managed to set aside the entire Weimar constitution—the Basic Rights of the Citizens, as it was called—and launch the process that would lead to total dictatorship. Although in the elections to the Reichstag of March 5, 1933, the Nazis did not gain a majority—they polled 44 percent of the vote—by the end of the month the Reichstag, intimidated, had voted to give the National Socialist party full powers.

Within its own small compass, the family of Arthur and Betty Scholem in Berlin provide a striking cross-section of the range of Jewish experience in that time of trial. The youngest of their four sons, Gerhard, who later took the

name of Gershom, had become a Zionist in the course of the First World War. Having decided to make his future in Palestine, he used his time at the university to study Semitic languages and philosophy and emigrated in 1923. The two middle sons, Erich and Reinhold, joined their father in the family printing business, while the eldest son, Werner, became a Communist. Arthur Scholem quarreled with Werner and Gerhard, who dissented from the bourgeois middle, as he was unable to see the slightest merit in either of their programs. Concerned about their capacity to support themselves, he wrote Gerhard that Hebraica and Judaica might be taken up as a hobby (*Steckenpferd*), but not as a life's work, and urged Werner first to get his university degree and then make his revolution. Neither son was to be moved, with very different consequences.

Arthur Scholem did not live to see Werner arrested in the first sweep against Communists in early 1933. The event that the Nazis turned to their advantage was the Reichstag fire of February 27, 1933. The cause of the conflagration is still debated, but the Nazis swiftly exploited it as an excuse to arrest Communists. Werner Scholem, among others, was taken into custody, released after a week, and then rearrested in April 1933. Despite tenacious efforts by his family on his behalf, he was never released again and was killed in Buchenwald in 1941.

What German Jews experienced was the steady building of pressure against segment after segment of their community. It began with robbing people of their livelihoods. Then in the six years before the outbreak of the war, the introduction of racial laws, the exclusion of Jews from civic life, and finally even from the streets and parks of the cities, isolated them from the gentile community. It divided families, separated friends, and turned those years into a time of desperation. As German Jews gradually understood, this was not a regime that could be ousted by peaceful electoral means; their life in Germany had come to an end. It became a time, as the Jewish Agency report of 1935 stated, "when it must be the aim of every German Jew to become a refugee."

The first blows by the regime immediately showed the Nazis' favorite techniques: the administrative decree, which worked quietly, and open violence, which terrorized not only the

The book burning organized by the Nazis, May 10, 1933.

Jews. With a third technique—the arrest of all active political opponents, including important Social Democrats as well as members of the Communist party—they realized their plan for consolidating their power.

Two months after the Nazis took over, they scheduled a boycott of Jewish business for April 1, 1933. The paramilitary sa force—the Brown Shirts—which had previously devoted itself to marching, singing, aggressively collecting funds for the party and beating up opponents, now sprang up everywhere in full uniform to jeer at those who dared to enter Jewish stores. Although many Germans defiantly went by these guards, the event itself cast a dark shadow. Betty Scholem reports that on the first evening of Passover in April 1933, a few weeks after the boycott, her brother-in-law Theobald Scholem attempted to reassure the assembled family, saying, "Jewry will overcome this persecution as it has others." But Betty Scholem wondered with sudden clairvoyance, "Jewry certainly, but will German Jewry?"

More drastic were the decrees that followed rapidly in April and May forbidding "non-Aryans" to hold positions as government employees, which meant teachers in secondary schools and universities as well as administra-

April 1, 1933, was a day of official boycott against Jewish businesses. Here Brown Shirts stand guard before a closed Jewish store in Berlin. The sign warns that the Jewish owners of this shop are "parasites and the gravediggers of German craftsmen."

tors; the elimination of "non-Aryan" doctors from health insurance programs; and the introduction of a *numerus clausus* in the universities. These actions soon seeped from the official to the private level as sports organizations also began to exclude Jews. In July, even the German Chess Organization joined in. Jews in the arts and in journalism found themselves unemployed as the opera houses, newspapers, and orchestras were purged. Then, in August, many towns began to post signs forbidding Jews to use municipal swimming pools or bathing places, and some even closed themselves entirely to Jews.

Once again Betty Scholem was in the midst of events; her sister Katie Schiepan, a physician, told her that she was losing most of her practice since Jewish doctors were no longer permitted to treat insured patients. Reporting all these events to her son Gerhard in Jerusalem, Betty Scholem concluded that with the free professions being closed to Jews, "they are being destroyed in this bloodless way just as certainly as if their necks had been wrung."

The escalation that had begun in the economic area moved into a new sphere in 1935 with the promulgation of the Nuremberg laws. These edicts attacked not only the functions of Jews in society but their very being. By creating elaborate distinctions among Jew, "Aryan," and *Mischling*—a person of "mixed blood"—and by requiring detailed research into ancestry for several generations, the Nazis created an atmosphere that successfully divided the nation into two parts, Aryans and Jews: accomplishment, virtue, and wealth all became irrelevant in a world where only race counted. When the Nazis took power in 1933, eleven of the forty German winners of a Nobel Prize in the sciences had been Jews. But they, too, were no longer regarded as anything but members of an "inferior race."

Three factors contributed to many German Jews' delaying to leave Germany until it was too late: the contradictory tactics of the Nazi regime, so that shortly after the boycott of April 1933 the government did not hesitate to order uniforms from Jewish textile and clothing manufacturers; a sense of disbelief that a legal government could destroy them; and the tight immigration quotas of most countries in the Western world, combined with the British cur-

"Jews are not wanted here" reads this sign posted next to a crucifix at the entrance to a village in Franconia, 1935.

tailment of Jewish immigration to Palestine. The contradictions and disclaimers by the government especially served to mask the ultimate menace in Nazi policy and to confuse Jews trying to decide about their future.

It gradually became apparent that the German Jews needed help—help to get out, help for vocational retraining in Germany, and help to meet their daily needs. For against every expectation, in a short space of time, a prosperous and self-sufficient community was reduced to indigence. Acting swiftly, a group of outstanding Jewish leaders came together in Berlin and founded the Reichsvertretung der deutschen Juden (Reich Representation of the German Jews) on September 17, 1933. Its purpose was to transcend the ideological differences that had divided existing organizations and to function as the single political representative of the Jews in Germany. In its two chief leaders, the Reichsvertretung chose men of such probity and commanding such respect in the community that they could hold together the many warring factions. They invited Leo Baeck, who had been a rabbi in Berlin since 1912 and was a distinguished lecturer and writer on Jewish philosophy, to be their president, and Otto Hirsch, a

lawyer and administrator in his native Stuttgart, to become executive director.

Both men had many opportunities to leave the country but refused, consciously sacrificing themselves for the community. Baeck, in reply to the offer of a rabbinical post in Cincinnati as late as 1941, replied, "As long as one Jew remains in Germany, my place is with him." In 1943, he was deported to Theresienstadt, but despite his sixty-seven years he managed to outlive the Nazi regime. Otto Hirsch, who had been in London in 1939 to negotiate for the emigration of the German Jews, returned to his post and in May 1941 was deported to the Mauthausen camp in Austria. There he was tortured and died a month later, on June 19, 1941.

The Reichsvertretung did not at first supplant the powerful community structures. On the contrary, at first its resources amounted to only a fifth of the combined community budgets. But with alarming swiftness the community began to collapse. In the winter of 1935–36, with 400,000 Jews left in Germany, nearly 84,000 received help, of whom 30,000 were in Berlin. The Jews left in Germany now began to desert their hometowns and flock to the cities in the hope of finding work or help or safety; by 1937,

The May 1939 issue of the Nazi newspaper *Der Stürmer* repeated the fifteenth-century blood libel claiming that Jews had murdered six boys in Regensburg for their blood. Note the Treitschke slogan at the bottom of the page: "The Jews are our misfortune."

Leo Baeck addressing
the Reichsvertretung,
1933 or 1934. Others
are, from left to right:
Dr. Franz Meyer,
Rabbi Jacob
Hoffmann, Dr. Sieg-
fried Moses, Dr. Otto
Hirsch, Dr. Rudolph
Callman, and
Heinrich Stahl.

Otto Hirsch (1885–
1941), executive
chairman of the
Reichsvertretung from
1933 until his death
in the Mauthausen
concentration camp.

Collection boxes for the Jüdische Winterhilfe campaigns in the 1930s.

two hundred of the sixteen hundred Jewish communities had gone under, and more than six hundred of those remaining required outside support to keep functioning.

The pressing need simply to feed people led to the revival of a charitable campaign known as Winterhilfe (Winter Help). Initiated during the Weimar Republic, it was designed to raise funds for immediate support to the poor by soliciting donations on the street. This appeal was also adopted by the Nazis, who used strong-arm methods to extort money from businesses and individuals in the name of Winterhilfe and then used the proceeds to line the party coffers. In the last winter before the war, a quarter of the 286,000 Jews still living in Germany received assistance from Jewish Winterhilfe.

Deprived not only of their livelihoods but also of their place in the life around them, the German Jews turned inward, building an admirable network of schools and expanding facilities for youth, the aged, and the indigent. Families more and more withdrew their children from the state schools so as to spare them exposure to anti-Semitism. By 1937, of the 39,000 Jewish children of school age in Germany, 23,600 were attending the 167 schools that had been im-

provised to teach them. In the meantime, the Reichsvertretung was working on programs to bring children out of the country to special schools or to live with families in England and Scotland. By June 1939, some 3,820 children under the age of fifteen had left on children's transports. These departures, often heartbreaking for both children and parents, were a measure of the parents' lack of confidence in their own ability to get out of Germany.

The shock of the Nazi takeover strengthened the Zionist movement. Although it had never been widely popular in Germany and in fact had been losing ground steadily through the 1920s, it suddenly developed a new appeal. Whether Jews had changed their minds about their place in Germany or whether it was an expedient measure in the attempt to migrate to Palestine is not certain, but membership jumped from 7,500 in 1931–32 to 43,000 in 1933–34 and rose again to 57,000 in the following year.

The Zionists did indeed initiate a program that helped German Jews who emigrated to Palestine to take some of their otherwise blocked funds with them. Under the terms of the Transfer, or Haavarah, Program, the German government permitted departing Jews to buy German

goods with their funds and ship them to Palestine. There the goods were sold, and upon arrival in Palestine the owner was reimbursed with whatever money had been realized. Originally the plan was surrounded by controversy because it required the purchase of German goods, but it proved a boon for Palestine, which needed raw and finished goods of every kind. It also provided start-up capital for the new arrivals. One way to enter Palestine outside the quota system was to get a "capitalist certificate" issued to anyone who had £1,000 sterling. Although German Jews could not take out £1,000 in money, they could ship the equivalent in goods and thus qualify for the coveted certificates. One-third of the German Jews who emigrated to Palestine, in fact, went as "capitalists."

Thinking of the future, the Zionists also initiated a program for German Jews between the ages of fifteen and seventeen. This special Youth Aliyah (Youth Immigration) movement enabled 3,400 young people to leave Germany for Palestine. Simultaneously a number of Labor Zionist organizations ran intensive agricultural training programs for youngsters between fourteen and sixteen who wanted to join the kibbutz

Old people receiving a meal at the Pestalozzistrasse synagogue in Berlin.

Students in the court-
yard of a school
maintained by the
Jewish community at
Rykestrasse, Berlin.
Shown here is an ex-
ercise hour during
the winter of 1936,
when many Jewish
families had already
withdrawn their chil-
dren from the public
schools.

A concert of the Jü-
dische Kulturbund or-
chestra in the New
Synagogue of Berlin,
1939.

movement and brought out perhaps an additional thousand.

Although emigration became the paramount preoccupation of the Jewish community, years often elapsed between the wish and the deed. Especially in Berlin, which still had a community of 176,000 Jews in 1933, Jews began to build a new world. One of the morale-building institutions, founded in 1933, was the Kulturbund (Cultural Union). In part it attempted to cope with the situation of 20,000 dispossessed musicians, artists, singers, actors, and others who needed theaters and audiences to continue their professional lives. But it also offered a friendly ambience to Jews who were increasingly unwelcome in public places.

Pointedly enough, the first production by the Kulturbund, presented on October 1, 1933, was Lessing's *Nathan the Wise*. The Kulturbund also produced operas, operettas, and concerts and sponsored films and lectures, establishing an extraordinary world of concentrated talent. The pioneer Kulturbund in Berlin was followed by others in cities around the country; by the beginning of 1938 there were seventy-six of them employing some seventeen hundred Jewish artists. But by 1938, despite the activity and community support, their monthly bulletin took on a despairing note: "Problems which only a short while ago were the subject of animated discussion have become illusory. The question is not any more that of an artistic competition between the various centers, but one of to be or not to be."

As the audience dwindled through emigration and its own hopes of a future diminished, the Kulturbund expected that its activities would be stopped. Strangely enough, even after the Night of Broken Glass (Kristallnacht) in November 1938 and the onset of the war ten months later, the Ministry of Propaganda kept it running. Then, in 1940, it was shut down; the artists were sent off to the camps and the grim fate that awaited them.

As the bulletin of the Kulturbund suggests, 1938 marked a turning point for the Jews left in Germany. Reduced to nearly half their number, those who remained began to feel a desperation inspired by long waits at consulates, refusals of entry from countries of even second or third choice, and increasing harshness by the Nazis at

home. Veterans of combat in World War I and their children had long been exempted from the measures taken against the general Jewish population. Now even they lost their special status in a final wave of dismissals of professionals; their children, in turn, were barred from attending state schools. Businesses were now forced to sell out, which meant in practice having their property confiscated and transferred to an "Aryan."

Then the tempo escalated. In July 1938, Jews were required to carry special identity cards; in August, each man was made to add the middle name "Israel," and each woman "Sara," in official papers. Beginning October 5, passports issued to Jews also carried a large red J stamped prominently on the identification page. Then on October 28, some 14,000–18,000 Jews of Polish citizenship were summarily expelled from the country. This order, which affected Jews who had lived for decades in Germany and their German-born children, was carried out with the utmost brutality: apartments were invaded in the early dawn hours by uniformed police ordering people to leave immediately. Some were not even permitted to change out of their nightclothes.

There were at this point 50,000 Polish Jews in Germany, and the foreign office was anxious to be rid of them. When the Polish government was sounded on this question at the beginning of October, they were not only not interested in having these former citizens back but went so far as to promulgate a decree denying entry to all Polish nationals after October 29 unless their passports had been approved. The day chosen by the Nazis to expel Polish nationals was perfectly timed to circumvent this decree.

At the border, the Polish guards, unaware of the negotiations in their foreign office, denied entrance to the expelled Jews, who were faced with drawn guns when they attempted to return to the German side. Five thousand lived for weeks in an improvised camp in a frontier town, Zbazsyn, until the Polish Jewish communities managed to intervene and find some form of shelter for them in Warsaw and elsewhere. Meanwhile, Poland was sending German Jews who had been living in Poland toward the German border. In a compromise, the Poles agreed to take 7,000 Jews from Germany, and the Germans accepted in return a small number of Jews

Passport of Kurt "Israel" Rubin, January 19, 1939. Notice the J stamp.

of German nationality who had been sent from Poland. The remainder were permitted to return home.

But this turn of events, which broke with lightning suddenness on Germany's Polish Jews, proved the trigger for a new wave of Nazi violence. On November 7, Herschel Grynszpan, a seventeen-year-old student in Paris, went to the German embassy intending to kill the ambassador in revenge for the deportations, including that of his Polish-Jewish parents. Instead he shot the third secretary, Ernst vom Rath, who died of his wounds two days later. The idea of retaliating by destroying Jewish property came from the Minister of Propaganda, Joseph Goebbels using thousands of SA members who turned the night of November 9–10 into a nightmare for Germany's Jews. During the Night of Broken Glass, twelve hundred synagogues were torched, Torah rolls and prayer books desecrated, and Jewish businesses systematically vandalized. Storefronts were smashed, the contents either destroyed or looted. At the same time 35,000 Jewish men were rounded up and sent off to three concentration camps—Sachsenhausen, Buchenwald, and Dachau—which had been well prepared for this influx. In the course of the night some ninety-one Jews were killed by the SA men. Several hundred more died in the camps of maltreatment and exposure or committed suicide.

The horror of the Jewish community at this "retaliation," which was described for the benefit of the international press as a spontaneous uprising of the German people against the Jews, was echoed in more measured terms by foreign governments. But it also caused trouble in the highest echelons of the Nazi party. Some officials objected to the pogrom on the ground that it discredited Germany's already shaky reputation in the world. Goebbels' way to rescue both himself and his idea was to top it. He suggested that the Jews be required to pay a fine of 1 billion reichsmarks, the equivalent of $400 million, for the death of vom Rath. To this was added 250 million reichsmarks to repair the damage to streets, lampposts, and storefronts, thus sparing the insurance companies the need to pay reparations while imposing an additional indignity on the Jews.

This organized pogrom, followed by extortion, naturally aroused the highest pitch of anx-

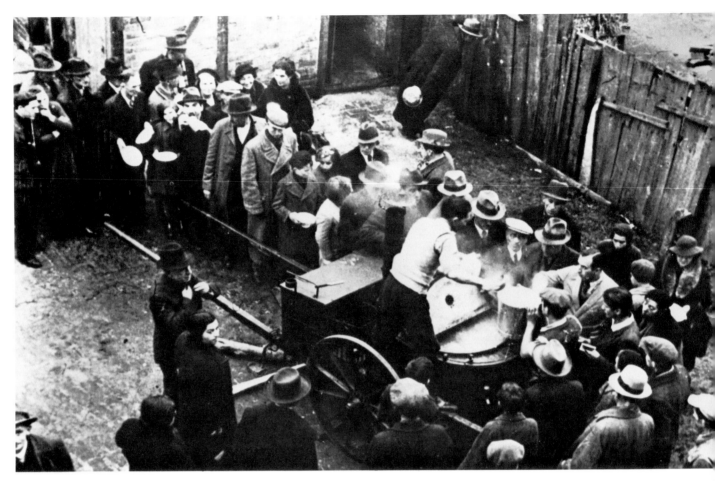

Stateless Jewish refugees being served hot soup while they wait at the border post between Germany and Poland, October 1938.

An account of the Nazi deportation of Polish Jews on October 28, 1938, written by a young Zionist who was on one of the trains but was later able to get to Palestine. This excerpt begins with his arrival at the border.

At night at a border railroad station—we are lined up in rows after untold confusion—we have all lost our heads, not astonishing in face of the fact that in a few hours we would be driven forward to nothingness. . . . To the right and left long lines of police and soldiers with bayonets at the ready. Everything works perfectly—they drive, push, curse; one doesn't yet take it all in consciously. . . . They drag old people forward; children cry, policemen swear. With us, the first, they still behave decently. With the later transports, they strike out with their gun butts, kick, stab with their bayonets, knock people's few possessions from their hands, and drive them through the muck. . . . One woman gives birth in the train. They are so "kind" as to ship her and her child to the border by bus. Shortly after we pass the German border barrier, the escort stops, takes aim, and calls out, "Go on, forward, keep running!" Only a short distance and we have reached the Polish border. . . . There no one has a clue. The crowd jams together in front of the [customs] house. Now I hear my Polish "mother tongue" for the first time. Our arrival in our homeland. What will happen? We have left Germany behind us—it pains my soul because I loved that country more than I wanted to believe. Admired it too much to have been driven from it in this way. . . .

Then a cat-and-mouse game unfolds, with five or six hundred people on the highway in the middle of the night. A commanding Polish police officer appears, vehemently gives orders. . . . On his command we array ourselves once again in rows of two and turn around. Armed patrols right and left; instead of going to Poland, we are to go back. We know perfectly well that the German border guards have set up machine guns. A horrible outcry; people throw themselves to the ground—he stops. This repeats itself three or four times. . . . Then we remain for the whole night, standing in the same spot in the rain. Out in the open, in the cold and wet, under guard, literally everyone who had come—the old, the sick, the weak, the simple-minded—it is enough to drive you mad! . . . . Then at six o'clock we march off . . . the Poles have relented—they are the weaker ones or perhaps the more humane.

" '*Es ertönen hebräische Gesänge. . . ' Polnische Juden auf dem Auszug aus Deutschland,*" *in* Mitteilungsblatt der Hitachduth Olej Germania, *Tel Aviv, [January 1] 1939.*

The Night of Broken Glass (Kristallnacht), Baden-Baden synagogue, November 9, 1938.

Jewish men in Baden-Baden being marched off to a concentration camp on November 9, 1938. They were forced to carry a large Jewish star with the words, "God will not forsake us."

A street in Magdeburg after November 9, 1938.

Austrian Jews in front of the Polish consulate in Vienna, April 1938.

iety in the remaining 250,000 Jews in Germany and the 150,000 in Austria, which had been annexed without resistance on March 13, 1938. Crowds formed daily in front of the Zionist offices in Berlin and Vienna as Jews sought places of refuge. How many must have thought with Betty Scholem, "It becomes more and more apparent how wrong we were to remain here after '33."

Emigration

One of the more disheartening events of 1938 was the conference which met in the French resort of Evian-les-Bains between July 6 and 15. Alarmed by Germany's annexation of Austria, President Roosevelt had sent invitations immediately to countries around the world that might receive Hitler's victims. Thirty-two countries accepted the invitation to the Evian Conference: six of Germany's closest neighbors, the United Kingdom and the Dominions, and nineteen Latin American countries. Uninvited, but permitted to make brief statements, were thirty-nine organizations already working on behalf of Germany's Jews, while representatives of the Reichsvertretung and the Viennese Jewish community, who had been allowed out just to make their plea, spoke for the potential refugees themselves.

As the newspapers quickly pointed out, Evian spelled backwards is "naive," and onlookers would have been naive indeed to have believed that any concrete action would come of the conference. A strong opening plea by Roosevelt's representative, Myron Taylor, stated the situation frankly: "Some millions of people as this meeting convenes, are actually or potentially without a country." This alarming prospect served, if anything, to stiffen the resolve of most countries to keep their borders closed. The United States, however, seemed about to reform. Taylor pledged that the full German and Austrian quota together—27,300 a year—would now be filled. In the five preceding years, as he neglected to mention, the United States had admitted a total of 27,000 persons on the German quota when they might have accepted 130,000. (Only 80–85 percent of those who had entered were Jews. Other Germans also had their reasons for leaving the Nazi state.) The only concrete result of Evian was an agreement among the participants to set up a permanent inter-governmental committee on refugees, which would attempt to "negotiate with the German Government" so that an "orderly migration from Germany may take place."

But no mass schemes ever emerged. Individuals found their way out as chance, family connections, and friendly help worked for them. After September 1939, when Nazi Germany went to war on Europe, emigration became even harder. In a world that was largely closed to them and hostile, German Jews accepted every likely and unlikely opportunity. Ten thousand German and Austrian Jews went to Shanghai, the only place in the world that had no quotas. Another 130,000 went to the United States; Britain took 50,000 and Australia, under severe conditions, 6,500. Four countries in Latin America—Argentina, Brazil, Chile, and Mexico—absorbed another 85,000, and Palestine accounted for 55,000, of whom some 12,000 were "illegal." Then, after the German armies conquered the Netherlands, Belgium, and France in May and June 1940, the 30,000 German Jews who thought that they had found refuge in Western Europe once again fell into the hands of the Nazis and met the same fate as their brethren in Germany.

What is missing from this recital of numbers, with their implication of a smoothly functioning process of mass migration, is the deliberate chicanery the Nazis practiced on their victims. They were intent on extracting as much money and goods from the departing Jews as possible and to subject them to every possible humiliation and delay, making them wait on line for hours, sending them from office to office, postponing and postponing moments of decision. A government that knew how to make things work efficiently was also masterly at operating its black counterpart. The calculated effect was to make the victims willing to do anything, part with property, goods, money—all they had—for that coveted passport.

In this atmosphere even so great a figure as the chemist Richard Willstätter, who had won a Nobel Prize in 1915, was driven to attempt an illegal flight to Switzerland. As he tells it, on November 10, 1938, several members of the Gestapo appeared at his house to take him away to Dachau. They did not think to look for him in his garden, where he was studying his roses, so

that he was temporarily spared. After this episode he decided to leave the country. "And then
it began," he recalled in his memoirs, "a situation
for which I was not at all prepared, one that
extended for months. The daily pursuit of many
officials, waiting on line at various city and state
financial offices, the customs duty office, the
foreign exchange office, the foreign exchange
supervisor's office; practically every day this
meant hours of waiting in corridors and humiliation by arrogant officials." Driven to distraction
by the endless waiting and uncertainty, he finally tried to cross the border, but was caught
and brought back.

Willstätter's story demonstrates that the exodus of German Jews was one of the most astonishing migrations in history. It included not only
Nobel Prize winners but thousands of other scientists, artists, academics, engineers, and professional men and women in every category. And
since this was an entire population and not the
usual young person in search of a fortune, it was
made up of whole families, middle-aged cou-
ples, and even the elderly, like Betty Scholem,
who settled in a small town in Australia, tending
a sweetshop with one of her sons. Driven out of
their country, they took their talent and skills
and culture with them and made the rest of the
world richer for it.

Delegates to the Evian
Conference in July
1938. Myron C. Tay-
lor is at the far right;
James MacDonald is
next to him.

Felix Nussbaum
(1904–1944), *Self-
Portrait with Jewish
Passport.*

**Here is Richard Willstätter's story of his attempted escape
from Nazi Germany in 1938.**

*Waiting for the American documents and doubting whether they
would come at all used up my patience. That was how I, an old man,
committed a fateful piece of folly. I drove to the Bodensee to a town
near the border, in order to see whether it was possible to leave the
country without a passport and without baggage. It was rainy and
stormy, and I tramped about, alone, for hours, in the end thoroughly
soaked and tired. Then I wanted to find a tavern or an inn where I
could spend the night. But everywhere I came upon the sign, "Entrance
to Jews is strictly forbidden." Thereupon I attempted to cross the border
in a rowboat. But it miscarried. Then there were examinations that
went on for many hours. Although dead tired, I held out until it ended
at midnight. The official who was summoned from the secret police
[the Gestapo] was just, and more than that, understanding, humane
and well-meaning. He listened and he understood. I was detained but
not arrested. After two days, as my statements were confirmed, I could
leave the prison and return as a free man to Munich. . . . After twelve
more difficult days, I received my passport. . . . I left my beloved German homeland, which had given me everything and was everything to
me, and found, as an emigrant* tolleranza per riposo *in Muralto-
Locarno.*

Richard Willstätter. Aus meinem Leben: Von Arbeit, Musse, und Freunden, *Basel, 1949.*

Emigrants on a ship
leaving from Bre-
merhaven, 1938. No
one is waving.

Palestine

Accepted everywhere else on sufferance, every head grudgingly counted, in Palestine at least German Jews felt they could consider themselves at home. True, the British authorities were curtailing Jewish immigration, presumably to buy Arab goodwill, but this was after all the Promised Land. Jews who had failed to reflect about their self-definition were shocked enough by the events in Germany to reconsider questions they had long thought settled. Not all who came to Palestine were Zionists, but for many their arrival marked a new awakening.

Upon reaching Palestine the German Jews found themselves in a marginal position both socially and vocationally. Although the founder of the Zionist movement, Theodor Herzl, had been a Western Jew, the heart and soul of the movement lay among the 7 million Yiddish-speaking Jews of Eastern Europe. The pioneers who had come to work the land and form the first collectives were from the East, and it was their voice and thought that put a stamp on the new, secular country that was developing under their hands. They propelled Palestine, which had lain asleep under the Ottoman Empire, into modernity. Even so, progress was late and little. The first electrical network was not established until the 1920s, and "industry" consisted largely of tiny workshops employing fewer than five persons.

Into this situation came the German Jews, speaking a language that grew to be more and more hated as Europe was plunged into war, and with skills meant for a different stage of industrialization. Most of these immigrants were shopkeepers and businessmen, but enough were professionals and intellectuals to over-fulfill many times the demand for doctors, lawyers, accountants, and university professors. What was clear immediately was that immigration to Palestine, far more than to any other country, meant a radical change in their lives.

The German Jews had not expected that they would be not only newcomers in the land but also at the bottom of the heap. Here the Ostjude to whom they had condescended for so long had established the norms of life, and suddenly the German Jew, referred to by the derogatory epithet *Yekke,* was no longer the model to which other Jews aspired. Instead he became a figure of fun: impractical, unadaptable, burdened by useless social forms, barely competent to make his way in the real world. Like many stereotypes, the vision of the bumbling *Yekke* far outlived the actuality of the struggling, self-sacrificing families who came and worked diligently at poorly paid labor.

Those who found a ready place for their skills in the country were, on the whole, rarer than those who struck out into new fields. By 1939, a survey by the Keren Hayesod (Palestine Foundation Fund) showed that 16,000 German Jews, 29 percent of the 55,000 in the country, were in some branch of farming. When they had arrived only 0.7 percent had listed agriculture as their occupation.

Whereas younger members of the immigrants formed or joined kibbutzim, older members, with families, preferred the *moshav,* or collective farm, where members shared risk, capital, and labor but lived independently. One of the more famous of these collectives was Ramot ha-Shavim, founded in 1933 by a group of newly arrived doctors, lawyers, and other professionals who decided that a mixed enterprise of egg farming and raising vegetables for market would be most appropriate for their level of experience. The amusement occasioned by these *Eier Jecken* (egg Yekkes) in their *Kikirikidorf* (Cock-a-Doodle-Do village) was bewildering to them in view of their arduous work under primitive conditions. But it was symptomatic of the benign if dismissive attitude with which they were received.

In this respect the *Landjuden,* or rural Jews, were better equipped to enter into a new life. In a unique case for those times an entire community of Jews emigrated en masse, from the village of Rexingen in Swabia, determined to stay with one another and settle together. Working with the Zionist Bureau for Resettlement, they bought sixty hectares of land north of Acco on the Mediterranean coast and in April 1938 established the fortified walls and the first houses of their village. Their moshav, which they called Shavei Zion (Returners to Zion), combined milk production with farming. While their children quickly learned to speak Hebrew, the adult business of daily life continued to go on in the mellifluous Swabian dialect they had brought with them.

A youth group from
Germany arriving in
Tel Aviv, April 1939.

A settler showers in water heated by the sun. Ramot ha-Shavim, 1930s.

Egg Yekkes preparing produce for market, Ramot ha-Shavim, 1930s. The man at the left still wears the sporting knickers he brought from Germany.

Building a protective wall around the perimeter of a new kibbutz, Kibbutz Alonim, June 1938.

The largest settlement of German Jews was the town of Nahariya, founded in 1934 and located three kilometers north of Shavei Zion on the coast. Here a visionary engineer and agronomist were the principal movers in the plans to build a model town especially to accommodate hard-pressed Jews from Central Europe. In the plans for a thousand settlers, each was to be given, with his house, a plot of land and all the tools and seed necessary to begin a subsistence farm. Living sometimes in shacks and sometimes even in the wooden packing cases in which they had shipped their worldly goods, the refugees rapidly gave even this frontier town a Central European character.

Most of the settlers originally intended to till the soil, but one prospective farmer was unexpectedly forced back into his original profession. Max Cramer, an eye doctor from Stuttgart, was besieged by importunate Arab patients, who camped for days outside his rather primitive house until they could see him. Neighborhood legend still celebrates his fairness and firmness in requiring that an insistent effendi also wait his turn.

As part of the development of Nahariya, the promoters laid out a grand central promenade leading to the sea and flanking the local river, whose banks were planted with eucalyptus trees. This measure was not only ornamental but also prevented flooding. There soon appeared on this promenade the ironically named Café Penguin, which was no more than a collection of wooden chairs and tables under an improvised shelter. But the small-plot farming that enjoyed a certain success gradually gave way to the demand for resort accommodations as Nahariya boarding houses became known for their cuisine and their attention to detail—the vase of flowers on the dresser, the newspaper on the breakfast table. Above all, they were known for a level of service quite exceptional in those egalitarian days.

The German immigration to Palestine brought capitalism and middle-class values to a society that had been polarized for millennia between rich and poor. With their modest capital, they established a new scale between the few large factories in existence and the tiny one-man workshops and began producing such fun-

Dr. Selig Eugen Soskin, one of the founders of Nahariya, explaining the plans for the town to potential settlers, 1938.

The "lift" (packing case) in which the Cramer family sent their household goods from Stuttgart housed them during their early months in Nahariya, 1939. Here they have arranged an outdoor dining area (note the tablecloth). Dr. Cramer carried on his ophthalmological practice in another such "lift."

Café Penguin, Nahariya, ca. 1939.

German immigrants,
members of a window
cleaners' cooperative,
Tel Aviv, ca. 1934.

Elderly couple in
Jerusalem, 1930s.

damental goods as baths, steel furniture, files, and nails, all of which had formerly been imported from Europe. In the retail trade they changed the look of city streets, introducing shops with carefully dressed windows, featuring fixed prices, and offering new levels of service. Their ubiquitous cafés with European pastries rapidly became one of the specialties of Tel Aviv life.

Perhaps the hardest hit among the refugees were the academics and other intellectuals and artists. In the 1930s, there were only two institutions of higher learning in Palestine—the Haifa Technion, founded in 1924 on German Jewish initiative, and the Hebrew University, founded a year later. Regarded from its inception as the treasure of the nation, the Hebrew University benefited immensely from the pool of talent provided by the refugees. The number of those who could be employed, however, was limited by the size of the university, which in 1941 had only a thousand students. Since there were 6,780 academics among the immigrants from Germany, it is not surprising that fewer than 1 percent of them ever found a teaching post at the university. These small numbers, however, cannot diminish the fact that the Hebrew University is one of the enduring monuments to the German Jews, who were among its first teachers and brought it international distinction.

Other academics managed to put their talents to use in publishing and in secondary education. In music, where language was not a barrier, German Jews practically filled the Palestine Symphonic Orchestra when it was founded in 1936. German Jewish culture, however, did not survive transplantation. The children of the refugees quickly took on the language and coloration of the country in which they were growing up. For all their talent and effort, German Jews have not left a strong mark on the kaleidoscopic Israeli culture. They are almost entirely absent from politics, and elsewhere the Central European culture seems simply to have evaporated in the Palestinian sun. Almost before its last members have gone, the German Jewish community has been fossilized. An exhibition in the Ethnographic Section of the Israel Museum displays a few rooms furnished with artifacts from the eighteenth to the twentieth centuries to show us how this people once lived—another exotic culture that contributed a scintilla to a complex land.

The End

The rest of the story is quickly told. On July 4, 1939, the Reichsvertretung was changed under orders from the Gestapo into the Reichsvereinigung der Juden in Deutschland (Reich Union of the Jews in Germany). This was not just a change in name: it meant that the organization was designated to become a conduit for Nazi directives to the Jewish community. Vain attempts were made by Otto Hirsch, who retained his position in the new organization, to protest the deportations that had begun in February 1940 and to bring back those who had already been deported to Poland. In October 1940, when Jews from southwest Germany were being deported to France, the Reichsvereinigung initiated an illegal campaign to warn those who were away from home not to return. But these limited measures and the proclamation of days of public fasting could not stop a monolith already in operation. Otto Hirsch was himself deported in 1941, and the organization was shut down in 1943 when Leo Baeck was taken to Theresienstadt.

Those who remained, trapped by the war, lived in a diminishing universe. Dismissed from every job and excluded from every profession, they were drafted to do forced labor in the war industries. They were permitted to shop for their needs only one hour a day and not allowed to use public transportation. On September 1, 1941, they were literally marked off from the rest of the population by the requirement that

Jews over the age of six wear the yellow star prominently placed on their clothes. On October 14, systematic deportation of the Jews to camps in the east began. In Berlin, the Levetzowstrasse synagogue was converted into an assembly point where Jews waited to be led to the trains. These transports took place at night, and the trains left from remote stations so as to make the disappearance of the Jews as mysterious as possible. The deportations continued until February 1943, which was the moment that Hitler had set for Germany to be *Judenrein*—cleared of Jews. The last Jewish armament workers were deported on February 27 from Berlin to Auschwitz.

After that, several thousand Jews who had gone underground or were passing as "Aryans" continued to survive in the Nazi Reich. It should be noted that for every Jew who lived underground, several non-Jews were responsible for his or her day-to-day survival. Even those who did not contribute food or shelter but knew and kept silent were involved in the rescue action. Some Jews were caught, some died, some were betrayed, yet 5,000 emerged at the end of the war. Another 14,000 maintained an open if precarious existence as spouses of "Aryans." When the counting stopped, it was clear that 170,000 German Jews had been killed in the camps.

Sixteen hundred years of German Jewish history were over. The members of the community were dispersed, its monuments and cemeteries silently marking their former presence and life. Its memory is preserved in diaries, letters, and pictures, in books, and in art, religious and secular; in the official records of the Nazi and other governments; in the records of the Jewish organizations; in the scholarly excavations that retell their history; and in the institutes, libraries, and museums that have gathered together the fragments and piece out the history of their sojourn.

Few Jews who live in Germany today would call themselves German Jews. The representative Jewish organization quite deliberately has taken the name Zentralrat der Juden in Deutschland (Central Council of Jews in Germany). That brief century when the Jews in Germany thought that they were creating a new symbiosis has become a historical curiosity. In Germany Jews live now, as they have lived for thousands of years, on an edge, in exile.

Z u m   A b s c h i e d.

Als die Kreis-Synagogen-Gemeinde Insterburg ihre Vorbereitungen für den 22. Mai 1938 traf und diesen Tag des Gedenkens an Einhundert Jahre Bestehen mit zahlreichen Ehrengästen aus den Provinzgemeinden im Gotteshause festlich beging, ahnte sie es nicht, dass das Jahr 1938 des einhundertjährigen Bestehens gleichzeitig das Jahr ihres Unterganges bedeuten werde.

Am 10. November 1938, sechs Monate nach der Jubelfeier war es in der Frühe zwischen 3 und 4 Uhr, als das schöne Gotteshaus, die Stätte einhundertjährigen jüdischen Lebens und Webens in der Stadt Insterburg, in Flammen aufging und es mit allem, was sie an Gedenktafeln und an sonstigen Denkwürdigkeiten aus der Zeit von 1838 bis 1938 enthielt, mit etwa 20 Thorarollen und ihren kostbaren Mänteln, mit wertvollen Vorhängen der heiligen Lade, mit der schönen Chuppa, mit einem klangvollen Harmonium, mit zwei Pianinos, mit zahlreichen Tallitim und Gebetbüchern von Gemeindemitgliedern, mit dem Ornat des Rabbiners, mit einer reichhaltigen Bibliothek u. a. in Schutt und Asche legte. - - - - - -

Einhundert Jahre jüdischen Lebens sind damit ausgelöscht, die Arbeit zielbewusster, kraftvoller führender Männer, die ihr Alles hingaben, der Gemeinde und dem Judentum zu dienen, sie ist umsonst gewesen; - eine Gemeinde, ausgestattet mit korporativen Rechten, mit einem Vorstande und einer Repräsentanten-Versammlung, die für eine ordnungsmässige Führung und Verwaltung sorgte, mit einem Rabbiner und einem Kantor, die jüdisches Leben und Wissen garantierten, - sie ist nicht mehr. - - - Ein von einem Bretterzaun umgebener, an zwei Strassenfronten gelegener freier Platz deutet z. Z. noch die Stelle an, auf welcher unsere erhabene Synagoge gestanden hat.

Nur ein winzig kleiner Rest von Mitgliedern unter Führung des Seniors der Gemeinde, des allverehrten zeitigen Vorstehers Herrn J o s e f K a d o r im biblischen Alter von 81 Jahren, bildet den Bestand einstiger Grösse der Gemeinde. Diesem Restbestande gelingt es einstweilen noch, an Sabbaten und Festtagen Gottesdienst abzuhalten, den der langjähr. frühere Schriftführer der Repräs.-Versammlung, Herr David Simon, in einem Betraume mit Sachkenntnis leitet.

Wie lange dieses zusammengeschrumpfte Häuflein noch eine jüdische Einheit bilden wird,

das liegt in Deiner Hand, Du grosser, erhabener Gott;

Erbarme Dich unser, erbarme Dich des ganzen jüd. Volkes!

Insterburg, 24. April 1941.

Josef Israel Wiessburg

"Farewell." This is the last entry in the record book of the community of Insterburg in East Prussia, dated April 24, 1941.

The last entry in the Minute Book of the community of Insterburg in East Prussia.

FAREWELL

As the synagogue of the District of Insterburg made its preparations for the twenty-second of May 1938, it did not suspect that this date, which was to commemorate the one hundredth anniversary of its founding and which was celebrated with festivities and with numerous honored guests from the Jewish communities in the surrounding area, would at the same time spell the year of its demise.

On the tenth of November 1938, six months after the jubilee celebration, in the early morning hours, between three and four, the beautiful synagogue, the site of one hundred years of life and being in the city of Insterburg, went up in flames. With it went everything contained within its walls. Some twenty Torah scrolls with their precious mantles, the costly hangings for the Holy Ark, the beautiful wedding canopy, the melodious harmonium, two pianos, large numbers of prayer shawls and prayer books that belonged to the members, the official robes of the rabbi and a rich library—all now in rubble and ashes.

One hundred years of Jewish life have been extinguished with it, the work of energetic leaders conscious of their goals, who gave everything they had in the service of Jewishness; it was all in vain. An organized community invested with corporate rights, with an executive body and a representative council, which concerned itself with an orderly leadership and administration, a rabbi and a cantor who guaranteed the continuity of Jewish life and knowledge—all of this is no more. An open space with a board fence on its two street fronts is the only sign that remains at this time of the place on which our noble synagogue stood.

Only a vanishingly small remnant of members make up the sum of a once great community . . .

How long can such a shrunken little band maintain a Jewish presence?

That lies in Thy hand, Thou great and exalted God;

Have mercy on us and have mercy on the whole Jewish people.

Insterburg 24 April 1941

Josef Israel Wilkowsky

Central Archives of the History of the Jewish People, Jerusalem, S 374/2.

Further Reading

The following list is intended as a guide for those who wish to read more extensively on one or another of the topics in this book. The works have been chosen with an eye to their general readability and availability. Although I have limited my selections to titles in English, readers who know German will find titles in that language cited in the monographs. In my own research I have, of course, used many specialized books, periodicals, and articles which are available only in large academic libraries and have therefore not listed them here in a book intended for general use.

The literature on German Jewry is understandably unevenly distributed through its history and tends to concentrate on the last hundred and fifty years of its existence, which gives a certain imbalance to this list. Readers who wish to pursue earlier topics will find additional references in the larger general works, which will take them into the areas of their special interest.

I would particularly like to draw the reader's attention to the publications of the Leo Baeck Institute. The *Yearbook,* published in London since 1956 with a special theme for each year, is an invaluable resource for the current scholarship on the history of the German Jewish community. In addition, a series of more than forty-five specialized volumes, most of them in German, already published by the Leo Baeck Institute with J. C. B. Mohr in Tübingen, pursue topics in modern Jewish history in depth. As a capstone to its program, in 1995 the institute will publish a comprehensive four-volume history of the German Jews from the Middle Ages to 1945. Written by a team of leading scholars, it will be an authoritative resource for all those interested in German Jewish history.

Abrahams, Israel. *Jewish Life in the Middle Ages*. London, 1896. Reprint New York, 1959.

Altmann, Alexander. *Moses Mendelssohn: A Biographical Study*. Philadelphia, 1973.

Angress, Werner T. *Between Fear and Hope: Jewish Youth in the Third Reich*. Translated by Werner T. Angress and Christine Granger. New York, 1988.

Arendt, Hannah. *Rahel Varnhagen: The Life of a Jewess*. London, 1957.

Aschheim, Steven E. *Brothers and Strangers: The East European Jew in German and German Jewish Consciousness, 1800–1923*. Madison, 1982.

Bolkosky, Sidney M. *The Distorted Image: German Jewish Perception of Germans and Germany, 1918–1935*. New York, 1975.

Cahnman, Werner J. *German Jewry: Its History and Sociology*. Edited with an introduction by Joseph B. Maier, Judith Marcus, and Zoltan Tarr. New Brunswick, N.J., 1989.

Chazan, Robert. *European Jewry and the First Crusade*. Berkeley and Los Angeles, 1987.

Elon, Amos. *The Israelis: Founders and Sons*. New York, 1971.

Finkelstein, Louis. *Jewish Self-Government in the Middle Ages*. New York, 1924.

Gay, Peter. *Freud, Jews and Other Germans: Masters and Victims in Modernist Culture*. New York, 1978.

———. *Weimar Culture: The Outsider as Insider*. New York, 1968.

Glückel of Hameln. *Memoirs*. Translated with notes by Marvin Lowenthal. New York, 1977.

Great Britain. *Palestine Royal Commission (Peel Report)*. Cmd. 5479. London, 1937.

Grunwald, Kurt. *Türkenhirsch: A Study of Baron Maurice de Hirsch, Entrepreneur and Philanthropist*. Jerusalem, 1966.

Hertz, Deborah. *Jewish High Society in Old Regime Berlin*. New Haven, 1988.

Jewish Agency. Central Bureau for Settlement of German Jews. *Reports—1935, 1937, 1939*. Jerusalem.

Kaplan, Marion A. *The Jewish Feminist Movement in Germany: The Campaigns of the Jüdischer Frauenbund, 1904–1938*. Westport, Conn., 1979.

———. *The Making of the Jewish Middle Class: Women, Family, and Identity in Imperial Germany*. New York, 1991.

Katz, Jacob. *From Prejudice to Destruction: Anti-Semitism, 1700–1933*. Cambridge, Mass., 1980.

———. *Out of the Ghetto: The Social Background of Jewish Emancipation, 1770–1870*. New York, 1978.

Krinsky, Carol Herselle. *Synagogues of Europe: Architecture, History, Meaning*. Cambridge, Mass., 1985.

Lamberti, Marjorie. *Jewish Activism in Imperial Germany: The Struggle for Civil Equality*. New Haven, 1978.

Laqueur, Walter. *A History of Zionism*. New York, 1972.

Liberles, Robert. *Religious Conflict in Social Context: The Resurgence of Orthodox Judaism in Frankfurt am Main, 1838–1877*. Westport, Conn., 1985.

Low, Alfred D. *Jews in the Eyes of the Germans: From the Enlightenment to Imperial Germany*. Philadelphia, 1979.

Lowenthal, Marvin. *The Jews of Germany: A Story of Sixteen Centuries*. Philadelphia, 1936.

Marcus, Ivan G. *Piety and Society: The Jewish Pietists of Medieval Germany*. Leiden, 1981.

Marcus, Jacob R. *The Jew in the Medieval World: A Source Book, 315–1791*. New York, 1938.

Mendes-Flohr, Paul R., and Jehuda Reinharz, eds. *The Jew in the Modern World: A Documentary History*. New York, 1980.

Meyer, Michael A. *The Origins of the Modern Jew: Jewish Identity and European Culture in Germany, 1749–1824*. Detroit, 1967.

———. *Response to Modernity: A History of the Reform Movement in Judaism*. New York, 1988.

Mosse, George L. *German Jews beyond Judaism*. Bloomington and Cincinnati, 1985.

———. *Germans and Jews: The Right, the Left, and the Search for a "Third Force" in Pre-Nazi Germany*. New York, 1970.

Mosse, Werner E., Arnold Paucker, Reinhard Rürup, eds. *Revolution and Evolution: 1848 in German Jewish History*. Tübingen, 1981.

Niewyk, Donald. *The Jews in Weimar Germany*. Baton Rouge, 1980.

Philipson, David. *Old European Jewries*. Philadelphia, 1895. Reprint New York, 1975.

Pollack, Herman. *Jewish Folkways in Germanic Lands, 1648–1806: Studies in Aspects of Daily Life*. Cambridge, 1971.

Poppel, Stephen M. *Zionism in Germany 1897–1933: The Shaping of a Jewish Identity*. Philadelphia, 1977.

Reinharz, Jehuda. *Fatherland or Promised Land: The Dilemma of the German Jew, 1893–1914*. Ann Arbor, 1975.

Reinharz, Jehuda, and Walter Schatzberg, eds. *The Jewish Response to German Culture: From the Enlightenment to the Second World War*. Hanover, N.H., 1985.

Richarz, Monika, ed. *Jewish Life in Germany: Memoirs from Three Centuries*. Translated by Stella P. Rosenfeld and Sidney Rosenfeld. Bloomington, 1991.

Ruppin, Arthur. *Building Israel: Selected Essays, 1907–1935*. New York, 1949.

Schorsch, Ismar. *Jewish Reactions to German Anti-Semitism, 1870–1914*. New York, 1972.

Shachar, Isaiah. *The Judensau: A Medieval Anti-Jewish Motif and Its History*. London, 1974.

Sorkin, David. *The Transformation of German Jewry 1780–1840*. New York, 1987.

Stern, Fritz. *Gold and Iron: Bismarck, Bleichröder and the Building of the German Empire*. New York, 1977.

Tal, Uriel. *Christians and Jews in Germany: Religion, Politics and Ideology in the Second Reich, 1870–1914*. Ithaca, 1975.

Trachtenberg, Joshua. *The Devil and the Jews: The Medieval Conception of the Jew and Its Relation to Modern Anti-Semitism*. New Haven, 1943.

Wertheimer, Jack. *Unwelcome Strangers: East European Jews in Imperial Germany*. New York, 1987.

Acknowledgments

A book such as this requires many hands, and in order to tell its history I would like here to note with heartfelt thanks the names of the people and institutions who have helped bring it into being. Above all, I want to thank Robert Slaughter for his advocacy and the Horace W. Goldsmith Foundation for a two-year grant which became the bedrock of my resources for travel and research. In this connection I also want to express my appreciation to Fred Grubel for opening the Leo Baeck Institute to me and to members of the staff who generously shared their special expertise, especially Evelyn Ehrlich, Marion Kaplan, Frank Mecklenburg, Aline Isdebsky-Pritchard, Michael A. Riff, Nusi Szneider, and Diane Spielman.

One of the pleasures of preparing this book has been the opportunity it has given me to meet people in various countries and to explore the resources of many archives and libraries. It is an additional pleasure now to be able to acknowledge their kindness, which often went far beyond the formal requirements of their work. Professor Bernhard Bischoff, who had first observed the lifelike drawing of the elephant in the ninth-century psalter of St. Denis and concluded that it was a portrait of Abulabaz, the only elephant in Europe, was kind enough to lead me to its present location. In Berlin I enjoyed the delightful company and sound advice of Heidrun Klein of the Bildarchiv Preussischer Kulturbesitz. Jürgen Landeck, head of the library of the Jüdische Gemeinde, and Jürgen Wetzel, director of the Landesarchiv, made me welcome in their congenial reading rooms. Veronika Bendt and Christiane Schütz of the Jüdisches Museum were learned and informative guides to the collection. In Frankfurt, I am indebted to Georg Heuberger, Helga Krohn, and Annette Weber of the Jüdisches Museum for their interest and active help.

At Hebrew Union College in Cincinnati, Dr. Herbert Zafren, Bernard Rabenstein, and Arnona Rudavsky helped unlock the rich resources of the college library, and I also owe special thanks to Professor Herbert Paper.

In New York, at the library of the Jewish Theological Seminary, Evelyn Cohen, then curator of prints, Sharon L. Mintz, and

Rabbi Jerry Schwarzbard provided patient guidance through their collections. At the Jewish Museum in New York, Norman Kleeblatt and Irene Schenck generously searched through their holdings for material on German Jews. At Yale University, Ingeborg Glier and Benjamin Harshav were loyal friends and invaluable in their willingness to decipher obscure texts. At Yale's various libraries, Barbara S. Gajewski, Linda Lerman, Barbara McCorkle, George Miles, and Christa Sammons were generous in sharing their knowledge of the sources in their special fields.

In Israel, Irene Levitt at the Israel Museum, Ruth Porter at Beth Hatefutsoth, Yitzhak Mais at Yad Vashem, Dr. Michael Heymann and Reuven Koffler at the Central Zionist Archives, Hadassah Allousine at the Central Archives for the History of the Jewish People, Miriam Broshee at the Wiener Library in Tel Aviv, and Leon Davidoff and Hagith Friedländer at Mishkenot Sha'ananim were hospitable guides to their country and their institutions.

I am also grateful for interviews granted by Shlomo Erel in Herzliya, Gustav Horn of Kibbutz Hasorea, Dan Fraenkel of Kibbutz Dalia, Hans and Resi Schwarz and Pinchas Erlanger at Shavei Zion, and Yisrael Shiloni, curator of the Museum of the German Jews in Nahariya, as well as Dr. Dov Lazar, also of Nahariya, who allowed me to use his photograph collection. In London, S. F. Hallgarten, Mr. and Mrs. Ronald Stent, and Dr. S. W. Nelki graciously gave me their firsthand observations of the Jewish student dueling societies in Germany during the 1920s and early 1930s.

Many others helped in various ways: Cécile Lowenthal-Hensel graciously permitted me to reproduce the portrait of her forebear Moses Mendelssohn. Alfred E. Laurence, a direct descendant of Süsskind Stern, was kind enough to provide me with a photograph of his portrait. The painting itself disappeared under mysterious circumstances in 1964 from the family's house in Soest, Westphalia. Monika Richarz of the Germania-Judaica Library in Cologne, Georg Syamken of the Hamburg Kunsthalle, Arnold Paucker of the Leo Baeck Institute in London, and Schlomo Meyer of the Leo Baeck Institute in Jerusalem provided advice and materials. It is a special pleasure to be able to acknowledge the efforts of my friend Elise Snyder in getting this project started. Also in New Haven, I am indebted to Jay Katz, James Ponet, Helmut Smith, Henry Turner, and George Warburg for their particular help. In Berlin, Silke Bernhard and Elisabeth Fischer were enthralling storytellers, while Martin Koerber and Richard Kostelanetz generously allowed me to listen to tapes of interviews with former Berliners made in connection with their film *Weissensee.* The Syndics of Oxford University Press have kindly permitted me to use William Rose's translation of a passage from Heine's *Baths of Lucca*, in his *Heinrich Heine: Two Studies of His Thought and Feeling*, 1956. All other translations are my own.

I have waited a long time to thank my beloved sister Shirley Gorenstein for years of patient listening and encouragement. I also owe special appreciation to my daughter Sophie Glazer, whose high editorial standards kept me alert to rhetorical perils.

Gladys Topkis, my editor at Yale University Press, was daring in her willingness to undertake this book and indefatigable in seeing it through the labyrinth of production. Ernst-Peter Wieckenberg of C. H. Beck Verlag in Munich, with whom I was delighted to discover a shared view of Jewish history, sympathetically and generously supported this project from its early stages.

To Richard Miller and Sylvia Steiner of Yale University Press, I offer heartfelt thanks for their expertise and patience in transforming a manuscript into a work of art. I am also grateful to Jean and Leo Staschover for incomparable breakfasts and a close reading of an early draft.

My husband, Peter Gay, as one of the survivors of the community celebrated here, was in a profound way the reason for this book. He was a steadfast friend as well as an unfailing source of advice and help during its writing. Finally, I want to thank Thea and Max Wolffsohn, in whose living room in Berlin this book was conceived.

Credits

Archive of the AEG, Frankfurt am Main:
p. 170

Photo Archive, Beth Hatefutsoth, Tel Aviv:
pp. 204 (courtesy Dr. Edina Meyer),
204, 227, 231 (photograph by Walter
Giercke), 236

Biblioteca Apostolica Vaticana: p. 5

Biblioteca Palatina, Parma: p. 19

Bibliotheca Rosenthaliana, Universiteits-
Bibliotheek, Amsterdam: pp. 25, 49

Bibliothèque Nationale, Paris: p. 7

Bildarchiv Foto Marburg: p. 46

Bildarchiv Preussischer Kulturbesitz,
Berlin: pp. 10, 88, 91, 93, 106, 111, 116,
126 (photograph by A. Pisarek), 130,
132, 136, 153, 163 (photograph by J.
Remmer), 177, 188, 190, 193, 204 (4),
215, 221 (photograph by Knut Petersen), 246, 251, 253, 257, 273 (photograph by H. Sonnenfeld)

Bischöfliches Dom- und Diözesanmuseum,
Trier: p. 24

British Library, London: p. 15

Busch-Reisinger Museum, Harvard University, Cambridge, Mass.: p. 242

By permission of the Syndics of Cambridge University: pp. 129, 147

Central Archives for the History of the
Jewish People, Jerusalem: pp. 37, 220,
282

Central Zionist Archives, Jerusalem: pp.
208, 209, 213, 214, 235, 266, 275, 276
(2), 279, 280

Edition Leipzig, Verlag für Kunst und
Wissenschaft: pp. 38, 44

Universitätsbibliothek, Friedrich Alexander Universität, Erlangen: p. 45

HAPAG-Lloyd, Hamburg: pp. 179, 180, 181

Hebrew National Library, Jerusalem:
p. 139

Hebrew Union College Library, Cincinnati:
pp. 16, 57

Hessische Landes- und Hochschul-Biblio-
thek, Darmstadt: pp. 58, 59

Historisches Museum, Frankfurt am Main:
pp. 66, 70, 138

Israel Museum, Jerusalem: pp. 34, 49, 53 (photograph by Reuven Milo), 60 (2) (photographs by Joram Lehmann), 61 (2), 225 (photograph by Avi Ganor), 228; pp. 14, 48, 52, 53 (2) (photographs by David Harris)

Jewish Museum, London: p. 123

Jewish Museum/Art Resource, New York: pp. 55, 56 (2) (photograph by Malcolm Varon), 124, 134, 135, 137, 227, 252

Library of the Jewish Theological Seminary of America, New York: pp. 25, 43, 69, 131, 155, 198, 201, 216; pp. 16, 78, 79, 101, 136, 145, 157, 164, 167, 222, 224, 225 (photographs by Suzanne Kaufman)

Judah L. Magnes Museum, Berkeley, Calif.: p. 104

Judaistisk Afdeling, Det Kondelige Bibliotek, Copenhagen: p. 19

Jüdisches Museum, Frankfurt am Main: pp. 72, 183

Courtesy of Dr. Jay Katz, John A. Garver Professor of Law and Psychoanalysis, Yale University: p. 187

Courtesy of Kaufhof AG Köln: p. 191

Courtesy of Kulturgeschichtliches Museum, Osnabruck: p. 272 (photograph by Hartwig Fender)

Kunsthalle Bremen: p. 110

Landesarchiv Speyer: p. 85

Landesbildstelle, Berlin: pp. 93, 94, 192, 194, 205, 249, 251, 255, 256, 262

Landesmuseum Mainz: p. 42

Landesmuseum Trier: p. 6 (photograph by H. Thornig)

Courtesy of Alfred E. Laurence: p. 70

By generosity of the Leo Baeck Institute, Jerusalem: p. 173

Courtesy of the Leo Baeck Institute, London: p. 173

Courtesy of the Leo Baeck Institute, New York: pp. 35, 43, 96, 97, 105, 113, 133, 136, 159, 174, 183, 196, 197, 199, 203, 211 (photograph by Pollitzer, Strong, and Meyer), 223, 241, 243, 259 (2), 261, 265 (photograph by Eric Pollitzer), 268; pp. 22, 24, 83, 89, 149, 168, 210, 230, 258, 260, 263, 268, 269 (2), 271 (photographs by Jim Strong)

Drawing by Laura Levy: p. 95

Library of Congress, Washington, D.C.: pp. 21, 114, 128

Courtesy of Dr. Cécile Lowenthal-Hensel: p. 100

Archives of the Municipal Museum of Nahariya. Reproductions by Dr. Dov Lazar: pp. 277, 278 (2)

New York Public Library: pp. 150, 206

Rheinisches Bildarchiv: p. 45

Ruprecht Karl Universität, Bibliothek, Heidelberg: p. 13

Staatliche Kunstsammlungen Kassel: p. 50

Staatliche Schlösser und Gärten Berlin, Schloss Charlottenburg: p. 93

Staatlichen Museen Heidecksburg: p. 47

Staats- und Universitätsbibliothek Hamburg: p. 33

Staatsbibliothek Preussischer Kulturbesitz, Berlin: p. 9

Stadtarchiv Augsburg: p. 34

Stadtarchiv Frankfurt am Main: p. 110, 119

Stadtarchiv Worms: p. 18

By permission of Max A. Warburg, Hamburg: p. 171

Warburg Institute, University of London: p. 248

Yale University, Beinecke Rare Book and Manuscript Library, New Haven: pp. 4, 11, 27, 31 (2), 63, 68, 73, 81, 82, 108, 120, 121, 148, 166, 176; pp. 51, 63, 142, 186 (Yale Collection of German Literature); p. 145 (Yale Collection of Western Americana)

Yale University, Medical Library, New Haven: p. 30

Yale University, Sterling Memorial Library, New Haven: pp. 22, 36, 39, 41, 67, 75, 77, 117, 140, 144, 151, 165, 171, 172, 175, 178, 182, 191, 200, 201, 207, 211, 217, 218, 219, 233, 238, 239; pp. 2, 3, 162 (Map Collection); p. 145 (Numismatic Collection)

Photographs by Walter Zadek: pp. 276 (2)

Index